Isle of Green Fire

Isle of Green Fire

Kaylee O'Shay, Irish Dancer

Rod Vick

Laikituk Creek Publishing

Isle of Green Fire

Kaylee O'Shay, Irish Dancer

Laikituk Creek Publishing
North Prairie, Wisconsin

This is a work of fiction. Names, characters, places, and incidents either are the product of the author's imagination or are used fictitiously. Any resemblance to actual persons, living or dead, events, or locales is entirely coincidental.

ISBN-13: 978-0692453780
ISBN-10: 0692453784

For my daughter and my son,
Haley and Josh.
Because of
you
my heart dances
every day.

One

She never had nightmares about the accident. This surprised her. Wasn't that how it always happened in the movies? After a traumatic event that forever changed the life of the main character, he would wake up at night in a cold sweat after reliving the terror in his dreams.

But Kaylee O'Shay never dreamed about the day almost a year earlier when a drunk driver in a pickup truck had smashed into Riley's car, crippling both of them. Riley's broken leg had healed, but his right eye was gone forever. The list of Kaylee's injuries had been considerably longer.

"Up on your toes! Up!"

Miss Helen urged her on, but the pain shot through her right leg like needles.

"Keep going!"

A few more seconds, and then she had to stop.

"I can't do it!" hissed Kaylee through gritted teeth. "You don't know how much it hurts!"

Miss Helen switched off the music. "Does it hurt more than not being able to compete in a feis?" asked Miss Helen, using the Gaelic word for a dance competition. "Does it hurt more than not being able to dance at Oireachtas? Does it hurt as much as it does to know you were so close to becoming a Champs dancer?"

Kaylee wiped a tear from one eye and straightened herself in the middle of the wooden floor, pointing her right toe. Miss Helen started the music again, which reverberated hollowly off the plaster walls of the aging church.

Since Miss Helen no longer taught at Trean Gaoth Academy of Irish Dance, she had persuaded the pastor at the Cream City

Church to allow her to use the area in back of the last row of pews. This makeshift dance floor spanned the forty-foot width of the church, although the other dimension—between the last pew and the back wall—was barely fifteen feet. The acoustics, too, were not the best, and the pounding of her hard shoes on the dark wood nearly drowned out the music from Kaylee's CD player. However, it was certainly better than trying to dance in Miss Helen's tiny living room.

"All right," said Miss Helen, her voice reflecting the futility of continuing to push her pupil—whose form was now deteriorating badly. "We'll walk back to my house and go again on Wednesday."

Kaylee dropped into a sitting position, relieved to get a respite from the pain, yet frustrated. She was grateful that Miss Helen had agreed to coach her again. And surprised. Before retiring six months earlier, Miss Helen had coached Kaylee ever since her first day at Trean Gaoth Academy six years earlier. When she had visited Miss Helen in early June, the old woman had been adamant about not wishing to resume her teaching. Yet, a few days later, Miss Helen had phoned Kaylee at home, saying that she had reconsidered. Perhaps she had remembered how much dance meant to Kaylee.

But it had been almost a month now, three days a week. Kaylee had hoped for more progress. Much more. She could finish her hornpipe, although the pain increased so dramatically during the last half of the dance that she found it difficult to concentrate on form and positioning. By the end of the dance, she suspected she looked a lot like a flailing, rhythm-challenged beginner. And she had never made it more than halfway through her slip jig without stopping. The leaps and twists were simply too much for bones held together by screws and metal plates.

In August, it would be a year since the accident. It still hurt to walk. It hurt even more to dance. Miss Helen had been her solution, her secret weapon. That was the thought that had kept her going ever since she had taken her first painful steps without crutches. She could overcome the pain. All she needed was to work harder, right? And Miss Helen would push her harder than anyone.

But weeks later, the pain remained undiminished.

Kaylee's eyes suddenly darkened and she grabbed the toe of one of her hard shoes, banging the heel five times—as fast and as forcefully as she could—onto the wooden floor. The sound rang off the walls like echoes of gunshots. Then she threw the shoe down the center aisle where it skidded to a stop against the base of the communion table. Miss Helen said nothing, and after a moment, Kaylee stood and trudged listlessly after it. She bent, retrieved the shoe, straightened, found her face directly in front of the open Bible resting on the center of the communion table. Luke. The story of the Good Samaritan, who had been there to help when everyone else had passed by. *I wish someone would show up to help me,* she thought, flexing her stiff right leg. *Yeah, right.*

The walk back was quiet, through a neighborhood wedged full of aging, neatly-kept bungalows. The silence was typical. Miss Helen always lit up a cigarette, which would be gone before the halfway point to her house. On some days, she smoked two. She usually limited herself to a single smoke on the trip *to* the church. Kaylee hated the smell and always tried to walk upwind of her teacher, but today the stench hovered around them, and so she was forced to endure.

Miss Helen finished cigarette number one, but before she could reach into her dark sweatpants for a second, Kaylee spoke up.

"When am I going to be able to dance in a feis?"

Miss Helen glanced quickly at her pupil but mostly kept her eyes on the neighborhood. "I am not a doctor."

Kaylee hated it when people used "I am not a doctor" to avoid giving her a direct answer.

"That's good," said Kaylee gruffly, "because the doctors keep saying I should quit dance and take up swimming or biking."

Miss Helen said nothing to this. Heaped atop Kaylee's frustration with her grudging progress at dance, the leg pain she felt as she trudged back to Miss Helen's, and the smell of cigarettes, the old woman's silence merely intensified her anger.

Kaylee pressed on. "Do you think I'll be ready by August?"

"I don't know," said Miss Helen, who momentarily seemed to have forgotten about the joys that a second cigarette might entail. "There is still much work to be done."

Kaylee slowed and glared at her teacher. "I've been working. For months. Ever since I got out of that stupid wheelchair."

"I know," said Miss Helen, but the tiny storm beside her roared on.

"I'm going to be a junior in high school! If I can't dance at Oireachtas in November, then I won't be able to qualify for the North American Championships in July! So how am I going to qualify for Worlds? After I graduate from high school, I'll probably go off to college somewhere and that'll be the end of my competitive career! I've been limping around for almost a year, trying to get back! What if another year goes by and I'm no better off?"

Miss Helen paused in front of a fenced yard in which two tiny girls chanted "Jack and Jill went up the hill to fetch a pail of water" as they danced around their brightly-colored plastic toys. How effortless they made it seem, full of joy, never giving a thought to bones in their legs that had been snapped and splintered and knitted together with metal and rivets. Their glee depressed Kaylee even more.

"You are still getting stronger, but you were hurt very badly," said Miss Helen. "Maybe you should not think about the World Championships and Oireachtas so much."

"But thinking about it keeps me going!" argued Kaylee.

"It also makes you so angry," observed Miss Helen.

Jack fell down and broke his crown . . .

"I thought you always wanted me to go to Worlds," cried Kaylee. "I thought that was why you pushed me so hard!"

Miss Helen said nothing.

"Why did you change your mind?" asked Kaylee hoarsely.

"What?"

"About coaching me. If it's not about getting to Worlds, then why are you here?"

Kaylee detected a look in her teacher's eyes that she had never seen before. Was it pity? Desperation? Fear? Or something else?

"It's not important," said Miss Helen quietly.

"You work me harder than anyone else," Kaylee continued. "You've always gotten me to do things I never thought I could do. And you were supposed to make the difference this time, too!"

"No," said Miss Helen. "*You* must make the difference. You expect too much of me."

Kaylee scowled even more menacingly. "Then I guess I'm just wasting my time coming here three times a week!" She turned and stomped off down the sidewalk, arriving alone at Miss Helen's house where her friend, Riley, waited in his car. Mrs. O'Shay usually dropped her daughter at Miss Helen's and then hurried to work at her store, leaving Riley to bring Kaylee home. She climbed into the front passenger seat, tossed her pack into the backseat and slammed the door.

"You don't look happy," said Riley.

Kaylee stared straight ahead. "Just drive!"

They proceeded in silence for awhile as Riley maneuvered through the residential side streets and then onto a main road that took them to the nicer western suburbs.

"I thought maybe we could stop for a burger on the way home," he suggested, speaking mostly to the back of Kaylee's head, for she had begun staring out the side window.

"I'm not hungry."

Silence returned for a few moments, and then: "Maybe just an order of fries?"

This time Kaylee sighed loudly. "I told you I'm not hungry." Couldn't he see that she was upset? Couldn't he understand that she needed some time to mend?

It was quiet again, but Kaylee could hear Riley grunting and fidgeting. Finally, he asked, "Maybe you'd just like to stop for a Coke then?"

This time she swung around toward him. "What's the big deal with you and food—"

Then she saw something. She hadn't noticed it at first, for everything had seemed so natural: his brilliant smile, the wavy brown hair, his dark eyes.

"Oh my God!"

Now the smile broadened. He pulled into the parking lot of a convenience store, stopped the car and faced her fully. "Huh? Pretty nice?" He pointed towards his face with both thumbs.

Since the accident, Riley had worn a patch to cover the space where his right eye had formerly been. Today, however, the patch was gone, and there was his beautiful brown eye. He looked just as he had before the tragedy.

"I wanted to surprise you," said Riley. "I've been trying out different prosthetics for a few months, but this is brand new. It uses magnets or something so that my new fake eye even moves right along with the real one!"

Kaylee could tell how excited he was, but she could not share it. Her dance world was in shambles. She could not satisfactorily complete even a single step, and she had just tossed away her last hope of ever competing again by walking away from Miss Helen. But here was Riley, who had also been injured in the accident a year ago, yet he had been able to throw away his crutches and resume dancing months ago. And now, with his new eye, he was perfect, something Kaylee would never be.

"I'm sorry," she said, facing away and leaning against the passenger window. "Just take me home."

"I don't believe this!" She assumed Riley was staring at the back of her head again. "I thought you'd be happy for me! Ever since the accident, I've been there for you whenever you needed me. I've tried to help you with everything! I can't believe you're being so selfish now!"

"Just please take me home!"

Not another word was spoken during the twenty-minute trip. Even when Kaylee exited the car, she did not turn to look at Riley who, after a moment, drove slowly away. As she walked toward the small Cape Cod which the O'Shays called home, she noticed both cars in the driveway. That was unusual on a Monday. At this time of day, her mother was usually at the Stitchin' Kitchen, the combination fabric store and coffee shop she operated in downtown Rosemary. And despite that it was late June, her father still had plenty of maintenance issues to keep him busy as a school custodian. Then she noticed a third car parked at the curb and recognized it as belonging to the parents of her best friend from school, Jackie Kizobu.

She broke into a run. Something was wrong. And as she burst into the kitchen, she saw them—Jackie and Mrs. Kizobu, her father, her brother Will—sitting or standing around the small table, her mother seated at the center, their eyes weary.

"Where's Grandma?"

Tom O'Shay stepped forward, gathered his daughter into his arms.

And Jill came tumbling after.

Two

Her grandmother's funeral was a blur of tears, grim embraces and organ music. Dozens of Grandma Birdsall's friends as well as some distant relatives whose existence Kaylee had scarcely been aware of made the slow march past the coffin. It surprised Kaylee that so many of her own friends came to pay their respects as well, including Caitlin Hubbard from dance. The one friend she did not see, however, was Riley.

Was this payback for that day in the car in front of Miss Helen's house? Would Riley really do something like that?

She hardly heard the eulogy. As the minister recounted Kitty Birdsall's days on the planet, littering the account with illustrations of her kindness, Kaylee drifted into her own remembrances.

Her grandmother teaching her to sew . . .

Secretly paying for her Irish dance lessons . . .

Sewing a beautiful school dress for her during Kaylee's first year of dance . . .

And when Kaylee had gone to visit after her grandmother had been hospitalized with chest pains or fainting spells, Grandma Birdsall would always be more concerned with Kaylee's well-being than her own.

That was what made it so hard. Her grandmother had been so good. And in return, Kaylee knew she had been a rotten granddaughter. Her guilt obscured everything else during the memorial ceremony.

She thought about the occasions when her grandmother had wanted to spend time with her—but Kaylee had made up excuses about being tired or having to hang out with friends.

She thought about how she had let the door knock down Grandma Birdsall at the doctor's office after Brittany Hall had splashed mud on her shirt.

But mostly, she thought of her beautiful, green Irish dance solo dress. Her grandmother had promised to make the dream dress for Kaylee, but her ill health and the side effects from her medicines had made the task seem to take forever. And Kaylee remembered the occasions when she had complained about the slow progress. Sometimes with a single sarcastic comment.

And now those comments stung *her*. A teacher had once told the class that sarcasm was a boomerang. Now she understood.

She knew in her heart that Grandma Birdsall had been working as quickly as she was able.

Poor Will, who was a year younger than Kaylee, seemed just as distraught. He had been there when Grandma Birdsall had suffered the heart attack. He had come down from his room where he had been scouring the universe of malevolent alien life forms using the latest video gaming technology. He had run out of cereal and, as he scrounged for a fresh box in the kitchen, Grandma Birdsall had come out of her room looking dazed.

"I'm not feeling quite right."

That was all she had said. Then she had sat down in a big, soft chair in the living room and died. Will had called 9-1-1 and the paramedics arrived in minutes. However, the doctor said later that no one could have saved her.

"Her heart, the way it was," he had told them, "she was fortunate to have lived to the age of seventy-six."

The day after the funeral, they buried Grandma Birdsall next to her second husband in the Rosemary cemetery. Her first husband, Grandpa Joey, had been cremated, and his ashes had supposedly been taken to Ireland and scattered in the street in front of a pub he had once visited.

As difficult as it was to watch everyone hanging their heads near her grandmother's grave, it was even harder for Kaylee to look at her aunt's tombstone nearby. Aunt Kat had died almost three years earlier, but Kaylee still felt a heaviness in her chest whenever she remembered her aunt's smile, her passion for life, her conviction that she would beat the cancer.

Kat had been fun, athletic and optimistic. Keep trying to reach the top of the mountain. That was her motto.

Yeah, right, thought Kaylee.

After a luncheon at the church, the O'Shays made the quiet ride home. Kaylee rode with Jackie, who had recently gotten her driver's license. The two girls went to Kaylee's room where Kaylee dug out photographs of family events that had included her grandmother. They talked about soccer, too, which took up a good part of Jackie's summer. She was on a team that traveled throughout Wisconsin and Illinois for games.

"It's nice being on a team without Brittany Hall for a change," said Jackie. "It's quite the thrill when someone actually passes you the ball when you're open!"

Kaylee smiled, remembering the awful things she had endured at Brittany's hands both on and off the soccer pitch. Brittany had purposely collided with Kaylee during a soccer contest and had broken her leg, causing her to miss her first feis. In middle school, Brittany had hidden Kaylee's school dress so that she was unable to dance in the talent show. She had even taken two hundred dollars from Kaylee in exchange for a solo costume, and then had stood by while her evil friend Heather had destroyed it. The list went on.

"Too bad she's such a good soccer player," said Jackie. "Maybe someday the weight of her enormous ego will slow her down so much that she'll get cut from the high school team. That would be sweet!"

"You'd still be stuck with Heather," Kaylee reminded her, referring to Brittany's best friend. "She's as bad if not worse."

In addition to being a good soccer player, Brittany was also a Champs Irish dancer. *Not that it matters much anymore*, Kaylee thought. At one time she had hoped to compete with Brittany on the Championship stage. Now that Kaylee had turned away from Miss Helen, any hope of a comeback seemed impossible. Even with Miss Helen's help, Kaylee had not seen much improvement. *I guess I was just fooling myself.*

But Aunt Kat's words kept coming back to her. *Keep trying to reach the top of the mountain.*

She wanted to cry out, "Where did it get you, Aunt Kat? You kept trying and now you're dead!" But she held it inside.

Jackie noticed the slight tremble in her friend's shoulders. "Are you okay?"

Kaylee nodded, but nothing was okay. Nothing would ever be okay again.

After Jackie left, Kaylee found the house quiet. She assumed her brother and parents had fallen asleep, despite that it was the middle of the day. Earlier, the phone had rung at regular intervals—friends of her mother's who had not been able to attend the funeral, offering their condolences. Each time the phone had sounded, Kaylee had held her breath, wondering whether her name would be called. *Kaylee, it's Riley.* He would tell her how sorry he was about her grandmother, how incredible circumstances had prevented him from coming to the funeral, and so he was calling now to let her know that he cared. She would understand completely. *You had no choice. No one could blame you. You'd have needed super powers.* She would apologize for her self-absorbed tantrum in the car. He would forgive her and say something wonderful and funny, and then he would tell her that he . . . he . . .

But the call did not come.

Kaylee herself felt exhausted now that the Jackie adrenaline rush had dissipated. Her mother had remarked about how emotionally draining the ordeal had been on all of them. As Kaylee sat in her room, staring into the thin atmosphere of this new world, listening, the house seemed quiet in a way it hadn't before. Her grandmother had never been a noisy person, and it had been easy to forget that she was nearby. Now, however, it was like sound behaved differently without Kitty Birdsall in the house, making the stillness more total.

Kaylee got up, stood for a moment in her bedroom doorway, gazing the short distance toward her grandmother's room. She felt drawn towards it, as if she might catch some fleeting wisp of her grandmother's essence before it drifted out of this world entirely, perhaps breathe it in, feel its warmth, hear it whisper "I love you" one last time.

In the room, however, she found her mother—who she suspected had been drawn there for similar reasons.   Mrs. O'Shay sat on the bed, taking in the remnants of her own mother's life: sewing machines, stacks of fabric scraps, boxes of memorabilia, knick-knacks, dozens of patterns.   All of these lined the walls.

"I keep expecting her to shuffle through this door, sit in her chair and start wondering where she put the last project she was working on," said her mother with a sad smile.

Kaylee sat next to her and leaned her forehead onto Bethany O'Shay's breast. "It's not fair. She was so nice to everyone."

Mrs. O'Shay squeezed her daughter.

"I wish I'd been nicer to Grandma," said Kaylee, her voice trembling slightly.

"What do you mean?" asked her mother.

Kaylee explained how she had been impatient with her grandmother and had sometimes avoided sewing by going off with friends.

"Kaylee, your grandmother understood," said Bethany O'Shay kindly. "She wasn't old all of her life. At one time, she was a teenage girl. She knew how important friends are in your life. Many times she told me she felt blessed to live with us because of the time she *did* get to spend with you. She knew that most grandmothers don't have it that lucky."

A tear slid down Kaylee's cheek. "Now I miss her even more!"

Mrs. O'Shay kissed the top of her daughter's head.

By the time Kaylee woke, it was late afternoon. She realized that she had fallen asleep on her grandmother's bed. Her mother had left, perhaps for a nap of her own, and so Kaylee sat on the bed alone.

She rose and moved to the bureau. Atop it sat pictures of her grandmother's important memories and people. School photos of Kaylee and Will—at various ages—were mixed into this collection. On a fabric pile, Kaylee found a quilt square. Was this one of the squares Kaylee herself had stitched two years earlier when she had spent Sunday afternoons with her grandmother?

Now she turned around slowly, taking in the whole room. Where would all of this go? Would her mother take the fabrics, patterns and sewing machines to the Stitchin' Kitchen? Would they load up the car and donate the items to charity? Or would her mother let the room stay as it was?

Kaylee opened the louvered door of the closet. One side contained hanging clothes, but the other was shelves filled with still more material, patterns and projects. One item caught her eye: a flattish, white box with KAYLEE written on it.

She wondered if she was ready to handle whatever might be inside. Kaylee suspected the box contained photographs and other memorabilia: Kaylee's kindergarten picture, a photo of Kaylee's first soccer game, an art project from second grade, a baby tooth that the "tooth fairy" had supposedly spirited away.

On the other hand, she considered the possibility that it might contain sewing projects that Kaylee had worked on years ago. She felt that seeing these would make her insides twist, for the projects would most likely be unfinished—a consequence of her lack of enthusiasm for the world of needle and thread. And now they would forever remain unfinished.

She was about to pull the box from the shelf when her mother's voice startled her from behind.

"You're awake."

Kaylee whirled around. "I was just—looking at Grandma's things. Remembering."

Mrs. O'Shay nodded. "We'll be doing a lot of remembering when we go through this room. But not for awhile. There's no hurry, and I need some time before I'm strong enough."

Kaylee nodded sympathetically.

"I've made some sandwiches," said Mrs. O'Shay. "Then I thought maybe we'd go out for ice cream afterwards."

"Ice cream?" There was rarely money in the O'Shay family budget for junk food outings.

Mrs. O'Shay noticed the confusion in her daughter's eyes. "I think Grandma would have wanted us to do something to cheer ourselves up. She wouldn't have wanted us to mope around thinking sad thoughts. There was a lot of fun and goodness in her life that we should be remembering."

At this particular moment, it did not seem to Kaylee that the words "fun" and "goodness" would apply to anything within the O'Shay household ever again. Nonetheless, she nodded to appease her mother and shuffled out to the kitchen.

"To Grandma Birdsall," said Kaylee's father, lifting his chocolate cone like a champagne glass. Will, Mrs. O'Shay and Kaylee tapped their cones against his and then sat back in the booth to enjoy the sweet coolness and their memories.

The ice cream shop in downtown Rosemary reminded Kaylee of her Aunt Kat, who had liked to treat herself to a cone after an especially hard run. Now it would remind her of Grandma Birdsall, too.

"Let's each share our favorite Grandma Birdsall memory," said Mrs. O'Shay. She tried to sound upbeat, but Kaylee could tell she was still exhausted.

Will chimed in first. "She made me pancakes on my birthday. And gave me a card with money, which I used to buy *Invader Quest*, the coolest video game ever!"

"Remember a few years ago on Halloween?" asked Mr. O'Shay. "She was determined that she was going to hand out the candy, and she was going to do it in costume. So she dressed up as a witch, complete with green makeup for her skin. And the first little girl to come to the door asked her if she was supposed to be a frog!"

Everyone laughed, and then Kaylee's mother offered a memory. "When I was a little girl, she was always there for me. I was sick one time and she missed work three days in a row to sit at home with me."

After a long pause, it was Kaylee's turn. She knew right away what her memory would be. "She made my first Irish dance dress. And it was perfect!"

"Thanks for the memories, Mom," said Mrs. O'Shay, the ghost of a smile on her face. They all raised their half-eaten cones again and tapped them together, except for Will, who had already finished his.

Kaylee seemed to be the slowest, and she noticed that her cone was starting to drip onto her hand. "I'm going to get some more napkins," she announced, and slid out of the booth to head for the condiment counter. The soft drink machine also stood in this area, and as Kaylee pulled napkins from a slot in the counter, she heard a familiar voice from the booth hidden on the far side of the drink dispenser.

"We played three games yesterday and two today. It was a really intense tournament. Coach told me that there'd be college scouts and I'd probably get lots of looks."

Brittany Hall. Hearing her voice was like sprinkling chalk dust onto an ice cream cone. Kaylee found herself unsurprised that Brittany would be bragging up her own accomplishments. At first she imagined that Brittany was probably talking to Heather, her best friend and possibly the only girl at Rosemary Senior High with a blacker heart. But Heather would have known all those soccer details, since she played on the same summer team as Brittany.

It's probably Michael Black.

He was the cutest boy in the school and had been eating out of Brittany's hand for years. The frustrating part for Kaylee was that, despite her nastiness, the boys all fawned over Brittany. Even Riley had spent two hours drooling when Brittany had sat next to him—and Kaylee—at a basketball game last winter. Brittany had flirted as if she'd been a spy after a top-secret rocket fuel formula, and Riley had invited her along when he and Kaylee went out for a burger afterwards. Blonde, built like a model, and full of self-confidence, Brittany could have any boy she wanted.

Except for her brother, Will. This made Kaylee smile. Brittany had unleashed her charms on Will on several occasions, but Will only had eyes for Jackie.

Kaylee sighed. That was another story.

She might easily have returned to her seat already, but it was too big a temptation to listen to someone's conversation when hidden behind a soft drink dispenser. Especially, thought Kaylee, if that person was someone with no redeeming qualities, and if the conversation might yield information that could be used against her at some point in the future.

"Did you see my last goal?" Brittany continued. "It was a header."

Did you see my last goal? Kaylee mimicked Brittany in her head. *She's pathetic. Whichever one of her loser friends she's here with, they deserve each other.*

But the next voice froze her.

"Yeah, that was pretty cool. The goalie never had a chance."

There was no mistake. The voice belonged to Riley. But she had to make sure. Cautiously, she peered around the edge of the soft drink machine. She saw the back of his head, but it was enough.

Now the tears moistened the corners of her eyes. It hurt to know that Riley was with someone else. It hurt even more that the "someone else" was Brittany Hall.

And then a more horrible realization occurred to her.

Did you see my last goal? The question meant that Riley had been at the tournament. And Brittany had mentioned that it had been a two-day soccer tournament. That explained why Riley had not been at her grandmother's funeral yesterday. Brittany's soccer tournament had been more important to him.

She turned and made her way back to the table.

"Can we go?"

Her mother stood, drew her into a hug.

"Of course we can, sweetheart. Oh, you poor thing. It's hard on all of us. We all loved her."

Her mother had no idea that Riley and Brittany sat in a booth on the other side of the restaurant.

"As time passes, it will hurt less," continued Mrs. O'Shay. "Things will get better. You'll see."

Kaylee nodded, but nothing that had happened during the past year gave her any reason to believe her mother's words.

Three

"Werewolves, witches and vampires . . . all in one movie! This is going to be awesome!"

Caitlin giggled and grabbed Kaylee's arm as they ran the short distance from the parking lot to the theater's entrance. They paid for their tickets, splurged on the monster bucket of popcorn and settled into seats in the back row.

"I've been watching clips of this movie on-line for three months!" said Caitlin. "It's supposed to be the biggest blockbuster of the summer!"

Kaylee wrinkled her nose at the silent screen. "Just what is a *blockbuster* anyway? What does busting blocks have to do with movies?"

Caitlin lobbed a puff of popcorn at Kaylee, hitting her on the forehead, and both girls exploded in laughter.

I haven't laughed like this in a long time, thought Kaylee. But Caitlin, her best friend from Trean Gaoth Academy of Irish Dance, always seemed to find a way to make it fun.

Why does life have to be so hard? Kaylee wondered. *Why can't it be like when we were ten?* There were no boy problems, no driver's licenses, no worries about qualifying for—she could hardly bear to think about it—the World Championships in Ireland. The biggest worry had been whether or not the next feis might be the one at which you earned your solo dress. How important it had seemed, the most important thing in the world.

But now the world was so much bigger.

"Did you read the first book?" asked Caitlin, snapping her friend back into the current pleasant moment.

Kaylee blinked. "Book?"

"*Beautiful Hopelessness,*" said Caitlin, giving her friend the "duh" expression. "I've read all five. *Beautiful Hopelessness, Beautifully Monstrous, Beauty and the Corpse, Beautiful Screams* and *Breathlessly Beautiful.*"

"I've only read the first two," said Kaylee, noticing now that the theater was more than half full.

"That's perfect," said Caitlin, all smiles. "Those are the books they based this movie on. I can't wait! How long now?"

Kaylee checked her watch. "Still ten minutes. We got here tons early."

Caitlin made a pouty face, but then she brightened almost immediately. "That gives us more time to catch up. It seems like I've hardly seen you at all this past year. I wish your parents would let you go online more often."

Now Kaylee scowled. "My mom doesn't trust those social networking sites."

"Maybe they could get you a cell phone. Then at least we could text."

"Cell phones are expensive," observed Kaylee. "Until they're free, you probably won't be seeing them at the O'Shay house."

Caitlin jingled her car keys in front of her friend's nose. "Well, now that I've got my driver's license, I can come pick you up any time!"

Kaylee smiled. Getting a driver's license. That was another way that last year's accident had left her behind most of her classmates. It's hard to practice driving a car when you're in a wheelchair or on crutches, Kaylee observed.

Three-quarters of the theater's seats were now occupied. Only five minutes separated them from the big event—assuming the surplus adrenaline in Caitlin's bloodstream did not send her into a coma.

"We should have gotten Raisinettes!" Caitlin blurted.

Kaylee laughed, covering her mouth to avoid losing her popcorn. She did not know why her friend's Raisinettes comment had seemed so funny. That's just how it was with Caitlin. Everything made her laugh.

Kaylee sighed. "I really miss hanging out with you. I was hoping that I'd be better by this time."

"You mean from the accident?" asked Caitlin.

Kaylee smiled weakly, nodded. "I mean, I know I was hurt pretty badly."

"Girl, I cried when I came to see you that first time. All the way home. You had bandages on everything! Your head was busted, and your ribs, there were a zillion pins in your leg . . ."

"But I never thought it would take so long," continued Kaylee. "When I was eleven and broke my leg, I was in a cast for six weeks and then everything was back to normal. I thought it would be like that."

Caitlin's eyes widened. "You could have died in that crash! You were a human jigsaw puzzle. If you thought you were going to be good-as-new in six weeks, they must have been giving you WAY too many pain drugs!"

Kaylee laughed. "I guess. But I was hoping that I'd at least be healed by the start of summer vacation so that we could dance together at feiseanna."

Now Caitlin's expression grew more serious. "Yeah. That would have been nice. That would have been really nice."

"Now that I walked out on Miss Helen, I don't know if I'll ever dance competitively again," said Kaylee matter-of-factly. "It's not how I expected things to end."

Caitlin sighed. "I know how you feel."

Kaylee eyed her friend skeptically, emitted a nervous giggle. "Yeah, right. You're going to be dancing at Worlds someday."

Now Caitlin shook her head. "No I'm not. I'll be dancing my last feis in August."

For a moment, Kaylee felt as though the padded seat had been snatched from beneath her, and she steadied herself with the armrests for reassurance. "Are you serious?"

Her friend smiled, shrugged, as if to imply that it was no big deal. They both knew differently.

"It's been fun. But I think I'm ready. I think I've gone about as far as I can go."

"But," argued Kaylee, "you're in PC! You're only one level away from Champs! You're so close to the top!"

Caitlin shook her head. "No. You were close to the top. You won the PC competition at the Gateway Feis last year. Everybody could see that you were going to win another one before too long. And then you'd be in Champs. But I just barely made it into PC. I've danced in nine feiseanna as a PC, and I still haven't placed in the top half!"

A terrible heaviness seemed to be growing inside of Kaylee, and she struggled to keep her voice level. "But I know how hard you work. Soon you'll be—"

Caitlin interrupted with another shake of her head. "I don't have your determination. I don't work nearly as hard. You were . . . psychotic!" Caitlin smiled at her own word choice, but when Kaylee did not return the smile, she plunged on. "I'm just not a Champs dancer. Besides, I've been getting more involved with history club at school. And I was thinking about trying out for the school play. Those things are going to take a lot of time, you know."

Kaylee nodded quietly.

Caitlin smiled suddenly and gave her shoulder a shove. "Hey, it's not like this changes anything. We're still best friends for life, right?"

Kaylee nodded again.

"And like you said, *you* can't dance competitively. So it's not like either of us will miss each other at feiseanna."

This time, Kaylee did not nod, but mustered a half-hearted smile.

"I guess it's time for both of us just to be normal teenagers," said Caitlin, as if she had shed an enormous weight or guilty secret. "There's lots of fun things to do instead of always practicing for Irish dancing!"

She leaned toward Kaylee and the two hugged, squeezing the monster bucket so that popcorn exploded onto both of their laps. Caitlin broke into laughter, and after a moment, Kaylee laughed, too.

But it was the sort of laugh a person laughs in order to convince others that she is enjoying the moment. There was no joy or humor at its heart.

Caitlin now began telling her friend what the fall play at Paavo High School would probably be. But Kaylee hardly heard a word. In her mind, she imagined the future without Irish dance. She had given up soccer for dance. In the process, she had upset her father's dream that his little girl would one day be a star. Instead, she had devoted thousands of hours to training herself to be a champion dancer, often practicing on her own.

But somehow, in the last year, everything had changed. Yes, the accident had been horrible. But it was more than that. She had resolved to work as hard as necessary to get back, to resume her place as a rising star of Irish dance.

Yet, at every turn, she had been beaten down and frustrated. If it had been only one or two things, she could have dealt with it. But it seemed that every setback relayed the same message: No.

There had been the accident itself. Not just an accident. An awful, crippling accident that did not simply break bones. It crushed them.

And sweet, good-natured Riley—she had driven him out of the picture. Now he was apparently seeing Brittany Hall, her evil nemesis, who would always be a better dancer than Kaylee.

Miss Helen might have helped her get back into dance, but Kaylee had walked away from her.

And because of her grandmother's death, Kaylee's solo dress would never be finished.

If Kaylee needed a final sign to show her the Fates had decreed that she was done with dance, Caitlin's announcement was it.

Suddenly, the screen burst into vibrant images of coming attractions.

"This is going to be so great!" Caitlin whispered loudly, giving Kaylee's forearm a squeeze.

Kaylee did not smile. In fact, she was not sure how she should feel. Everything had changed. But maybe change was good. Maybe she had been fighting a battle that could not be won. Perhaps she had been wasting hundreds of hours that she could have devoted to school and friends and . . .

And building a more solid relationship with Riley.

But she loved Irish dance. Didn't she? Or was that all in the past?

She did not know what to think. And so Kaylee sat there in the dark, watching the bright ghosts on the screen, feeling like a ghost herself. For the past year, she had been haunting her old life—there but not really there.

Now she knew it was time to let go.

Goodbye, Trean Gaoth Academy.

Goodbye, Miss Helen and feiseanna and beautiful solo dresses.

Goodbye Ireland.

Four

Three years earlier, Kaylee had sat on the Paavo College athletic field next to her Aunt Kat, watching the Fourth of July fireworks show explode around her. As with everything that had to do with Aunt Kat, this event brought back both pleasant and painful memories.

Kaylee could think of no one who had inspired her more. Aunt Kat had oozed confidence. In high school, she had been a track champion. She and Kaylee had run in a two-mile race together.

Only three years ago.

"If you work hard, you can overcome any obstacle," Kaylee had confidently told her friend April Lee that summer. "That's what my aunt taught me."

But Aunt Kat had not been able to outrun cancer.

"This is going to be fun!" said Jackie with a shiver, intentionally bumping shoulders with Kaylee as the two walked toward the athletic fields. "I love fireworks."

Kaylee mustered a smile and tried to shake away the memories. Under her right arm she carried a folded blanket that the two girls could spread on the ground. Jackie—who had driven the two of them from Rosemary—carried a second blanket for the two of them to huddle beneath in case the temperature dropped too drastically during the show.

"Here's a good spot!" called Jackie, halting abruptly and pointing at the ground. Kaylee spread the blanket and the two dropped down, watching others set up camp nearby.

Just like at a feis, thought Kaylee. Then she rolled her eyes at herself.

"Should be starting in about five minutes," said Jackie, consulting her watch. "This is so cool! We haven't hung out in, like, *forever!*"

"It's not my fault you're insane." A passerby might have interpreted the comment as an insult, but Jackie simply laughed.

"Because I do things with Will?"

Kaylee wrinkled her nose at the idea. "He's a cereal addict."

Jackie shrugged. "There's always rehab."

"And he's obsessed with video games."

"He never mentions them when he's with me," said Jackie, her smile growing wide. "He seems to have *different* obsessions."

Kaylee grimaced. "Oh, that's so gross! Don't ever talk like that when I'm around! That's my brother!"

Jackie laughed. "And best of all, he's an amazing soccer player. Not quite in Angelo Zizzo's class, but pretty amazing anyway," she said, referencing the pro soccer player whose posters papered the walls of Jackie's bedroom.

A sudden flash from above, followed by a loud pop drew their eyes to the night sky. Oohs and ahs erupted from the crowd. More explosions followed, sometimes sounding hollow and distant, and other times giving the impression that the two were camped in a war zone.

"That one was like a giant green and blue daisy!" cried Jackie. Kaylee smiled, stretched out on her back atop the blanket. She wished the night could never end. The fireworks were beautiful, breathtaking. The weather was perfect—cool enough to make her feel fresh and alert, warm enough so that she did not need the second blanket. And Jackie was there beside her. Jackie, who had been with her through all the years of soccer, who had giggled her way through a hundred sleepovers, who was one of the few girls brave enough to talk smack to Brittany Hall—even though Jackie cut a less-than-intimidating figure, weighing in at little more than one hundred pounds.

"Ooh, I love those squiggly ones! It's like they're alive!"

Now Kaylee laughed quietly. Was there any kind of fireworks that Jackie did not like?

Pop. Pop. Bam. Pop-pop-pop. Bam.

"This is *way* better than the fireworks they had at halftime of the Homecoming football game last fall!" said Jackie as the sky continued to erupt in electric color.

Kaylee remembered the game with very mixed feelings. She had been in a wheelchair at the time, hardly able to care for herself, the scars from the accident still fresh. But Riley had sat next to her in the bleachers. And they had kissed.

And Brittany Hall had seen it.

Kaylee smiled at this memory. But now the situation was reversed. Brittany Hall was prettier than Kaylee, was a better dancer, excelled at every sport and scored an eleven on the ten-point teenager popularity scale. And now she apparently had Riley, too. Kaylee felt a pain in her stomach, but it quickly subsided, and she tried to focus on the fireworks in the present moment.

Spiff. Pop-pop. Bam.

"What do you think junior year is going to be like?" she suddenly asked.

Without taking her eyes off the sky, Jackie replied, "Boring, pointless, occasionally interrupted by brilliant and exciting soccer-related moments. A lot like sophomore year was."

Kaylee knew that her friend was joking. Sort of. Yet, Jackie's vision of the upcoming school year bothered her. Kaylee had not danced in a feis in almost a year. Would probably never dance in one again. This admission made her shudder. What she wanted to hear—what she *needed* to hear— was that something else could matter.

"But Homecoming will be fun," offered Kaylee. "The parade . . . and we'll probably go to the dance, won't we?"

"I guess if Will asks me. Which he probably will."

Bam. Bam. Pop-pop-foosh.

Kaylee had imagined that she and Jackie would buy single tickets to the Homecoming dance, get all dressed up, dance the night away in the gymnasium, and then have a woefully misnamed sleepover, at which they would finally collapse into exhausted comas at five in the morning. But, of course, there was Will.

Bam.

And with Riley out of the picture, Kaylee had no one.

Bam. Bam.

And suddenly, Kaylee saw the long year stretching out in front of her, bleak and lonely. She felt herself flailing like a swimmer lunging for the rescue float.

"The football games are always a good time!"

Jackie grunted. "I just went last year because Will was going. He probably won't be able to go to many of them this year."

This statement puzzled Kaylee. "Why not?"

Poof-poof-bam.

"Duh! Will's like a tiny, non-Italian Angelo Zizzo! He's probably going to make varsity soccer!"

Now Kaylee understood. It was true that there had been talk that Will might be moved up to the varsity soccer team this year, even though he was only a sophomore. And the varsity sometimes played games on Friday nights—same as the football team.

Kaboom.

Somewhere deep inside of Kaylee there existed a rational core that knew the school year would have its pleasant moments, perhaps even scores of unexpected ones. But that core seemed far from the surface as she lay on her back, now hardly seeing the fantastic fireworks display above, smothered beneath the image of Riley and Brittany, beneath the thought of Caitlin dancing her last feis, beneath the scowling face of Miss Helen and especially beneath her own pain and physical shortcomings. And now even Jackie seemed to occupy a diminishing place in her universe, a universe whose stars seemed to flicker for a moment as if teasing, and then blink out.

"The entire world doesn't have to revolve around soccer, you know!"

Bam. Bam.

Rational thinking had nothing to do with this statement. *Of course* Jackie's whole world revolved around soccer—just as Kaylee's had revolved around Irish dance.

"What?"

Kaylee could not stop herself. "It's like everything's soccer, soccer, soccer!" She spat out the words as if they were bitter almonds.

Bam. Bam. Bam.

Now Jackie turned her head from the light show in the sky for the first time. The reflection of the exploding rockets flashed in her eyes.

"Yeah, I'm just awful. Wish I could be perfect, like you. You would never obsess about anything like that."

Kaylee felt her face redden and was thankful for the darkness. "It's different."

"How is obsessing over dance any different than soccer?" Jackie shot back. "Just because you pay a bazillion dollars for a dress?"

Boom-boom-wham.

"It's just different. Anybody can do soccer."

A silence grew between them, although the cacophony in the sky continued unabated. Both girls stared up into the chaos, which suddenly inspired no emotion, and then Jackie finally spoke.

"You know, if—" She stopped herself.

Kaylee turned toward her. "What?"

"Nothing. Forget it."

"Tell me!"

Woosh—bam.

Jackie sighed in resignation. "If you had stayed with soccer instead of Irish dance, everything would have been different!"

"Different?"

Jackie spoke bitterly. "You would have never had the accident!"

Kabam. Kabam.

This idea struck as if one of the rockets had plunged into Kaylee's heart. She had never thought it all the way through before, but Jackie was right. If Kaylee had continued to play soccer, so many things would have turned out differently. Most importantly, she would not have been coming home from Kenosha last August, because she would not have been dancing at the Gateway Feis. She would never have met Riley, and so she would not have been in his car. They would not have stopped for ice cream, pulled back onto the road and then been hit by the drunk driver in the truck.

Today Kaylee would be strong and whole and free from pain.

The realization hit her hard. Kaylee rolled to her feet and began to run.

"Where are you going?" Jackie called after her, but Kaylee did not reply, nor did she stop. With no destination in mind, nothing except the need to be in motion, Kaylee weaved between the tightly-knit islands of blankets and lawn chairs, like a soldier in mad retreat while an air battle raged overhead. The concentration of blankets thinned gradually, and Kaylee found herself crossing a street, cutting through someone's yard, then across another street. Her lungs burned and the pain in her legs was almost intolerable She now veered onto a sidewalk, stumbled on the uneven segments, flailed at the air and pushed ahead, taking another turn at the corner, and then another. Fatigue finally slowed her, as did the growing, grinding pain in her right leg. As she fell into a panting walk, Kaylee emerged into a dark, open area which she guessed was a small parking lot. She had crossed half of it when a fireworks explosion from Paavo College momentarily lit the scene.

Kaylee gasped. She stood in front of the old, converted bowling alley that for years had been home to Trean Gaoth Academy, her Irish dance school. Had some cruel coincidence drawn Kaylee to this place, she wondered? Or at the subconscious level, had she recognized the streets and landmarks that would guide her to the one spot that seemed to be at the heart of every one of her great dreams—as well as many of her greatest sorrows? Kaylee did not know, but the emotion of the night and of the place suddenly overwhelmed her and she sat on the front steps—steps long ago swept clean of Miss Helen's cigarette stubs, swept clean of Kaylee's championship dreams.

Overhead, the fireworks grand finale lit the sky with dazzling, simultaneous explosions that sent wave after wave of color onto the treetops, buildings and asphalt. Kaylee scarcely noticed the celebration as she sat on the steps of the darkened, locked building and cried.

Five

The drive home from Paavo seemed to take forever. Unfortunately, it had not.

After the fireworks, Kaylee had made her way back to Paavo College at a much less-frenzied pace than she had left. Most of the hundreds of cars had exited the parking area. She had found Jackie, who had been in a panic, worrying over Kaylee's whereabouts and whether she had any intention of returning. Upon discovering that Kaylee was unharmed, Jackie's mood had quickly changed to anger. The two had argued, and then an uncomfortable silence had descended on the drive home.

Nothing could be worse than this, thought Kaylee.

She was wrong.

"You are so grounded," said Mrs. O'Shay as her daughter walked through the front door. The calmness of this declaration sent a shiver up Kaylee's spine. Her father sat silently beside his wife on the sofa, his expression stern, saying little. He did not need to. Mrs. O'Shay let loose.

"Jackie waited. And then she searched for you for half an hour. I hope you realize how upset you made her!"

Kaylee did realize. It made her feel worse.

"She didn't know what to do," Mrs. O'Shay continued, "and so she finally called me. I had your father ready to drive to Paavo to help look for you when Jackie called again to say you had come back. Do you realize that I almost called the Paavo police?"

Kaylee stood there taking it. "I didn't mean to upset everybody."

"Well, what do you think is going to happen when you run off in the middle of the night?"

"It wasn't the middle of the night," muttered Kaylee. She knew she should have said nothing, that any rebuttal on her part would only worsen and prolong the agony, but the words seemed to tumble out of their own volition.

"Don't talk back, young lady," Mr. O'Shay said sternly, his first contribution.

"When you're sixteen years old, eleven-thirty is the middle of the night!" hissed Mrs. O'Shay. "And in a city like Paavo…"

Again, Kaylee could not help herself. "Paavo's not a city. It isn't any more dangerous than Rosemary."

"Stop it!" cried Mrs. O'Shay fiercely, causing Kaylee to jump. "If something would have happened to you, I don't know what I would have done!"

Something did happen to me, thought Kaylee. *Almost a year ago. And I still don't know what to do.*

"You can forget about any plans you've made," stated Mrs. O'Shay grimly. "If it's fun, cross it off your summer calendar. I don't think you realize how upset with you I am right now!"

Kaylee thought she had a pretty good idea. Then Mrs. O'Shay stood, as did her father a half-second later. The two turned to head off to bed. However, Mrs. O'Shay turned back almost immediately and gathered her daughter into a fierce hug, which surprised Kaylee. Then she found herself alone in the silent O'Shay kitchen, feeling as defeated and alone as ever in her lifetime.

No, that was not exactly true, she decided. Not alone. Her mother had hugged her. No matter what Kaylee did—good or bad—that hug was always there.

She walked toward her room, realizing how badly she had blown it tonight. Kaylee was grounded until—well, probably until adulthood. And now Jackie hated her, and that was big, since Kaylee's circle of friends had seemed to be shrinking even prior to this awful night. And sitting in the parking lot at Trean Gaoth had only served to remind Kaylee of her most maddening loss.

But the hug . . . *I'm not alone.*

However, as Kaylee passed her grandmother's room, the familiar pain of her loss seemed to suggest otherwise. If Grandma Birdsall were alive, Kaylee felt sure that she would have waited up and would have asked her granddaughter to come into her room. Kaylee would have told her all about her troubles and her mistakes, and Grandma Birdsall would have listened, providing a soft, lilac-scented shoulder for her tears. *I miss you Grandma.* Kaylee drifted toward the darkened room, switched on the light. *Maybe this was all a bad dream. Maybe Grandma will be there in bed, and she'll smile and . . .*

But the light showed an empty bed, and the room possessed that eerie stillness that it never had when Grandma Birdsall had been alive. Her grandmother was gone and could offer no help to her granddaughter.

Still, Kaylee stepped into the room, drawn by the familiar sights: the sewing machines, fabric stacks, framed photos. She breathed in the memories, hoping that these would somehow bring her closer.

Kaylee ran her finger across the top of a framed photo of Will. Dust. And how young her brother looked, smiling through the glass. Now he was almost a man.

She turned to a pile of blue and red fabric scraps stacked atop two cardboard boxes. Where were the projects that she had worked on with her grandmother? Most had gone unfinished. Kaylee opened the closet door. More patterns, fabric scraps and boxes jammed the shelves. It looked the same as it had the day of her grandmother's funeral. Someday her mother had promised to sort through all of these things, tossing some out, giving some to charity, keeping some as treasured mementos. The task would probably take weeks.

As she scanned the remnants of her grandmother's life, the box marked KAYLEE once again caught her attention. She pulled it toward her so as to not upset other items packed densely on the shelf. Then she set it on the bed. She was curious about the contents of the box, but she also longed to find items that connected her more intimately to her grandmother, something to combat the loneliness. A quilt scrap that she had crudely stitched six years ago under the loving eye of Kitty Birdsall would mean the world to her.

She removed the lid, and what she saw made her gasp.

"My green dress!"

It was true. The dress that Kaylee had always wanted, identical to the one in Aunt Kat's sketch book, it was right there in front of her.

Kaylee slipped out of the shorts she had worn to the fireworks, carefully lifted the dress from the box and slipped it on. She now noticed a few details that needed to be finished, although they were minor items.

The dress fit beautifully.

As Kaylee stood in front of her grandmother's mirror, unable to take her eyes away, she was filled with joy and longing and even hope. Now Aunt Kat's words came back to her as she recalled their conversation when Kat lay dying in the hospital in Paavo:

"Keep your eye on the top of the mountain," whispered Kaylee.

Aunt Kat mustered a tired smile. "That's where I've always kept mine. But not everyone reaches the top, you know."

Kaylee sniffed to keep the tears away. "Then why even try?"

"Because," said her aunt, "the view keeps getting better the higher you climb."

Kaylee hesitated, and this time a tear did slide down her cheek. "I just wish we could climb together."

Aunt Kat slipped an arm around her shoulders. "Just keep climbing, Munchkin. No matter how high you climb, you won't be alone."

And Kaylee realized again that she was not alone. *Thank you, Aunt Kat. And mom.*

And thank you, Grandma!

Six

She slumped onto the church floor, exhausted.

"That is enough for today," said Miss Helen. "You are looking better each time. Getting stronger."

Perhaps this was true. Perhaps the old woman saw subtle changes that Kaylee could not perceive. After all, she was a veteran dance instructor. She had assessed the miniscule assets and myriad flaws of thousands of dancers.

On the other hand, perhaps this was just the sort of thing a coach was supposed to say, whether it was true, or whether the situation simply necessitated giving hope to the hopeless. Doomed passengers on the Titanic had probably been offered a similar message.

Kaylee had to admit that she felt less tired now, three weeks after resuming her practices with Miss Helen. She had feared the old woman might reject her plea to continue with the work. Through the years, she had gotten the impression that her old teacher expected Kaylee to give up.

Yet, when Kaylee had called to apologize—the morning after discovering her finished dress in her grandmother's closet—Miss Helen had suggested that they meet the next day. And while Miss Helen's steady diet of merciless drilling had improved her stamina, the pain—especially in Kaylee's right leg—throbbed as horrifically as it had in workouts two months earlier.

"When am I going to feel normal?" Kaylee complained to her mother one evening. "It's been almost a year!"

"Be patient," her mother replied for the hundredth time.

"Maybe this *is* normal," her father had added.

This thought terrified Kaylee.

I've just got to work harder, she told herself. And so she laced on her running shoes the next morning and headed down Cranberry Street. The pain was immediate, although not as intense at the beginning of a run or dance workout as it would be as the minutes of exercise ticked away. By the time she reached the end of the block, the pain had grown from Nagging Ache to Banging on the Leg with a Rubber Mallet.

No pain, no gain, she muttered as she rounded the corner, which took her toward Water Tower Road. The two-mile round trip excursion into a newer residential development had been one of her favorites when she had trained to run the charity race with Aunt Kat three years earlier.

Water Tower Road started as a gradual uphill, but grew steeper as it neared the cul-de-sac where the rustic landmark water tower stood.

I've got to fight through this, thought Kaylee, her pain now equivalent to having her leg slammed repeatedly in a car door.

She had not run this far since the accident. At the start of the summer, she had walked three miles to the Grant farm to visit with Mrs. Grant and to see Trooper and the other horses she had cared for two summers earlier. But walking merely stiffened her legs. The jarring nature of running brought more meaningful pain.

Maybe I've just been babying myself. She had wondered if this might be the case. But the torture she felt now was enough to bring tears to a Marine.

After what seemed a marathon, the cul-de-sac came into view. *It's only been a mile?* But still she was proud of herself, making the turn and starting her descent. Instead of diminishing her pain, though, running downhill seemed to magnify it. Now Kaylee began to emit involuntary sounds, the sort an animal struggling in a steel trap might make. Despite the warm weather, goosebumps had broken out on her arms, and with each step, a subtle wave of nausea lapped at her throat. This level of pain she had never endured, unless it had been in the early weeks after the accident—but at that time she had been heavily medicated.

Until that tree. Until that mailbox. Until that rock up ahead.

She willed herself to keep going, envisioning herself onstage at a feis, at Oireachtas, in Ireland. She could no longer think in words. Mere images, raw concepts, emotions that, at their edges, were roughly framed in dance—these were what flashed through her mind.

Finally she reached the turn onto Cranberry Street, and the notion that she might finish the entire distance flickered momentarily.

But she could not.

Instead of energizing her, something about the closeness of her goal seemed to steal away her coordination, to turn her legs into applesauce, and she collapsed onto the sidewalk.

Her breathing came in rasping pants and she convulsed several times with dry heaves. Then, gradually, the breathing slowed. The pain diminished quickly, although her legs felt like sacks of wet flour. And when she pulled herself to her feet to walk the last block home, Kaylee discovered two disturbing facts. First, both legs as well as her right elbow were bloodied where she had skidded onto the concrete. Second, upon standing, the pain in her legs returned—not completely, but more than after a typical workout.

Did I make things worse? she wondered, beginning the slow walk to her house. Even if she had not, the pain she suffered in attempting to complete even modest workouts such as this raised a grim fear.

I'll never dance in Ireland.

Four women worked quietly at sewing machines, occasionally sipping from their paper coffee cups, occasionally making light chatter with each other. Kaylee fixed price stickers to fabric bolts in the sale bin, just one of her jobs at the Stitchin' Kitchen, her mother's combination fabric store and coffee shop.

"Lots of women like coffee," her mother had said years ago when she had first opened the business. "And my customers enjoy sewing, too. Here, they can do both."

The shop rested on a side street just off of Rosemary's main business corridor in the downtown area, a comfortable old building with a worn, brick façade, large front windows and a wooden floor that would have been perfect for dancing if Kaylee could have talked her mother into letting her move the shelves, sewing machines and coffee bar. The only thing the business seemed to be missing was a profitable bottom line.

Eight years ago, Kaylee's mother had quit her job as a teacher to pursue the dream of owning her own business.

"I didn't do this to become rich," Mrs. O'Shay had said, "but it would be nice to not have to worry about whether I could pay the rent on this place each month."

Some months were better than others, especially around the holidays, when people seemed more inclined to work on sewing projects as gifts, or to give their mothers or grandmothers gift certificates to stores like the Stitchin' Kitchen. But Kaylee could not recall a time when the business had not struggled, despite her mother's heroic efforts.

"Kaylee," Mrs. O'Shay called, and her daughter looked up from her work. "I've got to take a phone call. It's Dr. Jung. Can you come up and work the counter?"

She gathered her tags and markers and walked swiftly to the front. The women at the sewing machines smiled at her as she sailed between them and stepped behind the coffee bar. Her mother, who had been leaning her head out of the office on Kaylee's right, now disappeared again, presumably to resume her telephone conversation.

Kaylee's mouth felt suddenly dry as she considered the importance of this phone call. Then her thoughts were interrupted by a woman in her seventies who had risen from her machine and approached the counter.

"I'd like a mocha latte, decaf please, made with skim milk, dear."

Kaylee nodded, went to work at the stainless steel machines to her left. "What size?"

The woman, who was now digging in her purse, looked up. "Hm? Oh, large, please. And could I get whipped cream on that, dear?"

Again Kaylee nodded, continuing her work on the milk and coffee mixture.

The woman lowered her purse and rested a hand clutching several bills on the counter. "Are you home from college for the summer, dear?" she asked.

Kaylee had been concentrating on the latte production as well as on what Dr. Jung might be saying on the phone, and found it difficult to add this conversation to the mix. "Um, no, I'm going to be a junior. In high school."

A sixty-ish woman with red hair at one of the front sewing machines spoke up. "Dora, that's Bethany's daughter, the one who's an Irish dancer."

To everybody who knows me, I'm an Irish dancer, Kaylee thought. *Even though I haven't danced in a year.* The thought simultaneously made her proud and sad.

"It's *Kaylee*, right dear?" asked a third woman.

Kaylee smiled, nodded, brought forward the hot cup.

"Don't forget the whipped cream," reminded the first woman.

Kaylee brought the can from the refrigerator and dispensed a crown the size of half a snowball. The first woman smiled, handed over the money.

"Keep the change," she said. "I know you and your mother can use this."

"Thank you."

As the old woman teetered back to her seat, she added, "Yes, yes, I'd certainly hate to see this place close. It's the most comfortable shop I've ever seen."

Kaylee wanted to concentrate on what Dr. Jung might be saying, on the results of the tests that she had gone through the previous week, but she felt compelled to respond.

"I don't think the Stitchin' Kitchen will be closing any time soon. My mom works way too hard to let that happen."

The red-haired woman shrugged at this. "Your mother said maybe after Christmas. Depends on how things go through the holidays."

This was news to Kaylee. Or was it? Her mother had frequently talked about the financial woes of her business, but the subject of actually closing had always seemed to have been a rather abstract notion.

"Your wonderful mother's had such a rough time of it, poor thing," said the third woman, heavy-set and probably around forty. "It's tough enough to make ends meet in this economy. But she's had to close up the store so much in the last few years.

Her mother's poor health. Her sister dying. And the car accident last year." Her eyes flickered to Kaylee's face as she realized that the subject of this last incident was standing before her.

"I'm sure it'll all work out,' said Kaylee, and the women suddenly quieted and returned to their sewing. But the truth was, Kaylee was not so sure. It would be awful if her mother were to lose her shop, the dream into which she had poured eight years of her life.

But there was another concern. One that involved Kaylee.

Two weeks earlier, her mother had taken her back to Dr. Morse. After Kaylee had stumbled—bloodied and frustrated—into the house following her painful two-mile run, Bethany O'Shay had broken into tears.

"I can't watch you like this! I know it's so hard on you, and it's hard for me as your mother to see you suffer, to see you not be able to do what you love!"

Dr. Morse had referred Kaylee to an orthopedic surgeon who specialized in especially "problematic" cases.

"There are no guarantees," Dr. Morse had cautioned.

Last week, Dr. Susan Jung had examined Kaylee, her x-rays and medical history and had ordered a couple of additional tests. Dr. Jung was in her thirties with blonde hair tied back and a stern demeanor which occasionally melted into a friendly smile.

Kaylee liked her immediately.

"There are some physical therapy options we can take, but you may also be a candidate for certain surgical procedures," Dr. Jung had said. "For those who have the surgery, about seventy-five percent experience improvement."

"How much improvement?" Kaylee's mother had asked.

Dr. Jung did not hesitate. "Every patient is different. We can't predict how Kaylee would do. But with her youth going for her, and what you've told me about her desire to get better, those are two big positives."

"But it's also possible," said Mrs. O'Shay, "that Kaylee would be no better than she is now."

"Yes," said Dr. Jung. "And surgery can sometimes worsen a situation. You need to be aware of that, too."

And so Kaylee had gone home hopeful, yet fearful.

Maybe I can feel better! Maybe I can really dance again!
But maybe the surgery won't help. Maybe I'll be worse than I am now.

"You don't have to get the surgery, sweetheart," her mother had said as they had discussed Kaylee's fears on the trip home from Dr. Jung's. "It's entirely up to you."

Kaylee knew that. She knew that she could probably live a pretty good, mostly pain-free life without the surgery, as long as she did not attempt anything too physically extreme. She could probably even take up swimming or biking, as Dr. Morse had suggested, if she wanted exercise.

On the other hand, she knew she would always wonder. *What if I'd had the surgery? Would it have worked? Would I have made it to Champs?*

Her mother was certainly having a long conversation with Dr. Jung. Perhaps they were talking about the cost of the surgery. Kaylee knew that hospital stays and operations were expensive. That was another reason she had been troubled by what the women at the sewing machines had said. If her mother's shop was really in danger of closing, would they be able to afford Kaylee's surgery—assuming Dr. Jung gave her the green light?

"Kaylee?"

She had not even noticed that her mother had returned from her office and had slipped behind the counter next to her daughter. Mrs. O'Shay carried a scrap of paper in her hand and gave her daughter a hug.

"Oh, Mom," said Kaylee, her face clouding suddenly. "Is it bad news?"

Mrs. O'Shay kissed her daughter's forehead. "Next month. That's when they say you can have the surgery."

Kaylee's eyes widened. "August?" She did not know whether to jump up and down, or whether it might be better to wait and see whether the surgery worked before celebrating. "But, Mom, can we afford it?"

Mrs. O'Shay smiled. "Your father works for the school. Sweeping floors may not be quite as exciting as running a fabric shop—" This made Kaylee smile. "—but he's got good insurance."

Kaylee hugged her mother. "When in August?"

Mrs. O'Shay showed her the date, scribbled onto the paper next to some other notes about the procedure.

"Oh," said Kaylee, the slightest trace of disappointment coloring her voice.

"What's wrong?" asked her mother.

Kaylee smiled bashfully. "Nothing, really. It's almost poetic. But not quite."

Kaylee's mother raised an eyebrow. "Poetic?"

"It's the sort of thing my English teachers are always talking about," Kaylee explained. "Like in a story when there seems to be some pattern to how things turn out. It would have been sort of poetic if my surgery would have been on the same date as the accident. But it's a week later."

Mrs. O'Shay smiled wearily. "If you ask me, nothing about this past year has been poetic."

Seven

Every summer in late July, the carnies arrived in Rosemary. Their trucks and campers usually appeared in the park on Monday, and they spent the next three days assembling a variety of rides—tilt-a-whirl, ferris wheel, bumper cars—and midway games. Then, beginning on Thursday evening, the park would become a sort of alternate universe, a place awash in colorful flashing lights, the aroma of roasting corn, cotton candy and spilled beer, and the screams of hundreds of children and adults as they braved "The Scrambler" or "The Zipper" or whatever they were calling the year's craziest ride.

At the age of seven, Kaylee had thought the carnival was the most amazing thing in the world, and had even mentioned to her father once that it might be the sort of career she would be interested in pursuing.

By the time she reached middle school, most of the carnival's original luster had eroded, but Kaylee and her friends still screamed on "The Matterhorn" and ate massive quantities of hot dogs and popcorn.

Now, at the age of seventeen, Kaylee viewed the carnival as simply a diversion from the typical nothing-to-do summer evenings in Rosemary. Other than the ice cream shop and the community pool—which closed at 7:00 p.m.—Rosemary had little to offer the average teenager, and so many of them drifted to the park as soon as the carousel music began echoing through the town.

On the last Friday in July, Kaylee found herself drifting down the midway, too. When Jackie had called and asked if she wanted to go, Kaylee—celebrating her first un-grounded weekend since Independence Day—had leaped at the opportunity to get out of the house.

And at the opportunity to make up for being a jerk at the Paavo fireworks.

"I am so stupid," said Kaylee when Jackie arrived at the house.

"I'm the stupid one," said Jackie. "If I had any brains, I'd have left you in Paavo that night and we wouldn't have had a big argument."

Kaylee laughed. "All right, we're both stupid. It's a good thing we're friends, because no one else would have any chance of understanding us at all." She was glad Jackie had called.

Now that they were at the carnival, however, she wondered whether accepting her friend's invitation had been such a good idea.

She felt alone even though she was surrounded by people. Worse, she felt awkward.

Very awkward.

When Kaylee had agreed to go to the carnival, she had not known that Jackie intended to take Will along, too.

Absolutely disgusting, almost to the point of being a violation of the laws of human nature. At least that was Kaylee's take on it. Wasn't there a law somewhere that forbid relationships between a girl's best friend and a girl's brother?

The two had been "dating" since Homecoming last fall. Kaylee was impressed that they had lasted ten months in the wild-and-crazy, constantly-changing world of high school relationships. However, this did not make the situation any less revolting.

Now she watched as they walked three steps in front of her, talking in low tones, occasionally bumping shoulders. Then Will pointed to a game booth, fished in his pocket for money and accepted three baseballs.

If he wins her a big stuffed bear, I'm going to puke!

"I'm going to name him Zizzers!" squealed Jackie, bobbing her fluffy, teal-colored trophy in front of Kaylee.

Kaylee smiled at the gigantic teddy. "Neat."

I suppose I could walk home.   But she decided that abandoning her friend might make Jackie feel bad.   Kaylee would stay.   At least for awhile.   Or until things got worse.   *But things couldn't get any worse, could they?*

That was when she saw Riley.

She realized now that it had been about a month.   After he failed to show up for her grandmother's funeral, Kaylee had been furious.   Then, when Kaylee discovered that the two of them had gone to the ice cream shop together, she had been heartbroken and embarrassed.

So she had avoided him.   He had called the O'Shay house half a dozen times.   Kaylee had been fortunate to be gone for all of them and had neglected to return any of the calls.   He had contacted her online a couple of times, too, but Kaylee had kept the conversations factual and brief.   Now here he was with a couple of boys she did not recognize, smiling, laughing, looking way too good.

As she was deciding whether to dash off behind one of the game tents or to stand her ground, Riley saw her.   He said something to his two friends and then jogged over to where she stood.

"I was wondering if I'd run into you here."

"Yeah, well . . . I'm here."

Riley looked around.   "Are you with someone?"

Kaylee jabbed a thumb over her shoulder.   "Just my friend Jackie and her boyfriend, who happens to be my brother."

Riley glanced at Will who was now throwing darts at balloons while Jackie giggled.   "Awkward.   You want to get a drink?"

Of course she wanted to get a drink.   Even if the drink happened to be a glass full of swamp mud, it would be better than being sucked along in the wake of the Jackie-and-Will love boat.   And she had missed Riley.   He looked especially cute tonight in shorts and t-shirt and mussed hair.   But how could she forgive him for being such a jerk?

Then she heard Jackie's voice: "Will, maybe you and me and Kaylee can sit together on the Ferris wheel!"

"All right," Kaylee said, taking a step toward Riley, "let's get a Coke."

She waved to Jackie who made the OMG face, waved back and then headed toward the Ferris wheel with Will in tow. Kaylee ambled to one of the food stands where Riley bought two Coca Colas. They walked to where a man was swinging a large mallet, trying to ring a bell. Here they watched for awhile without really seeing anything until Riley broke the silence between them.

"How've you been feeling?"

How have I been feeling? She wanted to shout, *It depends on which feelings you mean. If you mean how am I feeling physically, well, I still can't finish a complete dance without looking like the scarecrow in Wizard of Oz. If you mean how am I feeling about you and me, I'm not sure you want the answer. In fact, you can probably guess that I'm not very happy that someone I thought was a really great guy just tosses me aside when I really need him. And if you only asked how I was feeling to make conversation because even though we've known each other for years, you couldn't think of anything better to say, then I'm not even going to bother to answer.*

Instead, she said:

"Okay."

Riley nodded, took a sip of his Coke, watched a short, pear-shaped man slam the mallet onto the bumper, raising the metal projectile about halfway to the bell.

"Did you really quit dancing with Miss Helen? For good?"

She decided she liked it better when his questions were less personal.

"No. I went back a couple weeks later."

Her mind raced. Maybe she should say something about school. They could talk about school for hours and never say anything meaningful. However, Riley spoke again before she could steer them into a bland conversation.

"Does that mean your leg is feeling better?"

Kaylee sighed. "I'm having surgery in a couple of weeks. On my right leg."

Now Riley's eyes widened. "Oh. Wow! Do they think it's going to help your dancing?"

No, stupid, they think it's going to make me a better piano player!

"It might. Could also make things worse."

Riley took a moment to consider this new information.

"So you'll be on crutches to start the school year. Again."

Kaylee nodded. "Sort of upsets my Master Plan." Riley pretzeled his brow in confusion and Kaylee explained. "Once I started working with Miss Helen, I thought it'd only be a short time before I'd dance in a feis again. Then I'd qualify for Oireachtas. By November, I'd be completely recovered and I'd smoke most of the Champs girls and qualify for Worlds. I must have been crazy."

"You *are* crazy."

Kaylee wondered if she had heard him correctly. "What?"

Riley smiled. "You've always been a little crazy when it comes to dance. In a good way. You set insane goals for yourself. No one works harder than you do. If Irish dance were the Tour de France, you'd be Lance Armstrong. Only female."

Why did he have to say such endearing things and be so fine looking on top of it? Kaylee had been determined to stay angry with him, but she felt her resolve melting.

"I'll be able to start training again in November," said Kaylee. "And if everything goes smoothly, I figure I'll be ready to dance my first feis in January. If I earn another first in PC right away, I'll be able to dance at Nationals in July and possibly qualify for Worlds!"

Riley's smile broadened in response to her enthusiasm. Kaylee almost felt like nothing had ever come between them. His face looked just as it had that day when they had been alone on the upper deck of the ferry coming back from the feis in Michigan . . .

. . . on the afternoon he had bought her ice cream on the way back from the Gateway Feis.

. . . at the Homecoming football game when he had kissed her.

As these thoughts passed through her mind, Riley took a step closer. "Just let me know how I can help. I'll be there for you, Kaylee."

The pleasant images dissolved, and Kaylee responded sullenly. "Yeah."

She could tell her response puzzled Riley. "What's wrong?" he asked. "It sounds like you . . ."

"Don't believe you?" Kaylee said, finishing the thought. "I guess I'm just a little skeptical after what happened."

"What do you mean?" asked Riley. "I tried to be there for you. I've called your house, but you never—"

"My grandmother's funeral!" Kaylee spat out the words like weapons. "You weren't exactly there for me then, were you? And you knew how much she meant to me, how badly I felt! But you didn't even come! You went to a soccer tournament with Brittany Hall instead!"

Riley's mouth dropped open and his eyes revealed both confusion and disbelief. He seemed to struggle as if trying to remember.

"But . . . I *was* at your grandmother's funeral."

Kaylee shook her head. "I remember everyone who came through the line."

Riley's features seemed to harden at this.

"I didn't go through the line. You're right. I got there later and there were so many people and I could see how bad you felt. I didn't know what to say, and it looked like it was mostly your family getting ready for the service. So I just sort of hung around the back of the room. Just to be there for you."

"No!"

"Check the guest book or whatever they call that thing you sign when you arrive. You'll see my name!"

This had to be impossible. Could Kaylee have been wrong about Riley? Had she wasted the past month on a petty misunderstanding? Then she recalled the overheard conversation at the ice cream shop.

"You were at soccer with Brittany," she argued. "I heard you talking about her tournament. At the ice cream shop."

Riley's eyes widened. "Spying?"

"I was getting a drink and you were sitting right near the machine! I couldn't help hearing."

Again Riley struggled to remember details. "It was a two-day tournament."

Kaylee nodded. "And the first day was the same day as my grandmother's funeral!"

"That's right," agreed Riley, "but I only went to the second day."

Now Kaylee tried to remember precisely what she had heard. Could she have jumped to the wrong conclusion?

"A buddy of mine dates a girl on Brittany's soccer team," continued Riley. "I went with him."

Kaylee felt relieved, wary, embarrassed and angry all at the same time. "But you were at the ice cream shop."

Riley's gaze on her narrowed. "With Brittany? Sure. We've known each other forever through dance. You know that. We're friends. And she's fun. We were just having a cone. I didn't realize you'd be so paranoid about it."

Kaylee stared at the ground.

"I like you, Kaylee," said Riley, and Kaylee's eyes rose to his face, though the tilt of her head was still downward. "I really like you. But if you're not going to trust me . . . I don't know if I can handle that."

Kaylee took a deep breath. "Yeah, well, it's been a tough year. When so much gets taken away from you, you wonder where it's going to stop."

"I know," said Riley, and now he hung his head. "I know." Then he said goodnight and walked off, presumably to find his friends.

Jackie dropped off Kaylee and Will about ten-thirty. "Is everything okay?" she had asked, noticing Kaylee's quietness and dour expression. Kaylee simply shrugged, for she did not really know the answer to the question. Was Riley done with her? Did he want any sort of relationship? How did *she* feel about *him*?

Will disappeared upstairs almost immediately, but Kaylee lingered in the kitchen where Mrs. O'Shay appeared in her bathrobe.

"You're still up?" asked Kaylee.

"Mothers rarely fall asleep before their children are home," said Mrs. O'Shay. Her voice seemed to have some odd tension to it that surprised Kaylee. Or perhaps it was simply imagination. "How was the carnival?"

"Awkward. Odd. Frustrating." She described in detail her conversation with Riley.

"Everything seems like it's changing," she added. "I can't wait for the surgery so my life can get back to the way it was before!"

Her mother took a deep breath. "That's another reason I waited up. Kaylee, Dr. Jung's office called tonight."

The tone of her mother's voice suggested bad news. But what bad news could there be? Dr. Jung had told Kaylee herself that she seemed an excellent candidate for the surgery. Maybe the date had been changed. Maybe she would not be having the surgery until mid-September. That definitely would be bad news. Kaylee did not know if she could wait two more weeks. And it would push back her whole timetable for qualifying for Nationals.

"Don't tell me they're changing the date!"

Mrs. O'Shay pulled her daughter into a hug. "Sweetheart, I'm afraid there's been a change of plans. There isn't going to be any surgery."

Eight

Kaylee's father rarely swore. On those widely-spaced occasions when he had uttered a vulgarity, it typically involved a hammer and his thumb, a wrench and a stubborn bolt, or some other impertinent soldier in the never-ending home maintenance war.

On Saturday morning, however, Tom O'Shay swore freely and enthusiastically, his ire directed at one target:

"Insurance! What a joke! What's the point in having it if they won't let you use it when you need it?"

Then a string of vulgarities.

Kaylee had slept fitfully the previous night after her mother had broken the news to her. Her father had filled in the details in the morning.

"The way it works," he had explained angrily, "is that you notify the insurance company when a doctor recommends surgery. Then the insurance company—in its *infinite wisdom*—decides if you really need it!"

Kaylee's pillow was still damp from the previous night, yet tears threatened at the corners of her eyes as she spoke. "If a doctor says you need surgery, why wouldn't the insurance company take her word?"

"That's a heck of a question, sweetheart!" said her father, who then hugged her, poured himself a cup of coffee and, instead of drinking it, began another verbal onslaught.

"The insurance company is classifying it as elective surgery," said her mother.

"Which means they think I don't really need it," sniffed Kaylee.

Her mother nodded. "Because you can function normally, without pain, doing routine daily tasks, they won't pay. They don't consider Irish dance . . ."

"Necessary?" Kaylee finished the sentence. "Vital? A matter of life and death?"

The kitchen remained quiet for a few moments. Then Mrs. O'Shay said:

"We're going to file an appeal. There's always a chance that the insurance company will change its mind."

Tom O'Shay snorted derisively. "Oh, right!"

Kaylee slumped into one of the kitchen chairs. "There must be something we can do! Maybe if we got another doctor to talk to the insurance company!"

Mrs. O'Shay shook her head. "I don't think that'll do any good."

An idea came to Kaylee. "If the insurance company won't pay, we could pay for it ourselves!"

Her mother smiled sympathetically. "Honey, I told you before we don't have the money. You know how it is with the store." Kaylee recalled the older women talking about the Stitchin' Kitchen closing at the end of the year. "And we have other expenses. We're still paying off this house, you know."

"And keeping enough cereal in the house for your brother costs a fortune in itself," added her father. Under different circumstances, Kaylee might have laughed.

"What about the money I got from Aunt Kat?" asked Kaylee.

A concerned look clouded her mother's face. "Oh, dear, you know that Kat explicitly stated that the money was to be used for college."

Kaylee's voice rose in anger. "For college? What's the point of college? What's the point of anything if I can't be . . . me!"

"Sweetheart . . ."

"Aunt Kat would have understood!" argued Kaylee. "If she were here right now, she'd say *Use the money for the operation!* I know she would!"

"Calm down," instructed Tom O'Shay, who seemed to have gotten his own emotions under control. "I don't know if the money Aunt Kat left would even be enough to cover the surgery.

And even if it would, I don't know if we could justify trading college tuition—your future, Kaylee—for maybe another year of Irish dancing!"

Now Kaylee's anger darkened. "You'd do it if I were playing soccer!"

This statement seemed to shock her mother. "Kaylee, that's not true!"

"If I still played soccer and the operation would let me continue, dad would use the money!" repeated Kaylee. "Anything for soccer! But not for Irish dance! You've never forgiven me for choosing dance over soccer!"

Now the energy seemed to have drained from her father's face and he stood at the counter, helpless. "Kaylee, that's not true."

"It is true! You've always hated Irish dance! Well, congratulations! You finally got what you wanted! I'm not a dancer anymore!"

With that outburst, she raced to her room, slamming the door.

The breeze invigorated her but did not change her mood. Kaylee pedaled her bike toward Jackie's house as she had so many times over the years when she needed someone to talk to. *I'll bet I'm the only sixteen-year-old in Rosemary who still uses a bike. Just another example of how messed up my life is.*

Kaylee told herself that Brittany Hall would not be riding a bike to her friend's house. She would probably have a brand-new car. Probably a Porsche or a Jaguar. Definitely a convertible. And she would not be upset, either, because her father would have plenty of money to pay for her daughter's surgery. In fact, Brittany would never need surgery to begin with, because nothing bad ever seemed to happen to her.

This line of thinking did not make Kaylee feel better. First, she understood at some level that it was inspired by self-pity. Second, she knew that it was not true.

Yes, Brittany Hall was beautiful and attracted the attention of almost every boy in Rosemary. Yes, her family had money and lived in the ritzy Oakton Heights neighborhood. On top of that, she was an ace at Irish dance, basketball, soccer or whatever else she tried.

But Kaylee knew that the Halls had problems, too. Brittany's mother was a drunk. She ran an antique shop near Aunt Kat's former apartment, a shop that did not seem to attract many customers. Kaylee got the sense that Brittany's father poured money into the business to keep it open so that Mrs. Hall would have something to occupy her days. Even so, Kaylee had seen Mrs. Hall, stone drunk in the middle of the day, spewing nonsense at befuddled and ultimately offended customers. Brittany worked part time at the store, attempting to hold the business together and limit the impact of her mother's behavior on customers, but Kaylee suspected the ordeal had to be embarrassing.

Of course, it did not end at the antique store. When Kaylee had visited the Hall residence, Brittany had mentioned that her mother frequently drank vodka martinis and passed out by eight o'clock each evening, giving Brittany the house to herself. Kaylee thought of her own mother, who either worked diligently at the Stitchin' Kitchen or cooked, cleaned and mothered at the modest O'Shay home. She could not imagine her own mother behaving like Mrs. Hall.

And Mr. Hall had to hold down two jobs so that his family could continue living in their mansion in the nice neighborhood. She had discovered his night job—working maintenance at Paavo College—three years ago. She remembered how Brittany had been either too embarrassed to admit that her father held the same sort of employment as Mr. O'Shay, or else she did not know about it. Kaylee had suspected Mr. Hall might have taken the second job without his daughter's knowledge, knowing that it would have mortified her.

So Brittany's life was not perfect. Kaylee surmised that no one's was. Yet, that did not mean she had to be happy about an insurance company ruining the rest of *her* life.

Kaylee dropped her bicycle on Jackie's front lawn. When Jackie opened the front door, her first response was to give Kaylee a hug.

"Your mom told my mom about the surgery," said Jackie. "That stinks!"

Usually when Kaylee needed Jackie's therapeutic ear, the two girls talked in her friend's bedroom. However, Jackie was helping her father shuck corn in the kitchen, and so Kaylee thudded onto a chair at the table and spilled the details. Jackie passed her an ear of corn, and so Kaylee joined the Kizobus in peeling away the husk and plucking the silk as she ranted.

"I can't believe an insurance company could do something like that," said Kaylee at the conclusion of her narrative. "Why don't they just let the doctors make those decisions?"

Jackie nodded in disbelief. "They're basically ruining your life! Don't they know how much pain you're in when you dance? There should be a law against what they're doing!"

Mr. Kizobu, who had helped coach Kaylee's soccer team years earlier with Mr. O'Shay, and who had been listening quietly up to this point, suddenly spoke up. "Insurance companies have different policies about what is necessary surgery and what is not. If your father was insured by a different company, they might pay for your operation."

Kaylee brightened. "So all we have to do is change insurance companies?"

Mr. Kizobu shook his head. "No. If you have a pre-existing condition, and you get new insurance, they usually won't cover it either."

Kaylee frowned deeply. "Don't they want people to get better?"

Mr. Kizobu shrugged. "It's especially hard if you have something like heart disease or cancer and you're looking for insurance. Since you already have your injury, your surgery might not be covered by a new company even though they would cover it for someone who had been their customer for years, but who just got injured."

Kaylee rested her elbows on the table, dropped her head into her hands. "I think my brain is going to explode."

"Careful," Jackie cautioned her, "they probably won't cover that either."

The two girls laughed, but after a moment, Kaylee grew glum again. "Thanks for listening. It really helps. But I guess there's nothing I can do."

Now a slight smile played across Mr. Kizobu's face.

"What?" asked Jackie, noticing her father's expression.

"Well," said Mr. Kizobu, "I guess there is one thing you could do."

Both girls waited expectantly.

"You could sue the insurance company."

Nine

"Hello, I'm Deena Strong."

"And I'm Ty Andrews, and this is the WPAV evening news. We've got a report on that new mall being built on Paavo's north side coming up later in the newscast."

"And a look at which gas stations in the suburban area have the lowest prices as we approach the middle of August. But first, a story about a local girl who's taking on the insurance companies. Sixteen-year-old Kaylee O'Shay of Rosemary is suing for her right to dance. Here's WPAV's Marietta Martinez with the report."

"Thank you, Deena. I'm standing outside the courthouse, but the real story is what will be happening inside next week. Kaylee O'Shay, an Irish dancer for the past seven years, was severely injured in a car accident about a year ago. Following surgery and months of therapy, she still has not been able to resume her passion because of the extreme pain. A doctor has apparently told the O'Shays that another surgery could help, but Mr. O'Shay's insurance carrier initially denied the operation, classifying it as an elective or unnecessary procedure. I think we have a clip of Mr. Thomas O'Shay, recorded earlier outside his home in Rosemary:"

"Um, yeah, we just want to, you know, do what's best. For my daughter. She wants to dance."

"We also had an opportunity to talk with Mr. Nathan Wendowski, the Paavo attorney representing the O'Shays:"

"Our argument is that this little girl is still suffering, and the insurance company has an obligation to address that situation. Insurance companies provide a valuable service, and while most of their actions are based on sound reasoning by right-thinking men, we believe this decision was a serious error."

"That again was Mr. Nathan Wendowski, the attorney representing the O'Shays. As I mentioned before, there will be a preliminary hearing right here next week, Ty and Deena. This is Marietta Martinez for WPAV news."

"Thank you, Marietta. Let's hope that little girl gets a chance to dance again. And now, let's take a look at the Paavo Hills Mall project, that from its start, has been plagued with . . . ."

Ten

She pushed off the wall and let herself glide through the tepid, over-chlorinated water. She would finish the mile soon, which was good, because the morning was warm and sunny. On cool, overcast days, Kaylee had the Rosemary public pool almost to herself and could swim laps unobstructed. But on warm days, the stay-at-home moms would begin bringing the rugrats to the pool shortly after it opened at nine, and then Kaylee would have to dodge small, writhing bodies as she attempted to complete her workout.

Today, Jackie had come along. She lay in a deck chair near the pool edge, her new, yellow one-piece swimsuit almost dry now after an earlier dip, her eyes covered with sunglasses—working on her tan.

Jackie never tanned.

Sometimes older kids would come to the pool on sunny days, and they were often worse than the little ones. They wrestled with each other in the water, threw spongy footballs and plastic disks, not noticing or not caring whether someone was trying to swim laps. And when one of them collided with you, you noticed *and* cared.

When Kaylee had started coming to the pool a week earlier, she had worried that the staff might recognize her and throw her out. Three years ago, Kaylee had been banned from the pool after bullying a group of younger swimmers—at the urging of Brittany Hall. When the lifeguards had kicked out Kaylee, Brittany and Heather, the other two girls had laughed about it as if it were a big joke. Kaylee had been mortified. She had never been kicked out of anything before.

On the other hand, she had never attempted to form a friendship with someone like Brittany Hall before. What a misguided idea that had been. Kaylee had lied to her parents to attend a drinking party at Brittany's—although Kaylee had managed to avoid consuming any alcohol. She had nearly been arrested. She had actually been grabbed by a police officer while running through the woods, but then the cop had been distracted and she had escaped.

And she had pushed kids into the pool.

Of course, she realized that these were not the sorts of offenses one is sent to prison for. Still, that sort of behavior was not how she normally behaved, nor how she normally saw herself.

Kaylee soon discovered that her fears over being recognized and kicked out by the pool staff had been unfounded. After three years, the guard staff had changed completely. Most of those who had sat in the watch chairs three years earlier had probably moved on to college or other summer jobs. In addition, Kaylee knew that her appearance had changed in the past three years, and so any staff that remained might not even recognize her. Her copper-colored hair had darkened just slightly, and she wore it somewhat shorter—though it was still an unruly mass of curls most days. Some of her freckles had seemed to fade, although a sprinkle still played across the bridge of her nose, spilling onto her cheekbones. And while she had been merely skinny three years ago, now she looked more like a sixteen-year-old. True, her figure lacked the swimsuit-model proportions that Brittany Hall seemed to possess, but there was also no longer any chance whatsoever that she might be mistaken for a boy.

"How many more laps?" called Jackie as Kaylee swam past her chair.

Kaylee paused, popped her head out. "Six."

Jackie nodded, lay back. Her sunglasses masked whether or not she closed her eyes, but Kaylee guessed that she did. Then Kaylee resumed her swim.

Since running had been so painful, Kaylee had decided on the pool. Dr. Morse had suggested it soon after the accident, and Kaylee now supposed that she should have tried it sooner.

The backs of someone's thighs bashed into her shoulder and she surfaced to catch a breath and orient herself.

"Sorry!" called the boy, about fourteen, chased by a friend. He continued through her wake and Kaylee resumed swimming. The teenagers were starting to arrive, which meant she needed to finish quickly.

A few minutes later, she sat on the pool edge, letting the warm rays dry her.

"I really hate swimming," she said to Jackie, who adjusted the back of her lounger so that she sat upright.

"Then what are we doing here?" asked her friend. "Other than getting a tan?" Jackie touched her own triceps with two fingers, looked pleased, even though to Kaylee her friend still looked like a glass of milk.

"Conditioning," said Kaylee. "Cardio work!"

Jackie frowned. "But you're supposed to have your surgery in a couple of weeks, right?"

"If things work out in court," replied Kaylee.

"But then you'll be on crutches again for weeks. It's like you're doing it all for nothing."

Kaylee squinted across the pool at the slowly-growing hoard of splashing bodies. "I read somewhere that the better shape you're in before an operation, the less time before you get back in shape after."

Jackie shook her head. "Boy, I hope the judge makes them pay for your operation."

Kaylee shuddered. "Don't even think about the alternative!"

A shadow passed across the two girls, and Kaylee twisted around to see Brittany Hall and Heather Chandler standing nearby sipping from gigantic iced soft drink cups from the pool concession stand. It was almost as if the horrible thought that the judge might not approve her operation had been a magnet for additional evil.

"Hey, it's O'Shrimp!" said Brittany, loudly.

Jackie lay back on her lounger. "Might want to try a new tune. Last I checked, Kaylee was as tall as you, O'Hall."

Kaylee had not realized it before, but Jackie was right. At one time, Brittany had seemed to tower over Kaylee like an Amazon. Kaylee observed, however, that she still could not possibly fill out the barely-a-bikini that Brittany was wearing in the same all-the-boys-will-be-drooling way. Heather, however, was at least six inches taller than either of them and skinny but athletic-looking.

"Maybe we'd better not talk with the big celebrity," said Heather, who always seemed to think that she was far more funny than she actually was.

"That's right," said Brittany more earnestly, taking a sip from her enormous drink. "I heard on TV that you're suing some big insurance company so you can dance again. Way to go!"

There seemed to be genuine respect in Brittany's observation, which Kaylee attributed to the fact that she was an Irish dancer, too.

Kaylee shrugged. "They're not even sure if the surgery will work."

"I'm sure someday they'll be ready to try it on humans," said Heather with a smirk. "Until then, just be proud of the service you're performing for medical science."

"Hey Heather," said Jackie from her recliner, "when they finally perform that transplant and give you a normal-sized brain, just be proud of the service *you're* performing for medical science."

Heather's eyes radiated dark, anti-matter lasers at Jackie.

"So what do you have to do to convince the judge?" asked Brittany.

"You see, if Kaylee had *your* father," Jackie chimed in, "she could just pay off the judge."

Brittany ignored the jab and Kaylee explained. "We all had to make statements. You know, explaining our side of it. And Mr. Wendowski—our lawyer—is doing what's called discovery. I guess that means looking at similar cases. Finding out what our insurance company has done in the past. Anything that could help out the case."

Brittany nodded. "And the trial starts next week?"

"The preliminary hearing," stated Kaylee. "We're trying to move fast. Every week we wait is one week less to recover in time for Oireachtas." Then she added, "I mean next year's Oireachtas."

Brittany shook her head, apparently able to appreciate how far in the future next year's Oireachtas was, yet how quickly it would pass for someone who had endured major surgery and who was attempting to make a comeback as an Irish dancer. "Wow, O'Shri—" She stopped herself. "Wow. Maybe it would have been better if you'd stayed with soccer!"

Of course, Brittany had no way of knowing that Jackie had said this same thing, and that it had hurt Kaylee immensely. Kaylee saw Jackie stiffen but kept her composure, like a circus performer on a high-wire riding a unicycle while attempting to balance a dozen delicate wine glasses on her head..

Then Heather spoke and everything crashed to the ground. "Yeah, if you'd stayed with soccer, you'd be dead. No worries!" She laughed stupidly, as if this might lead others to the punch line.

Jackie had never been able to resist a follow-up jab where Heather was concerned.   "I'd think that death would be preferable to having to listen to another minute of junk from that open sewer you call your mouth."

Again, Heather's eyes darkened, and suddenly she thrust her giant soft drink cup toward Jackie. The plastic lid popped off and dark cola soaked Jackie's hair, face, and her bright, yellow suit.

"Ooh," said Heather with mock concern, "I think that's going to leave a stain!"

Jackie's face contorted in rage. "I hear blood is even harder to get out!"

Although one of the school's top athletes, Heather was completely unprepared for Jackie's lunge. The two toppled over an empty deck chair which followed them into the pool—and onto a group of nine-year-olds playing with inflatable animals.

A few minutes later, all four girls stood outside the chain-link fence that surrounded the Rosemary public pool.

"You guys are done for the summer!" barked the square-chinned guard, his nose hidden under a thick layer of zinc. "If I see you back here, I'll call the cops!"

Jackie, still seething, headed toward the parking lot. As Kaylee followed, Brittany called after her.

"Hey, O'Shay!"

Kaylee turned back.

Brittany grinned smugly, gave a thumb's up, and said, "Just like old times, right?"

Eleven

Kaylee sat at the wide table between her parents. Mr. Wendowski, their attorney, sat next to Mr. O'Shay. She was more nervous than she had ever been at an Irish dance competition.

This fact did not prevent her from noticing that this courtroom did not seem very much like the ones on television. The lights here seemed much dimmer, giving everything and everyone a dingy appearance, as if they had been slogging it out for days, despite the fact that they had just settled into their seats a few minutes ago. No one looked like an actor, either. The women were definitely not gorgeous models, which is what the attorneys, jurors and female court reporters looked like on TV shows. The men wore ill-fitting suits with creases where they had sat on the backs, and most were a few pounds overweight and looked like they had said yes to cheap haircuts, but no to styling gel, blow dryers and tinting. And people spoke so quietly here. On TV, everybody spoke like Abraham Lincoln delivering the Gettysburg Address. Here, people mumbled, repeated themselves and sounded utterly human.

The courtroom was not crowded, either. Kaylee had half expected it to be like the movie *To Kill a Mockingbird*, where the room had been jammed with noisy spectators to hear Atticus Finch defend Tom Robinson. When her own father had been interviewed by a TV reporter on their way into the building, this had further convinced her that the event would be standing room only. But it was just her family and Mr. Wendowski, a representative of the insurance company and his attorney, a court reporter, a uniformed officer, two people who sat halfway back and who Kaylee could not see what their connection was to the case, and—of course—the judge.

Judge Samuel T. Brooks.

"Where's the jury?" Kaylee had asked her father after they had settled into their seats.

Hearing her question, Mr. Wendowski had smiled and offered the explanation. "Not all cases are settled before juries. In our case, the only one we have to convince is Judge Brooks."

"Hm," Mr. Kizobu had said when, before the hearing, Kaylee had mentioned who was going to oversee their case. "That could be a good thing. But it's hard to know for sure."

"What do you mean?" Kaylee had asked.

"Brooks is pretty family friendly," explained Mr. Kizobu. "That goes in your favor. He has real strong opinions when it comes to money issues. Usually likes to make a show of standing up for the underprivileged."

"That's good, right?" Kaylee had said.

"Like I said, it could be," continued Mr. Kizobu. "But that's the funny thing about court. No matter how clear a case seems when you walk through the doors, you never can tell for sure how it's going to turn out."

"They should just flip a coin and save us all the drama," suggested Jackie.

"Another thing," added Mr. Kizobu, "Brooks has a reputation for going with his gut."

Kaylee frowned. "What's that mean?"

"He gets a feeling about a case, and this sets the whole tone for how he proceeds. He likes to make a public statement, something that'll send a message."

"How do you know all this stuff?" Jackie had asked.

"I just do," Mr. Kizobu had smiled.

Mr. Kizobu did seem to know a lot. In some respects, Kaylee wished that he were sitting at the table with her family. The meeting with Mr. Wendowski had not inspired as much confidence. The O'Shays had driven to his office in a strip mall in Paavo after Kaylee's father had found his ad in the phone book.

"It says if we don't win the case, we don't pay anything," Mr. O'Shay had said, pointing to the ad. "What have we got to lose?"

Kaylee's mother had been less than enthusiastic but had eventually thrown in her support. "If it gets my baby her surgery, I'm for it."

After Kaylee had offered the basic details, her father and mother had fleshed it out for Mr. Wendowski. Then, the short, balding, sweaty-looking man had sat with his elbows on his desk and his fingers laced together for at least two minutes, saying nothing. At one point, Kaylee wondered whether he had forgotten they were there and was daydreaming about some favorite vacation spot. Finally Mrs. O'Shay had asked, "What do you think? Can we sue them?"

At this, Nathan Wendowski had smiled confidently. "Anyone can sue anyone for anything. That's a fact. Of course, that doesn't mean every lawsuit is successful. That depends on the merits of the case. On the rule of law. And on historical precedent."

Kaylee was not sure what all of that meant, exactly, but it certainly sounded like Mr. Wendowski knew the law. He spoke in a nasal tone, but quickly, as if there was so much legal knowledge inside just waiting to spill out. She had begun to feel better.

"A case like this will make the insurance company look bad," Mr. Wendowski had explained. "They don't want that kind of publicity. My guess is that they'll settle once the suit is filed, before it goes to trial."

"That would be nice," Mrs. O'Shay had said.

"But before there's a trial, there will be a hearing at which we will ask for a writ of mandamus," Mr. Wendowski had added. "Basically, we'll be asking the court to keep the insurance company from causing permanent damage to you by requiring them to pay for your operation now. By getting the writ, you can get your surgery now, when you need it. A lawsuit can take months, even years."

Now they sat at the hearing in the dingy, too quiet courtroom, watching Judge Brooks fidget at his bench, looking over papers, shuffling them, clearing his throat occasionally. Finally he addressed the two attorneys.

"Mr. Wendowski, Mr. Van Dorn, I think we can dispense with this matter quickly."

Kaylee was relieved to hear this, although she wondered what it was about the case that had led the judge to this conclusion.

"Mr. Wendowski, if I understand correctly, your clients wish to have Mr. Van Dorn's client pay the cost of their daughter's surgery."

"Yes, Your Honor. The insurance company has classified the surgery as elective, and we are challenging that decision."

"But why a writ of mandamus?" asked Judge Brooks. "There doesn't appear to be anything of an emergency or life-threatening nature about this young lady's situation."

"Your Honor," explained Mr. Van Dorn, "Miss O'Shay possesses unique athletic gifts. Recovery from surgery will take months. Returning to competitive form will take even longer. But in a little more than a year, Miss O'Shay's window of opportunity to qualify for the World Championships will close. The clock is ticking. She does not have months she can afford to waste while a trial drags on."

Judge Brooks adjusted his glasses and addressed the man seated next to attorney Van Dorn. "Mr. Klein, your company insured Mr. O'Shay and his family at the time of the original accident in August of last year, is that correct?"

"Yes sir," Mr. Klein replied.

"And you covered the cost of all initial surgeries, hospitalization and follow-up therapies, is that correct?"

Another yes.

"At any point prior to their most recent request did you deny any of the O'Shay family's medical claims?"

This time a no.

A curt nod from the judge, and then: "Mr. Klein, why do you classify this current surgery as elective, while the earlier surgery was not."

Kaylee sensed that the judge already knew the answers to all these questions from reading the documents in front of him. Perhaps he thought he might hear something in the verbal responses that had not communicated itself clearly in written form. Or perhaps this was just a formality, a way of making sure the basic facts were on the official record. Or maybe something else.

"Without the earlier surgery, Your Honor, Miss O'Shay would have been unable to walk," said Mr. Klein. "And she had other injuries, including broken bones and internal injuries that, if left untreated, could have resulted in limited mobility, chronic pain or even death."

Despite the fact that nearly a year had passed, hearing that she had come close to dying sent a shiver up Kaylee's spine.

"Today, Miss O'Shay is able to walk without limping, endures no unusual chronic pain, and enjoys what most people would describe as a normal life," said Mr. Klein.

The judge peered over his glasses. "Normal." Then Judge Brooks exhaled noisily, glanced over papers in front of him and looked directly at Kaylee—or so it seemed. "Mr. O'Shay, it appears your insurance carrier has provided for your daughter nicely up to this point. Would you agree?"

"Yes. Yes Your Honor." Kaylee could tell her father was nervous.

"Would you agree with Mr. Klein's assessment of your daughter's current state of health?" asked the judge. "Doesn't limp. No pain. A normal life."

Tom O'Shay looked like a man being interrogated under a bright light by guys with brass knuckles and rubber hoses. "Er, yes and no."

Judge Brooks scowled. "Either she's normal or she isn't."

"Well, what he said is true," said Mr. O'Shay.

Before he could continue, Mrs. O'Shay stood and blurted a clarification. "Her life's not normal. Not for her."

Judge Brooks continued to scowl but said, "Go on."

Mrs. O'Shay now seemed conscious of her place in the spotlight, and her enthusiasm dwindled. However, she plunged ahead.

"My daughter loves Irish dance. Since she was ten, it's been her life. I've never seen anyone who works at it so hard. She puts in hours dancing, stretching, running, all so that she can go to Ireland someday and dance in the World Championships. But since last August, she can't dance. Not for very long. The pain is too intense. That's why we were so hopeful when Dr. Jung told us about the surgery." She paused for a moment, and Kaylee could see that her mother's eyes had grown moist. "Since the accident, my daughter's life has definitely not been the same. It hurts her so badly to see her dream slipping away." Now she cast a glance at Mr. Klein and her resolve stiffened. "I always thought that it was our right to expect our insurance company to fix the damage when we got hurt. Well, Kaylee is still hurting. If a writ is what Mr. Wendowski said—to make whole someone whose rights have been violated—then it's what we need. My daughter has not been made whole. There's a part of her that was taken away by that accident, and this surgery could give it back to her."

She sat down suddenly, dug into her purse for a tissue. Kaylee had never been so proud of her mother. She heard Mr. Wendowski lean close to Mrs. O'Shay and whisper, "Have you ever thought of a career in law?"

Then Mr. Wendowski stood and said, "Your Honor, I think Mrs. O'Shay said it quite articulately. We're looking to restore *status quo ante*—"

"Yes, yes," interrupted Judge Brooks, "I know what you're looking to do." Then he glanced alternately at the papers in front of him and at Kaylee's father. "Mr. O'Shay, it says here that you're employed by the Rosemary school system."

"Yes, Your Honor."

"Do you own or rent?" asked the judge.

"Our house?" asked Mr. O'Shay, surprised by the question. "Own. Well, sort of own. We have a mortgage."

"Everybody has a mortgage, Mr. O'Shay," responded Judge Brooks. "*I* have a mortgage."

Now Mr. Wendowski spoke. "Your Honor, I don't see—"

"Relax, Mr. Wendowski," said the judge. "I'm entitled." Then he turned his attention to the O'Shays. Often Kaylee could read a person's feelings by the look on his face. Facing Judge Brooks, she was clueless.

"Irish dance." Judge Brooks let the words hang in the air for a moment before continuing. "I have friends whose daughters

are Irish dancers. In fact, my neighbor's granddaughter dances.
He talks about it all the time."

Kaylee breathed a sigh of relief, which she managed to
mostly hide from those around her. The judge's neighbor's
granddaughter was an Irish dancer. That meant he understood.

"Before the accident last August," Judge Brooks continued,
"did you travel to Irish dance competitions—oh, what's that
name you call them . . ."

"Feiseanna!" blurted Kaylee.   And then more softly:
"Feises."

"Right," said the judge. "As I was saying, did you travel to
competitions? My neighbor's granddaughter does."

Mrs. O'Shay answered. "Yes, but—"

"To different states?" asked Judge Brooks. "Where?"

Mrs. O'Shay clearly did not understand the relevance of the
question, but Mr. Wendowski simply shrugged and she replied.
"Oh, Chicago, a couple in Indiana. Michigan. St. Louis. We
did the Quad Cities Feis a couple of times."

"Is that it?"

Mrs. O'Shay sighed, rubbed her right temple. "I don't
know. I may have forgotten some."

Judge Brooks stared at her, then shook his head as the
silence grew. "I sat on a case a few years ago. A man who
worked as an electrician. Blue collar fellow. It got so he
couldn't hold his tools. Hurt terribly, although when he wasn't
working he was fine. Insurance company denied his initial
request for surgery. Can you believe it? The man could no
longer put food on the table for his family because he couldn't
do his job, and his surgery is denied!"

To Kaylee, this sounded something like her own situation.
This man did not have pain all the time, and so the insurance
company would not pay. Was Judge Brooks building to a
decision in her favor?

Then Judge Brooks continued, addressing Kaylee's father.
"But this isn't about putting food on your family's table, is it,
Mr. O'Shay?"

Tom O'Shay's confusion registered on his face as he spoke.
"Your Honor, I don't understand."

"Your daughter is an Irish dancer," said the judge. "As I said, I've got a little experience in this area, and I know it's not cheap. In fact, it's one of the most expensive activities you can let your kid be involved in! Dresses that cost thousands of dollars! Wigs, shoes, makeup, lessons! And then you travel all over the Midwest!"

"Your Honor," interrupted Mr. Wendowski, "I don't see the relevance. Personal income is not an issue here. The O'Shays should be entitled to fair treatment by their insurance carrier regardless of whether they are millionaires or paupers."

"I agree," replied Judge Brooks. "Fair treatment is what they deserve. But not extraordinary treatment! If this were a question of life or death, of providing for one's family, of not being able to live normally, that would be one thing. But we're talking about people who own their own house, who own their own business, who travel all over the country engaging in an expensive hobby. And you're asking me order an insurance company to pay tens of thousands of dollars so that they can continue with this *hobby*?"

"You've got it wrong," said Mr. O'Shay.

"We're not like that!" cried Mrs. O'Shay.

"Not everybody is fortunate enough to have the things you have, Mr. and Mrs. O'Shay," the judge continued, and now he looked toward Kaylee. "And I do sympathize with you, young lady. But I have to look at the big picture. Not just what people with houses and businesses and expensive hobbies like Irish dance want. That's what *fair* treatment is all about. Awful, isn't it? To have to accept the same as everybody else?"

Judge Brooks suddenly appeared vaguely disgusted by his audience. "Here's the deal. When people take advantage of the system to try and get more than their share, *everybody* gets hurt. Insurance companies have to raise their rates. Pretty soon, regular folks can hardly afford coverage anymore. And so the insurance companies do their best to address the reasonable needs of everyone. It's reasonable to want to be able to walk, to live without undue pain, to do everything that a normal young girl can do."

He paused here and looked again at Kaylee.

"But spending $3000 on a dress, chasing all over the country to compete, dancing in Ireland? An insurance company is under no obligation to guarantee you an extraordinary existence. And to expect it to do so is elitist and arrogant! I'm denying your request for a writ, and, Mr. Wendowski, if you advise your clients to pursue this lawsuit, I'd say you're a fool. In my opinion, it is completely frivolous and without merit!"

With that, Judge Brooks left the bench, and the only sound was crying. The loudest came from Kaylee's mother.

Twelve

It was over.

Kaylee stood just off the left corner of stage number two, watching the smiling girl in the shimmering blue dress bow to the judges, bow to the musician. Then she walked swiftly to the edge of the stage, hopped down to the floor and headed toward the camping area in back of the last row of chairs.

Caitlin Hubbard had finished her final dance. She had started Irish dance only months before Kaylee. The two had connected immediately, had spent hours together at feiseanna, practices, sleepovers, shopping trips. Now the thing that had brought the two of them together was over.

For both of them.

"You looked really good!" said Kaylee, catching up with her friend.

"Thanks," said Caitlin, pulling off her ghillies, still smiling. It seemed to Kaylee the sort of smile intended to tell people one is happy even though one is not. "It'll be at least an hour before they announce results. Let's get some nachos!"

Caitlin slipped out of her solo dress, zipped it carefully into her garment bag, and then turned to her mother, who had only just picked her way through the crowds from where she had been standing at the opposite side of the stage. Tears trickled down her cheeks, a consequence of watching one's child say goodbye to a meaningful part of her life.

"Oh, darling, you were beautiful!" Mrs. Hubbard gathered her daughter into a hug. "I think that's the best you ever danced!"

"Let's hope the judges think so," said Caitlin brightly, now standing in shorts, a t-shirt and sandals. "It sure would be nice to recall in my very last feis!"

When had it happened? How? Kaylee recalled that the two of them had always been so similar, both bringing home a handful of medals in most Beginner Two, Novice and Prizewinner competitions. But about two years ago, Kaylee had quietly left her friend behind. Both finished near the bottom of the group in their first Preliminary Champion competitions, but then Kaylee had begun to recall. And even though Caitlin seemed to work equally hard in practices at Trean Gaoth, she had never finished in the top half.

But today she had danced very well. As a best friend, Kaylee had sometimes been obligated to say things like, "You looked good!" even on days when Caitlin had served up a less-than-stellar performance. This day's comments had been sincere, and she was certain her friend would get her wish. Although it would not be quite like dancing at nationals or at Worlds, recalling in Caitlin's final feis would make a nice ending.

Now Caitlin took her mother's proffered cash and the two girls walked briskly toward the food court.

While Kaylee was happy that her friend had danced well, it reminded her that there would be no happy ending in her own case. With surgery, Kaylee had possessed a small chance of being able to return to competitive dance.

But there would be no surgery. Judge Brooks had made sure of that.

And without surgery, there was no chance that Kaylee would ever dance in a feis again. Oh, technically she could probably suck it up, grimace, muddle through her dances, growing more and more clumsy with each bar. But she would never recall.

To recall meant to place in the upper half of the competition, an indication that you were among the better dancers at a feis. Because of Kaylee's awkwardness, her inability to suppress the pain even for one complete number, she could not imagine herself finishing ahead of even a single competitor, much less finishing in the top half.

And if she could not recall, she could not dance at Oireachtas. And it was at Oireachtas where she would need to place not just in the top half of all the best dancers from across the Midwest, but probably in the top ten or fifteen dancers. Only then could she qualify to dance at the World Championships in Ireland.

But there was no point in even thinking about it. She was as far away from that feat as a toddler, learning to walk, is distant from winning a gold medal in the Olympic marathon.

Caitlin brought the plastic nacho tray to a table. How many nacho boats had the two shared over the years, Kaylee wondered? As they sat down, two girls rushed over and smothered them in hugs.

Jordi and Hannah, who were a year younger, danced for Golden Academy. Kaylee had tried to recruit them to help saw off her foot cast so that she could dance at a feis five years ago. Jordi was short and radiated one of two expressions perpetually: either a beaming, heartfelt smile or naïve incredulity. Hannah was much taller and more slender with large, dark eyes that reminded Kaylee of a stuffed toy she had once had.

"We hardly ever see you anymore!" said Hannah to Kaylee. "But we sometimes see Caitlin."

"Are you better now?" asked Jordi. "Can you dance?"

Hannah elbowed her friend. "Jordi, she's not wearing her wig or makeup! Remember what we saw on TV?"

A light seemed to click on behind Jordi's eyes. "Oh yeah! We heard them talk about you on the news!" Then her amazing eyes grew troubled. "But I didn't hear how everything turned out."

Kaylee explained how the hearing had gone, touching only on the high points, as she had no desire to completely relive the experience. The two girls listened rapt, occasionally emitting small gasps or expressions of astonishment.

"That's so unfair!" said Hannah.

"So what are you going to do?" asked Jordi.

Kaylee shrugged. "Guess I'll have to get my driver's license so I can come to more feiseanna and hang out with you guys!"

This brought smiles and laughter and more hugs, but it also made Kaylee sad, for she knew it would never happen. Getting her license was still months away. And then there would be school. She might make the effort if the feis were close enough. But then other things would take center stage in her life—things that she could more fully participate in—and the world of dance would begin to fade away.

"We'd better get back!" cried Caitlin as the last of the nachos disappeared. "They might do awards soon!"

Goodbye-hugs were exchanged and Jordi and Hannah headed off to their own stage. Caitlin returned to the camp area and Kaylee helped her into her dress.

"Wish me luck!" said Caitlin, taking a deep breath.

Then Kaylee stood facing the empty stage where Caitlin had earlier danced, around which dancers and spectators now loitered or rested on folding chairs, waiting for results. How wonderful to be able to step onto a stage again and dance the way she had danced before. For the past six years, every time she had paused in front of an empty stage—or any flat, hard surface that in some remote way might resemble a dance floor—she had imagined herself on a stage in Ireland, a huge trophy cup in her hands, a sash draped across her shoulders. Ireland, the birthplace of her dance. Wasn't that where every little girl dreamed of dancing?

But Kaylee was no longer a little girl. No longer a dancer. And Ireland was just a place on a map. She might someday visit, tour the shops and picturesque towns, listen to music at a rustic pub, watch sheep create a traffic jam on a country road. All of these things might cause her to smile, too, for it would be Ireland.

However, a part of her would remember her dance dream, and how close it had all seemed after the Gateway Feis so many years ago, and this part of her would always be sad in a way that she would not be able to describe to anyone. A sadness of the soul.

Kaylee was shaken into the moment by the sound of a woman's voice, amplified by the stage's speaker system, beginning the results for Caitlin's competition. She realized she had been dancing in place while daydreaming.

Oh, please, let her recall! It would mean so much!

"There were twenty-eight dancers in this competition," said the nicely-dressed woman at the microphone. "We will be recalling fourteen."

"In fourteenth place, competitor number 1109, Vicki McKenzie from the Lakes Area Dance School."

Applause as a cute girl in a pink dress stepped forward to claim her modest trophy and take a place in the recall line.

Please, please, please...

"In thirteenth place, competitor number 478 . . ."

The list continued. Kaylee could see her friend across the dance floor where the hopefuls stood, a wide smile across her face, ready to be gracious if her name were called. But each time a name other than her own boomed out, Kaylee could see it in her friend's eyes—the effort to conceal the sort of sharp pain that might be inflicted by a tiny stiletto.

By the time the announcer reached tenth place, Kaylee's hope had begun to flag, and she felt the beginnings of disappointment in her stomach like a sack of wet flour. Caitlin had never recalled. The odds of her placing in the top nine would be pretty slim.

On the other hand, she had danced well. Kaylee clung to her hope, but as ninth place was announced—not Caitlin—she looked across, and she saw that her friend struggled mightily.

Eighth place. Seventh. Sixth.

Perhaps this is going to be like in the movies, thought Kaylee. *Just when all seems lost, they'll call Caitlin's name. She'll smile and cry and accept one of the enormous top-three trophies, and then she'll stand up there with all the best dancers and we'll talk about her last feis and how great it was forever and ever!*

"And in first place, competitor number 1277, Kara Milligan from Golden Academy!"

Now Kaylee saw that her friend's eyes had grown red, and there were tears streaming down her own cheeks as well. She met Caitlin at the camp area. Her friend wiped her cheeks with the back of a hand and began extricating herself from her dress.

Kaylee gave her a hug, and so did Mrs. Hubbard, who arrived a moment later.

"Oh, honey . . ."

"It's okay," said Caitlin, doing her best to bring back a smile. "I didn't really think I was going to place. There were a lot of good girls in my competition today."

Mrs. Hubbard wiped her own eyes but stood back, knowing when to give her daughter space. "But you danced so well!"

Caitlin folded her dress into the bag, stood up, shrugged. "That's life, I guess."

Thirteen

Kaylee sat in her room, gazing at the floor—the actual floor. Six years ago, she had torn up the carpet to expose the wooden boards underneath so that she could train for dance.

She was too tired to pull her gaze away. Kaylee had worked all day in the Stitchin' Kitchen. She wanted to lie in front of the television and watch a movie and not move a single muscle.

The work was not that hard—sweeping, stocking shelves, making coffee. But Kaylee realized that the events of the past few weeks had worn her down. Last week's dismal court result. Caitlin's feis on Saturday. And then today her mother had told her she should call Miss Helen and inform her that she would not need private dance lessons anymore. There had been a strange quality in her mother's voice and her expression when she had said this, something Kaylee could not quite decipher. But then it had passed.

Miss Helen seemed to have always known this day was coming, at least after she learned of Kaylee's involvement with soccer. Even though forces beyond Kaylee's control had ultimately bullied her out of dance—and in her heart, she knew Miss Helen would understand this—giving her teacher this final pronouncement would be difficult.

She lifted her head, looked to her shelves for a movie to watch. Most of the shelves were filled with trophies and medals from various feiseanna. These would have to go, too, wouldn't they? For some reason, she enjoyed having them surrounding her. Rather than resenting them as a mockery of her shattered dance dreams, the awards seemed more like old friends—friends she had accumulated on a long journey, and who understood and grieved with her.

Tucked away here and there were odd movie cases. Kaylee picked up a classic animated film about a princess. Not in the mood. She selected another, a comedy. Didn't feel very funny. Then she found *Isle of Green Fire* in her hand. For years, this had been her favorite DVD, the friend she turned to when she needed inspiration or when her mood was glum. She flipped to the back panel and read the words:

At twenty-four, Elena McGinty formed her own company and developed *Isle of Green Fire,* a breathtaking re-telling of Ireland's historic struggle for social justice— brought to the stage in dance! Ms. McGinty, who is honored to have danced the lead in every performance of *Isle of Green Fire*, electrifies audiences everywhere she goes with dance movements that seem to defy gravity and dare the human eye to keep up!

When Kaylee had first seen the dazzling footwork and costumes, she had known she wanted to be an Irish dancer. She had watched the DVD at least one hundred times.

Kaylee sighed, realizing that she was not in the mood for this movie either. She wondered if she would ever be in the mood for it again.

Moving to her desk, she pawed open the center drawer and pulled out another DVD, rolling her eyes and tossing it onto her bed. Brushing aside pens, half a pack of peppermint gum and an earring she thought she had lost, she found the battered school folder with MATH written across the front. Her real math folders usually went into the recycling bin immediately after the school bell on the last day in June. This one was a ruse, a secret hiding place.

By writing the word MATH on the cover, Kaylee had guessed that neither Will nor her parents would have any interest in it should they ever decide to go poking through her desk. At least that had been her theory. Two years ago, someone had removed one of the prized objects from the folder, and Kaylee had not seen it since. Opening the folder now, a math worksheet stared at her from the pockets on either side. These were decoys, placed there to complete the deception, although since the sanctity of the folder had been violated, Kaylee wondered why she had continued with this subterfuge.

She removed the worksheet tucked into the left pocket. Behind it was a treasured photograph of Aunt Kat as a senior in high school, resplendent in her track uniform, her arm around her sister, who was, of course, Kaylee's mother. The two young girls smiled brilliantly, unaware of the triumphs and tragedies that lay ahead—for one of them, not far ahead.

Behind the photograph was the thick booklet from Kaylee's first feis—before many feiseanna had "gone green" and stopped printing voluminous booklets for their events. Tucked into this was a picture of Kaylee and Caitlin, little pixies still in grade school, already feeling like champions in their first dance dresses. Life had been simple, joyful, unspoiled.

Kaylee replaced those items and the worksheet, digging behind the math paper from the right pocket. A paper clip held a ticket stub commemorating the ferry ride to the feis in Muskegon. She had stood on the top deck of the ferry with Riley. A pang of remorse stabbed through her and she was reminded of how much she missed him. There was also a ribbon from the Paavo Hospital run to benefit cancer research—the run she had completed with Aunt Kat.

The big item in the right pocket, however, was Aunt Kat's sketch book, filled with drawings from Kat's college days as well as more recent portraits of dancers from various feiseanna that she had attended with Kaylee. Kaylee's favorite sketch, though, was a drawing imagining what Kaylee herself would look like in a beautiful green solo dress—a dress very similar to the one that her grandmother had ultimately sewn.

This sketch exerted a double pull on her heartstrings.

Up until two years ago, Kaylee had kept the mystery letter from Lizzie Martin tucked into the sketch book. Even if someone had discovered that her math folder was not really a math folder, it was unlikely that they would page through the sketch book and stumble upon the hidden letter. Yet, that was apparently what had happened. Kaylee had suspected Will, of course, but he had never poked around in her room previously and had seemed to have no idea what she was talking about when she had questioned him. She found it hard to imagine that her parents would search her room or take the letter. And it made no sense at all that someone might break into the house only to steal an obscure letter written nearly two decades earlier. Kaylee acknowledged the remote possibility that she herself had misplaced the note, but this seemed even more unlikely than the other scenarios, for she always exercised such care with it. And so it remained a mystery.

In more ways than one.

When Kaylee had started taking Irish dance lessons at Trean Gaoth at the age of ten, she had quickly learned that Miss Helen hated soccer. This had been bad news for Kaylee, who at the time had been attempting to juggle dance and playing soccer on the Green Storm, a team coached by her father.

Miss Helen's hatred of the sport stemmed from a betrayal of sorts. Sixteen years earlier, Miss Helen had coached a more-than-promising dancer named Lizzie Martin. Lizzie, a natural athlete, had performed brilliantly at the Champion level and many felt she would finish among the top three at the World Championships.

But Lizzie had been a soccer player, A good one. Ultimately she had quit dance in favor of playing on an elite team. Miss Helen had been crushed.

Then, just four years ago, Kaylee had discovered that her mother had known Lizzie Martin at Northland College where they had both been students. Lizzie had been a star on the school's soccer squad, and Kaylee's mother had been, well, doing whatever it was she did. This knowledge had come to her accidentally when, as she had sifted through a box of old papers in her mother's office, she happened upon a note to her mother from Lizzie:

Hey,

Thanks for inviting me for pizza with you and the gang, but I can't on Friday. Big soccer game. What can I say? It's my life! We'll do the pizza some other time!

Lizzie Martin

Even before finding the letter, Lizzie Martin had fascinated Kaylee. She had always wondered how someone so close to the top of the world in Irish dance could toss it all away. It had also become Kaylee's mission to show Miss Helen that she was not like Lizzie Martin. As a result, the letter naturally intrigued Kaylee. She even theorized that it explained Miss Helen's animosity toward Kaylee, for it was possible that the old woman also knew of the long-ago friendship between Mrs. O'Shay and Lizzie.

The letter had also convinced Kaylee that she might be able to track down Lizzie and ask her why?

Why did you give it up? You were so close!

And what had killed the friendship between Lizzie and her mother? Something must have happened back in those college days, Kaylee surmised, for her mother had been upset that Kaylee had found the letter, and refused to answer questions about Lizzie.

Except to say that Lizzie had died in a car accident.

For awhile, this had ended the quest. But then Jackie had conducted some online research which revealed that Lizzie Martin had indeed been injured in a car crash, but the result had been a crushed foot—and the end of her Northland College soccer career.

Why would her mother lie?

Kaylee had been afraid to ask, and this had led to more detective work with Jackie. Unfortunately, the result had been a series of dead ends, including an embarrassing case of mistaken identity just a few months ago with a Mrs. Hartenstein, who ended up definitely not being Lizzie Martin.

Who had taken her letter? Where in the world was Lizzie Martin? Why did she quit when she might have been a world champion? None of that mattered anymore. Irish dance was yesterday. Tomorrow would be . . . biking . . . or swimming . . . but not at the Rosemary public pool. Kaylee grimaced.

All of these movies are boring. Kaylee sighed. Nothing exciting ever happened to her.

Correction:

Nothing exciting in a *good* way ever happened to her. She sat heavily onto her mattress and flopped back onto the comforter.

The doorbell rang.

I can't move. I don't have the strength.

Kaylee heard urgent, light footsteps and knew that her mother had taken care of it. Then she heard something she had not expected.

"Tim! This is a surprise! Come in!"

Kaylee peeled herself off the bed, intrigued. She did not know many Tims. If it were the one she was thinking of, she could understand her mother's astonishment.

She pushed open her door, padded through the living room and found Uncle Tim already seated at the O'Shay kitchen table, a fresh cup of coffee in his hand. Kaylee's father sat across from him, but Mrs. O'Shay fluttered around nervously.

Technically, Kaylee supposed that Tim was not really their uncle anymore. He had been married to Aunt Kat. She had poured herself into her blossoming art gallery in Chicago. Tim had immersed himself in the world of advertising. Ultimately, neither of them had time for the other. They divorced when Kaylee was six.

Tim sent a letter or card occasionally, but not with any regularity. Three years might pass between Christmas cards. He had stopped in at the Stitchin' Kitchen once shortly after Kaylee's mother opened her doors, and Kaylee remembered him visiting Kat near the end at the hospital.

And at her funeral.

Then he had vanished again. Although there had been a card at Christmas.

Tim had seemed, in Kaylee's limited encounters with him, extremely nice. And Kat seemed to like him, despite the fact that they had divorced. The relationship had fascinated Kaylee, who often saw divorces framed by anger and vindictiveness.

"So," said Mr. O'Shay after the opening pleasantries had been exchanged, "are you passing through on a business trip?"

"No," said Tim, who seemed a bit ill-at-ease, unusual for him. He stood about six-two, had broad shoulders and biked religiously in his free time. With his wavy brown hair and square chin, he and Kat had seemed the perfect storybook couple. Except for the part in the story where they were supposed to devote themselves to each other rather than to their careers.

"I came to see all of you," he continued. Then he spotted Kaylee in the doorway. "Hello, Kaylee," he said warmly, and then to Mrs. O'Shay: "She looks just like you when you were her age. Kat showed me pictures."

Mrs. O'Shay smiled, but then her eyebrows dipped in confusion. "You drove all the way from Chicago? Just to see us?"

"Well, I do have an ulterior motive," said Tim. "A proposition, I guess you could say."

"If it involves buying something, or us making an investment, you made a long trip for nothing, Tim," said Mr. O'Shay.

"Oh, nothing like that," said Tim solemnly. "It's just, well, I know how much all of you meant to Kat. When she and I divorced, it was because we were heading in different directions and didn't know how to make it work. Or maybe we were too stubborn or lazy to make it work. On some level, though, I'll always love her."

Mrs. O'Shay's gaze dropped to the floor, and Kaylee felt that warm heaviness that often accompanied memories of her aunt.

"I also know she had a very special relationship with her niece, Kaylee," Tim continued, turning his attention to her. "Kat and I never had kids, and so you were the closest thing she had to a daughter. I hope you know how much you mattered to her."

Kaylee felt hot tears slide down both cheeks as she nodded.

After a moment of silence, Tim resumed. "You can imagine how surprised I was when I turned on the TV a couple weeks ago and heard Kaylee's name on the news. I guess they fed it all over the country. 'Irish dancer takes on the big insurance company.' I was sorry to hear that your case got thrown out."

Both O'Shay parents nodded solemnly.

"It got me thinking though," said Tim, and now he seemed to grow uncomfortable again. "When Kat passed away, a portion of her estate came to me, as she had promised, because of some financial help I had given her in setting up the gallery. And that's when two thoughts occurred to me."

It seemed to Kaylee that neither of her parents was breathing. And then she realized that she, too, was holding her breath.

"First, I realized I didn't really need the money. I'm in advertising and I'm doing pretty well. No, make that extremely well. Second, I realized I knew someone who did need the money to pay for her surgery."

Kaylee's heart pounded as if she had just run a mile.

"Tim," said Mrs. O'Shay, her own cheeks wet with tears now, "we really can't—"

"Of course you can," said Tim gently. "And I'll tell you why. Because everyone in this room loved Kat dearly. And everyone in this room knows what Kat would say if we asked her what I should do with this money."

The room was silent for a moment. Then Tim reached into a pocket and retrieved his checkbook.

"All right, then," he said, a cautious smile breaking onto his face. "Does anybody have a pen?"

Fourteen

"Déjà vu!" said Jackie, meeting Kaylee at the curb in front of Rosemary Senior High, where Mrs. O'Shay had just deposited her.

"Déjà not quite," Kaylee replied, attempting to position her backpack in such a way that she could use her crutches without falling on her face. "Last year I was in a *wheelchair* on the first day of school. It took weeks before I graduated to crutches."

"I hope you realize," said Jackie, "that I'm giving up the opportunity to walk to class with the cutest sophomore guy in the whole school just so I can make sure you get to class without popping all your stitches!"

For a moment, Kaylee felt a stab of surprise, as if she had missed some major development in her friend's life. Then she frowned as she realized that this was a new school year and her brother was now a sophomore.

"Unless you want to add nausea to my list of medical issues, you'll never refer to my brother as cute in my presence," said Kaylee.

Jackie laughed and pulled her schedule from between the pages of a spiral notebook she carried. "What've you got first period?"

Their class schedules had been mailed weeks earlier so that appropriate school supplies could be acquired. Kaylee balanced on her crutches while retrieving hers from a shallow pocket. "English. Boring. Especially so early in the day."

"I've got chemistry. Even more boring! If not for soccer, I'd probably drop out of school, go to Nepal, become a sherpa. I mean, if not for soccer and Will." Jackie smiled slyly.

Kaylee grimaced. "Remember? Nausea?"

Jackie held the glass-and-steel front doors and Kaylee hobbled through into the bustling main hallway. "Now that we're juniors, I thought it would look . . . *different*," she said. "Oh well."

"How much time before class?" asked Kaylee.

Jackie flipped open her phone. "Twelve. No sense getting there too quickly." She led her friend to a table in the large common area that doubled as a cafeteria, and both took seats.

Kaylee noticed that posters advertising Homecoming week activities already peppered the walls, even though the Homecoming dance was still a month away. "Actually, Homecoming week is a lot of fun," said Jackie as her eyes followed Kaylee's gaze to the posters. "Homecoming, soccer and swordfish. They almost make up for the zillions of just plain boring and ridiculous aspects of high school."

Kaylee wondered if she had heard her friend wrong. "Swordfish?"

"Well," said Jackie smugly, "you said you didn't want to hear me talking about Will anymore, so I made up a code word so you wouldn't vomit. Whenever I say *swordfish*, I really mean *Will*."

"You're weird," said Kaylee, shaking her head.

Jackie shrugged. "Hey, I'm not the one related to the hot swordfish!"

Both girls laughed, and then high school returned to normal.

"Are you clumsy, or are you such a wimp that you break every time somebody bumps you in the hallway?"

Heather Chandler stood over the two friends, wearing the most amazingly fashionable white and yellow outfit, as well as an amazingly large quantity of makeup.

"Hey Heather," said Jackie casually, "did you mean to wear that much makeup or were you standing too close when a clown exploded?"

Heather's lower lip curled in a way that suggested a very scary clown. Then she ignored Jackie, turning her full attention on Kaylee. "Seriously. Weren't you on crutches last year at the start of the school year?"

"Seriously," retorted Jackie, "are you a total moron? Remember her accident?"

"I just had surgery to try and fix things that still weren't quite right," explained Kaylee, although she was not sure why she cared to justify anything to Heather.

Heather emitted a grating trill of a laugh, glaring hatefully at Jackie but speaking to Kaylee. "It's just one thing after another with you! I remember when you bumped into Brittany during a soccer game and broke your leg!"

"She ran into me!" Kaylee corrected her, annoyed. She heard Jackie sigh noisily and suddenly realized what Heather was up to. It wasn't about insulting Kaylee at all, at least not today. In attacking Kaylee, Heather was trying to get to Jackie.

And it was working.

Although Brittany and Heather had singled out Kaylee for years, Heather had gradually developed a special loathing for Jackie. While many people found Heather intimidating and retreated from her caustic attacks, Jackie seemed to delight in sparring with her. And Jackie's erudite wit often left Heather shredded and seething. The fact that Jackie and Heather both still played on the high school soccer team only intensified Heather's hatred. But despite her limited intellectual resources, Heather had deduced one thing: While she could not hurt Jackie in a direct verbal skirmish, she could wound her mortally by attacking Kaylee.

"And didn't you break your nose in gym class one time?" Heather continued.

"It wasn't broken," said Kaylee, growing angry, remembering how Heather had left the base line and purposely plowed into Kaylee like a runaway tank during a softball game. She knew she should not allow Heather's taunting to get to her, that she was only playing into her trap. Yet, it was so difficult to simply let her statements wash over her.

Heather shook her head. "Soccer was too tough for you. Then dance was too tough for you. Even gym class was too tough for you! Now you can barely make it to school!"

Although Kaylee could not see her friend at the moment, she could hear the involuntary sounds that one makes as she attempts to control her temper, could sense the fidgeting.

And she could see Heather's eyes flicker to where Jackie sat, see the muscles on her face subtly contort in cruel pleasure as she observed that her remarks were having the desired effect. Worst of all, something in Heather's expression suggested a still untapped cesspool of sociopathic glee, suggested that she had still not delivered the masterstroke—but that she was ready to.

"It's no wonder," said Heather, almost as if bored, "that you can't even hold on to a one-eyed boyfriend."

Jackie vaulted over the table top and would have had her hands around Heather's throat, except that Kaylee managed to grab her around the waist and wrestle her toward the ground. As she did so, a searing pain shot through Kaylee's right side. "Jackie, stop!" She was not supposed to be engaging in strenuous physical activity at this stage of her recovery. *No, please, don't let it hurt my surgery!*

Jackie's efforts subsided slightly, but Kaylee still struggled to hold her, and another pain shot through her. "Think about soccer!" she said through gritted teeth. "Homecoming!"

All three girls knew that a suspension for starting a fight could jeopardize Jackie's spot on the soccer team or even get her suspended from Homecoming activities—not to mention being booted out of school for several days at the start of the term. Jackie relaxed a bit more.

Then Brittany Hall stood only a few feet away. "Heather! Let's cruise!" Her voice had been neither angry nor mocking, simply a matter-of-fact command to her pet rodent.

Heather smiled broadly at Jackie and Kaylee. "Let's do this again real soon!" Then she flounced off with Brittany.

Jackie straightened, lowered herself to the seat beside Kaylee and then noticed the pained expression on her friend's face. "Oh, Zizzers, I didn't hurt you, did I? I know I shouldn't have— Are you okay?"

The pain seemed to have disappeared, and as Kaylee shifted position gingerly, she noticed nothing that felt like a chunk of bone that had been torn out of its appointed spot.

"I think I'm okay."

Jackie sighed. "I've got to stop letting her get to me. She's an idiot, but when she gets me like that, I'm the one who looks stupid."

"Looking stupid would have been the least of your worries if some teacher had seen you pounding on Heather," said Kaylee.

"It would have almost been worth it," said Jackie, her angry eyes glazing momentarily.

Kaylee smiled and shook her head at her friend. "This is going to be a great year! We don't want to get off on the wrong foot!"

The bell sounded as if to punctuate this thought, and Kaylee hefted herself up and onto her crutches as Jackie followed with her backpack.

Last year, I started off the year in a wheelchair. Crutches is an improvement, I guess.

They plunged forward into the swirl of students in the main hallway, Kaylee attempting to avoid the torrent of feet with her crutch tips.

Fourteen weeks. That's how long it was until I could take my first steps last year. Dr. Jung says I'll be off crutches this time in six weeks.

Around the corner they veered, into the language arts hallway.

According to Dr. Jung, the surgery had gone well. Kaylee was not certain of all the details—although she was sure her mother would know everything—Dr. Jung had apparently removed lots of scar tissue, had tried to relieve pressure on some nerves, had removed some nerve endings that had been damaged and had done something with the bolts in her leg. "You might have some numbness," Dr. Jung had said. "But hopefully you'll have less pain."

Now the two girls stood outside of Kaylee's English classroom. "Hi, I'm your teacher, here's your textbook, let's go over the class rules. Get ready to suffer through that routine six times today! I already know my teacher, because I can read my schedule! The rules are the same every year! And getting a textbook takes two minutes! This day is going to be about as much fun as . . . a conversation with Heather Chandler!" Both girls laughed.

The second bell sounded and Jackie rushed off in the direction of chemistry.

Hopefully you'll have less pain. Dr. Jung's words both fortified and frightened Kaylee. *Hopefully.* Even though everything seemed to have gone well, there was no guarantee that Kaylee's pain would diminish nor that she would dance again. From boys to Lizzie Martin to her surgery, Kaylee observed that life seemed to be filled with uncertainty.

"Hello everyone, my name is Mr. Hillis," said the middle-aged teacher, doing his best to broadcast a winning smile. "I'm going to be handing out textbooks in a minute, and then we'll go over the class rules."

Life was filled with uncertainty—except where school was concerned.

Fifteen

The plan was simple: Six weeks on crutches, then start training again, dance her first feis in January. After that, it would be a steady climb back to her old form, which would put her right on track for qualifying for Oireachtas, Nationals and Worlds.

"Slow down," said her mother when Kaylee explained her timetable. "Let's take things one step at a time. You don't even know how your leg is going to feel yet."

Dr. Jung recommended caution, too.

"Everything looks fine," she said at Kaylee's two-week check-up. "But everyone responds a little differently, especially when we're talking about nerve damage and scar tissue. We should start getting a clearer picture when you begin physical therapy next week."

Kaylee hated physical therapy. And she hated the fact that everything she really wanted seemed to take such a long time.

Jackie could not conceal her exasperation when she talked with Kaylee on the phone. "Once again, you won't be able to *dance* at the Homecoming dance."

"But I'd still like to go," said Kaylee. "And it would be nice to actually have a date this year!"

Riley seemed to be back in the picture. After a few bumpy moments during the summer, he had come to see her before her surgery, and then had visited her at home a few days after. During that visit, they had talked about the start of the new school year. Football had been mentioned. This had resulted in an awkward conversation about the Rosemary vs. Paavo game, which would be at Paavo this year, and how they were probably looking forward to it and how they could go together.

Probably.

The ride to Paavo High School from Kaylee's house was the quietest time she had ever spent in a car with Riley. Before the accident, their conversations had been so free and natural. Now it seemed like they were strangers again.

I'm being so stupid, thought Kaylee. *I know Riley better than almost anyone outside of my own family. And possibly Jackie and Caitlin.*

They had gone to feiseanna together. Had shared the most passionate kiss. Had almost died together.

But now, even though he sat next to her in the car, it felt like he was on the opposite side of the world. And she did not know how to get him home.

Or am I the one who's lost?

They settled into the Paavo student section, and as Kaylee tucked her crutches beside her, she suddenly could not help but smile.

"Well, this is a lot better than last year," she said. "I've only got crutches, and my mom isn't planning to sit next to us the whole game."

Riley raised an eyebrow. "I don't remember her sitting next to us last year."

"That's because I chased her away before you got there!"

Riley looked at her sideways, smugly. "One thing's the same: Paavo's going to kill Rosemary again this year!"

And suddenly, it was as if they were on the same side of the planet again. They talked about dance, movies, which of their schools had the inferior lunch program, music, chamber pots— neither was certain how that particular subject had been broached—wireless stuff and school dress codes. When they finally refocused on the game, they found that Riley's prophecy seemed well on its way to being fulfilled, for Paavo had a 20-0 lead.

"Well, it's halftime," said Riley, watching the game clock tick to zero. "At least that'll stop the bleeding for awhile. You want anything?"

Kaylee smiled. "Maybe something to drink."

"I'll run," he said, popping to his feet. "It'd probably be easier than you trying to make it through the crowd with your crutches."

Kaylee nodded and Riley disappeared down the metal steps, joining the tide of fans heading toward the restrooms or concession stand.

With Riley gone, Kaylee felt a bit like a foreigner. Although several of Riley's friends had stopped by to trade high-fives or yell things like "Paavo rules!" the conversations had generally been conducted as if Kaylee had been a pleasant-looking potted azalea.

She listened to the Paavo marching band for a few minutes, and then the crowd in the walkway at the front of the bleachers grew thicker as fans headed back to their seats with popcorn, hotdogs and drinks. She spotted Will and Jackie—holding hands, of course! Jackie seemed to be talking a mile-a-minute, which was not unusual. What caught Kaylee's attention was the genuine happiness that seemed to radiate from her friend's face.

Kaylee smiled. Although she frequently informed Jackie of how revolting it was that she was dating/seeing/even having kind thoughts about her brother, she privately was glad for the joy it seemed to bring her friend. And for that matter, for the joy it seemed to bring Will. For a brother, he was not awful. After all, he had helped her to find the track medal that Kaylee had inherited from her Aunt Kat—after Brittany and Heather had knocked the treasured symbol of her aunt's strength into the brush at the soccer park.

Someone plopped down suddenly on the seat beside Kaylee, and she squealed when she recognized her friend, Caitlin. "I thought you'd probably be here!" cried Kaylee, giving her friend a hug. Caitlin, after all, attended Paavo High School.

Caitlin looked around. "What are you doing sitting all by yourself in the Paavo student section?"

Kaylee explained that Riley had gone to get her a drink. This provoked a wry smile from Caitlin and a flurry of conversation. "Yeah, I'm sort of hoping he says something about the Homecoming dance," said Kaylee nonchalantly.

The word "dance" caused Caitlin's eyes to flicker toward Kaylee's crutches. "Has the surgery helped yet?"

Kaylee shrugged. "Won't know for awhile." She explained about the physical therapy and her plan for returning to competition.

"Oh, I hope the surgery works!" said Caitlin, giving her friend another hug. "Dance just isn't the same without you there."

Kaylee thought she had heard wrong. "But you quit dance. August was your last feis."

Caitlin gave a little gasp as she grasped her friend's meaning. "I didn't quit dance. I just quit dancing in feiseanna. I'll still be taking classes—just once a week. And I'll be dancing in the big shows, like on St. Patrick's Day."

Kaylee smiled, which is what she had intended to do. But then a strange sensation overwhelmed her. It started as a sudden warmth at her core, spreading rapidly to her extremities. Then a strange tightness in her throat and a stinging at the corners of her eyes. Tears came quickly, and the Kaylee fell into her friend's arms, sobbing.

"What is it?" cried Caitlin, her eyes wide and uncomprehending. "Is it your leg?"

It took a moment for Kaylee to lift her red eyes level with Caitlin's and answer. "No, I'm fine. I'm really fine. The best I've been in a long time." She tried to smile, though her cheeks were still wet with tears. "It's just that I'm happy."

Caitlin held Kaylee by both shoulders. "You call this happy?"

Kaylee blubbered a meager laugh, wiped her eyes with her sleeves, and the words rushed out. "It's just that you're one of my best friends, and when you said you weren't dancing at feiseanna, I thought I'd hardly ever see you, but you'll still be at classes and shows and . . . and . . ." The tears came again. "It's just that I'm so happy because nothing really good has happened for such a long time, and now finally it has!"

And this, of course, made Caitlin cry, too, and the friends embraced for a third time.

Finally Kaylee felt her control returning. She noticed that the marching band had retired, replaced by the two football squads, warming up for the second half.

"I was sitting with some friends up there," said Caitlin, pointing to a spot a dozen rows higher and to the left. "Do you and Riley want to come and sit with us?" Then she remembered the crutches. "Or we could maybe move down here with you."

"I can make it up there," said Kaylee. "I'll wait here for Riley and meet you!"

With a fourth hug, Caitlin swept off to join the Paavo group, and Kaylee scanned the moving throng for Riley. *What's taking him so long?*

Then she saw Brittany Hall, walking back toward the bleachers, talking, smiling. It figured that Brittany would be at the game, as she was one of the *popular* people, and thus apt not to miss any sort of social occasion. *It's a wonder, after all these years, that I can't sense when she's nearby*, Kaylee thought, only half-joking with herself. Wasn't that, after all, how it happened in the movies? The hero always sensed when her mortal enemy was close, and consequently could find a way to nullify the evil-doer's mischief and save the day.

Somehow, she did not seem to possess that sixth sense. Kaylee glanced at the crutch sitting next to her. *Maybe I'm not the hero.*

When she raised her eyes to the crowd again, she noticed who Brittany was talking to: Riley. She was smiling, gesturing, and Riley seemed to be enjoying the conversation as well.

Is that why he's been taking forever? This angered Kaylee, for Riley knew she had no one to talk to. He should have been hurrying. And he certainly knew how she felt about Brittany, so it had been thoughtless of him to leave Kaylee alone in order to flirt with Little Miss Wears-her-tops-too-tight.

It was the embrace, though, that made Kaylee boil. She watched as Brittany threw her arms around Riley's neck and pulled him into a major hug, and Kaylee felt like tossing a crutch at both of them. If they had been exploding crutches, she would not have hesitated. Riley then continued pushing through the crowd—alone—to their section, climbed the stairs, and in moments was seated beside Kaylee again.

"Here's your Coke," he said, offering the drink with a smile.

"You were gone a long time," said Kaylee coolly.

Riley shrugged, still holding out the Coke cup. "Just taking care of some student government stuff."

Student government stuff? While it was true that Riley was the vice-president of Paavo's student government, that would hardly have required a hugging liaison with Brittany, who did not even attend Paavo High School. While she had not particularly enjoyed watching Riley hug Brittany, it was lying about it that set her off.

Kaylee gazed at her feet, her face devoid of expression. "I'm not feeling well. Could you take me home?"

Riley's smile disappeared. "But you were fine a minute ago."

A minute ago! A minute ago the Skank Queen had you wrapped up in her slimy tentacles!

"Well, I'm not now."

Riley nodded, rose from the bench as Paavo kicked off to start the second half. Kaylee grabbed her crutches and hobbled to her feet.

"Touchdown, Paavo!" cried the game announcer, sending the Paavo section into a frenzy—again.

I'm on crutches, my high school is getting killed, and I still don't have a Homecoming date. Kaylee sighed. *I'm definitely not the hero.*

Sixteen

"All right, let's get full range of motion . . . that's it, nice and slow."

Robert, Kaylee's physical therapist, seemed like a nice guy with a gentle personality. Underneath it all, she decided, lurked a sadist.

He works me as hard as Miss Helen!

Privately, she was glad of this. The harder she worked, the sooner she would get back. Not that she was sure what "back" meant anymore. Even when she started competing again—not if; *when*—she would not be *back* to the level at which she had been dancing before the accident. It seemed hard to believe that thirteen months had now passed since her first-place finish at the Gateway Feis. It was almost as if she had been asleep, a prisoner of some awful dream, and was only now waking up to her real life.

"Do each of those exercises ten times," said Robert. "Don't rush them! I'll be back in a minute." He moved off to check on another client.

But "back" would be difficult to define in other ways. Without Caitlin at feiseanna, things would never be *back* to the way they were. Not exactly. And seeing Riley at feiseanna would be awkward, considering how their so-called relationship was constantly morphing into something else.

And Miss Helen had retired, so things at Trean Gaoth would never quite be *back* to the way they had been—although her old teacher had promised to continue the private lessons whenever Kaylee was ready.

That was odd, too, Kaylee had decided. Before the accident, Miss Helen would have never volunteered to do anything to help

Kaylee. But after the latest round of surgery, Miss Helen had called to see how she was doing.

No, Kaylee thought, squinting in concentration as she worked her healing leg. Miss Helen had changed, but it had not happened right after the accident. It was not until June—ten months later—that her disagreeable old teacher had seemed to change her attitude toward Kaylee, coming out of retirement to coach her privately.

She probably just needs the money, thought Kaylee. *Most retired people are on fixed incomes.*

But she knew it was more than that. Something in the way she looked at Kaylee as she tried and failed repeatedly. It was not pity, nor disgust. There was almost a kind of hope in the expression. But why had she suddenly been able to read this in Miss Helen's face in June, but not in May? Or February for that matter?

"How are we doing?" asked Robert, smiling benignly, the happy dungeon master. "Grab your crutches and follow me over here." He pointed across the wide room filled with work stations designed to rehab virtually any damaged muscle group or joint. Kaylee followed and Robert continued talking. "I've got another patient over here who needs to learn this same group of exercises, so I'm going to teach you both at the same time."

Kaylee figured the other patient would be some seventy-year-old man who had just had a knee replaced. There seemed to be a lot of old people in physical therapy. She was surprised when Robert sat her down next to a dark-haired high school-aged boy. She was even more surprised to find she knew him.

Michael Black.

"This is Mike," said Robert, and he introduced Kaylee.

Mike smiled, but only slightly.

"We go to school together," said Kaylee awkwardly. "I mean, we have some classes together, not all of them. At Rosemary. Actually just math. That's one class."

"Great," said Robert with exaggerated enthusiasm. "Let's learn those exercises, shall we?"

After a few minutes of instruction, and a few more making sure that Kaylee and Mike were putting themselves into sufficiently painful states, Robert left them on their own to complete the set. A few minutes elapsed, silent except for their occasional grunts. As they sat breathing between sets, the awkwardness of the situation finally reached an unbearable level, and so Kaylee asked, "What happened? To your leg, I mean."

"Football," Mike grunted. "First game of the season. ACL."

Kaylee had heard scores of high school football players, wrestlers and gymnasts talk about their ACL—anterior cruciate ligament—surgeries. It was the classic blow-out-your-knee injury. Most recovered, although some injuries ended careers.

"I'm probably done for the season," explained Mike. "But my doctor says everything looks good. And I've still got senior year."

Kaylee paused in her stretching. "Senior year! That seems like such a long time away!"

Mike nodded. "You had that bad accident last year," he said. "And then you just had more surgery, I heard."

Kaylee felt her face redden, and she quickly resumed her stretching. Michael Black, whose wavy dark hair and chocolate eyes had weakened the knees and fluttered the hearts of hundreds of girls ever since fifth grade, he actually knew what was happening in her life. She had always assumed that people like her were beneath the notice of the popular crowd, but Michael Black had noticed.

"Um, yeah, just a few weeks ago," said Kaylee. "I'm hoping to be able to dance again."

Mike smiled, and Kaylee almost forgot how to do the exercise she had just learned. "You'll do it," he said. "Brittany says you're nuts."

Now Kaylee suddenly felt embarrassed. She might have run out of the room if running had been physically possible.

"She says you work like a crazy person," Mike continued. "Says she's never seen anybody work so hard at being a dancer as you."

She was glad she had not run—or rather, that it had not been possible. This had the sound of a compliment to it. A compliment from Brittany Hall, delivered by Michael Black. The world was full of surprises.

Occasionally, good ones.

Robert returned and frowned. "Perhaps it was a mistake putting you two together."

Kaylee rested on her crutches in the lobby of the professional building which housed the physical therapy center, glancing at her watch twice just to make sure. Her father would not be there to pick her up for half an hour.

She sighed, stared out at high clouds that peppered an otherwise ocean-blue September sky.

"Need a ride?" Mike had hobbled up behind her on his own crutches, his leg in the characteristic post-surgical brace. He held up his cell phone. "I'm supposed to call my mom when I'm ready."

Kaylee shook her head. "My dad's going to be here in half an hour."

Mike frowned. "That stinks." Then he brightened. "Hey, there's a coffee shop one floor up!"

Seventeen

"You're going to Homecoming with who?"

Kaylee laughed into the phone, partly because Jackie's response was exactly what she would have predicted, partly because the whole thing was exciting, amazing, even ridiculous.

"But . . . it's beyond human reasoning!" said Jackie melodramatically. "It's like the laws of nature have been scrambled! What about Brittany Hall?"

"I guess she and Mike have been kind of off-and-on for a couple of years," explained Kaylee, hardly able to keep the glee from her voice. "They've been off now for about half a year."

Which, in retrospect, helped explain Brittany's interest in Riley, Kaylee thought.

"But," continued Jackie, still struggling with these new concepts, "Brittany has always hated you. Anyone else, she'd probably be okay with it. But you going to Homecoming with Michael Black! She could go super-nova!"

Kaylee had considered this, and it worried her somewhat. However, she preferred a different scenario.

"Hey, we're sixteen now! We're almost adults! Did you ever think that maybe we're past treating each other like animals or mortal enemies?"

Jackie laughed a mirthless laugh. "Need I remind you that Jack the Ripper, Adolph Hitler and Cruella DeVil were all adults."

Kaylee rolled her eyes. "Cruella DeVil was a cartoon character."

"My point," continued Jackie, "is that sixteen is pretty much the pinnacle of malice! It's the last chance to degrade and debase another human being before you enter the adult world and the defamation lawsuit!"

Kaylee had no answer for this except to say, "We'll see."

Jackie moved on to her next concern. "What about Riley?"

Kaylee explained what had occurred at the football game. "He lied right to my face! *Student government business*! And from the hug Brittany gave him, it's pretty clear that there's something going on there." Even as she made these accusations, however, Kaylee felt an unpleasant heaviness that seemed to start at the back of her throat and sag into her chest. She tried to ignore the feelings. *You're an idiot,* she told herself. *Riley's not interested. Besides, Michael Black is much cuter than he is. And he really likes you. Riley's got Brittany. Case closed.*

"So," said Jackie, "maybe we could double-date!"

Now Kaylee offered a mirthless laugh.

Homecoming week.
"Remember, class, we still have notes to take,
homework to complete,
tests to study for.
Just because it's
Homecoming week,
don't think that we're going to ease up blah blah blah . . ."

Signs taped to lockers.
Crepe paper streamers in the lunch room.
Posters everywhere.
GOOD LUCK TO THE VOLLEYBALL TEAM!
SCORE, BOYS SOCCER!
OUTRUN THEM, CROSS COUNTRY RUNNERS!
But mostly . . .
FOOTBALL THIS FRIDAY!
CRUSH 'EM!
SMASH 'EM!
TACKLE 'EM!
Spirit days, spirit contests, spirit . . . everywhere!
Where have they been hiding all of this spirit? Usually it's

I hate this school.

School lunch is terrible.
Too much homework.
This building is so ugly.
Too early in the morning!
Boring classes.

Not this week, though, because it's
Homecoming week.

Are you going to the dance?
Have a date?
There's still time!
Bonfire!
PEP RALLY
Cheerleaders, poms, class competitions
And the football coach introduces the team.
Homecoming week.
PARADE
Class floats club floats marching band classic cars carrying the Homecoming court waving
And then
THE GAME
Homecoming week.
And then
The Real Game
Homecoming Dance
The finishing touch on
Homecoming Week

It had been a week out of a dream. On Monday after school, Mike had driven her to the Cream City Mall in Milwaukee to pick out a dress for the Homecoming dance. "I'm glad that linebacker didn't take out my right knee," said Mike during the drive. "Otherwise my mom would have to drive us everywhere."

"Nothing too expensive," Kaylee's father had said, opening his wallet before they left.

When he had mentioned the approximate amount of money that she should limit her spending to, Kaylee had cried, "Dad! You can't buy a pair of jeans for that!"

Prior to her first day at physical therapy, Kaylee had entertained an image of Michael Black as an extremely cute boy whose thoughts were limited to sports and Brittany Hall.

"Yeah, she was my first girlfriend," he told Kaylee on the trip to the mall. "But we went together for so many years that we knew each other too well. It got sort of old."

Kaylee nodded as if she understood. "You seem . . . different."

Mike raised an eyebrow but continued to focus on the road. "Different? Different than what?"

"Than when I'd see you and Brittany together," said Kaylee. "You seem nice. You talk more."

"There's a compliment a guy doesn't get every day," said Mike.

"You know what I mean," said Kaylee, blushing. "At that party in the woods, you hardly said a word. And you ignored me." She pictured the secluded fire pit in her mind. Located in a clearing behind Brittany's house, it was a popular place for teen parties because of its secluded setting and because Brittany's father was always at work, while her mother was frequently passed out drunk.

"How many years ago was that?" asked Mike, smiling wryly. "What was I, like, ten?"

"Thirteen."

"So you expected a thirteen-year-old boy to be Mr. Smooth-talker?"

Kaylee felt herself blushing again. "No. I think you were drunk, too."

Mike shook his head, still smiling. "Didn't you ever do anything stupid when you were thirteen?"

Kaylee's lower lip jutted. "Tons. And I didn't stop at thirteen."

"We used to get a big kick out of having beers over at Brit's," continued Mike. "It felt like we were getting away with something. Like we weren't kids anymore. Yeah, it was dumb. But I never got drunk. Never liked the taste of beer. I'd sit there with one can all night, taking little sips."

"But some of the others—"

"Really *were* idiots," said Mike. "Don't get me wrong, they're my friends, but even friends sometimes do dumb stuff."

"Like Brittany?" asked Kaylee.

Mike shook his head. "It's funny. She hosted a lot of the parties, but she didn't drink any more than I did. Heather was bad, though. She drinks like she's trying to prove something."

How can you be friends with someone like Heather? Kaylee wondered.

"I'm sure you know what it's like when you've got friends who don't know when to stop," said Mike thoughtfully.

Kaylee nodded, although in truth, she had never faced the problem in her circle of friends. Jackie had talked about having wine at her grandmother's house a couple of times. And Caitlin had told Kaylee she had sneaked some sips of her father's beer now and then when he wasn't looking. "I only keep doing it because I keep thinking that one of these days, it's going to taste better," Caitlin had told her. "But it's always awful! How can so many people drink so much of that stuff?" She wondered for a moment about Riley, and then they had arrived at the mall and her thoughts vaulted back into the moment.

She had found a simple, green dress on the close-out rack in one of the larger chain stores. She had modeled it for Mike at the store, and he had whistled his approval.

On Wednesday, Mike and Kaylee attended the powder puff football game together.

"Oh, the two of you are so cute together with your matching crutches," Brittany had said with an exaggerated smile before taking the field with the junior girls.

Kaylee was not certain she could have returned the compliment. Brittany wore smudges of black grease-paint high on her cheekbones the way the boys sometimes did. She also had an "R" for "Rosemary" painted in red on each cheek. She wore a floppy football jersey and a headband as well as striped socks that came up to her knees.

It's like the circus is in town, thought Kaylee.

The powder puff game pitted a team of junior girls against a squad made up of girls from the senior class. The seniors usually won, but everybody knew that two of the school's best athletes—Brittany and Heather—could tip the scales to the younger team this year.

As many had expected, the juniors won—35-7. And as expected, Brittany and Heather had provided most of the heroics—just as they had in soccer and basketball over the years.

On Thursday, Mike took Kaylee to the bonfire. More and more people seemed to be whispering about them. Kaylee tried to imagine what they might be saying. Was it something like, *Wow, he's taking her to the Homecoming dance and not Brittany! She must be way cooler than we thought!* Or was it something mean, like, *Why is he taking someone so plain and pathetically nerdy? Did he lose a bet? Is this a pity date?* The thoughts Kaylee imagined them directing toward her made her anxious, and she rested her weight on her crutches, letting her feet move lightly in an approximation of her dance steps—like a teenage boy drumming on a desktop with pencils.

Friday was a big day, of course: pep assembly, parade and game.

"What are you wearing?" Jackie asked, staring at Kaylee's attire when the two met in the morning at the front of the school.

Kaylee blushed. What she was wearing was Mike's "away" football jersey, white with the red number thirty-three on the front and back, and the name BLACK in red letters across the shoulders. She felt a bit like a celebrity.

School was dismissed an hour early and the vast majority of the student body crowded into the gymnasium where they sat in groups by class. Kaylee and Jackie sat with the rest of the junior class, although Mike was with the football team in folding chairs on the main gym floor. Even though he was injured, he was still considered part of the team, and so attended all team meetings and sat with his teammates on the sidelines during games.

Will was not seated beside Jackie, and so Kaylee settled next to her friend. As a sophomore, Will had to sit with the other tenth graders. But he was also a member of the varsity soccer team, and so Kaylee found him seated in the folding chairs in the middle of the gym reserved for fall varsity athletes.

"Why are you smiling?" Jackie asked, seeing Kaylee gazing toward the center of the gym.

"I'm just so proud of Will," Kaylee replied. "Sitting with the varsity!"

Jackie nodded, but then she turned to Kaylee. "But you know what stinks? You should be sitting down there, too."

"Me?"

"You're a better athlete than ninety percent of them," explained Jackie, waving a hand toward the folding chairs. "A sprinter on the track team wins a race against seven guys and everybody gets so excited that they want to name a street after him! But you've won dance competitions against like thirty girls! And you've danced at the Midwest Championships! How many of *them* have competed against athletes from thirteen different states?" She waved toward the chairs again. "And before you got injured, you were on the verge of qualifying for Nationals! And maybe Worlds!"

Kaylee smiled broadly at her friend. "This is why I love you, Jackie!" But as she returned her gaze to the athletes seated on the folding chairs, she did find herself thinking how nice it would be to sit with the elite, to be recognized for her dance accomplishments. But even if she were World Champion, she knew that would never happen.

After the class spirit yells, the coach of each of the fall sports took a turn at the microphone, saying a word about his own team, and then wishing the football team good luck in the night's big game. Last was Coach Harrington, who introduced his football starters, bellowed a few inspirational sports homilies, and exited to a thunderous standing ovation.

Jackie yawned. "Is he done? Good. Now we can get on to the exciting stuff. Like who's going to be this year's Homecoming queen!"

A school-wide vote had determined the twelve boys and girls who would be on the Homecoming court. All juniors and seniors were eligible. Jackie and Kaylee had voted for each other. "At least that will guarantee we'll each get at least one vote!" Jackie had said. The top vote-getters would be named Homecoming king and queen. Of course, no one would know the results of the school-wide vote until Mrs. Ross, the senior class adviser, stepped to the microphone and read off the names.

Which she now seemed poised to do.

"This year's Homecoming is the most exciting I've seen since I started teaching at Rosemary Senior High twenty-eight years ago!" said Mrs. Ross.

"She says that every year," whispered Jackie.

"Almost twelve hundred votes were cast," Mrs. Ross continued, "and let me tell you, I think the student body chose some wonderful candidates for this year's court!"

Celebratory whoops and applause.

"She says that every year, too," whispered Jackie.

"Shall I read the names now, or should I let you wait until the dance to find out?" asked Mrs. Ross, with a wide, conspiratorial smile.

The crowd roared, imploring her to read the list.

Jackie rolled her eyes. "She does that every year, too."

Everyone in the gym knew that Mrs. Ross would not wait. Reading the list was just as exciting for her as for the students. In addition, the members of the Homecoming court rode in the parade in shiny convertibles that community members had volunteered to drive in the event, so they had to be announced beforehand.

Mrs. Ross cleared her throat. "Our first couple is Kristen Bell and Bobby Wasikowsky."

The gymnasium shook with cheering and applause. The two students stood and walked to the front near Mrs. Ross, where Kristen was given a bouquet of roses.

"Next," said Mrs. Ross, "is Heather Chandler and Carl Stanley."

Of course Heather was on Homecoming court, thought Kaylee. She was one of the *popular* people. Kaylee watched her stand from amongst the volleyball team and walk to the front, smiling smugly, basking in the ovation, as Carl joined her from the football section.

"Our third couple is Jennica Duerst and Jarod Plum," Mrs. Ross announced. Kaylee clapped along with the others.

"Couple number four," began Mrs. Ross, clearing her throat.

"Is probably as boring as couple number three," said Jackie, taking advantage of the pause.

Mrs. Ross continued. "Excuse me. Couple number four is Kaylee O'Shay and Michael Black."

Jackie's eyes went wide. "I stand corrected!"

As the applause grew, Jackie hugged her friend and motioned her to go—and after a moment, Kaylee did, hobbling to the front on her crutches as Mike met her on his. This seemed to endear them to the crowd even more, Kaylee observed, and the cheering swelled to a new level. Mike wedged his crutches under his arms and gave Kaylee a hug, and then the two joined the other couples.

Wow! Kaylee thought, smiling widely, gazing out at the packed, wildly-cheering mass of teen enthusiasm. *I never would have believed that Riley and I would be on Homecoming court together!*

Then with a gasp, she caught herself.

Mike and I.

Eighteen

"Mom, you're not going to believe it!" That had been the start of the phone call Kaylee had made after borrowing Jackie's cell phone at the conclusion of the pep assembly. Then, after delivering the astonishing news about Homecoming court, Kaylee had been whisked off with the other court members to the parade staging area near the faculty parking lot.

"Don't worry about it," said Jackie as her friend was drawn away. "I'm meeting Will. We'll wave when your car comes past!"

Mrs. Ross escorted the court members to a line of cars and then instructed them to wait while she flitted off to check on details. The weather was fairly warm for September, mostly sunny with a scattering of high clouds, and Kaylee took it all in like a kid on her first visit to the toy store. The dozen floats produced by classes and clubs rested off to the right. Rosemary's opponent would be the Drumlin High School Dragons. Many of the floats featured Medieval settings or knights-in-armor situations, often involving dragon slayings. The Rosemary Senior High marching band warmed up on the left. A few businesses had created simple floats, too. And, of course, there would be fire trucks. Four stood ready to be inserted at intervals in the parade lineup.

"All right, everyone, I'll be taking you to your cars now!" called Mrs. Ross, fluttering back in front of them. "Brittany! Let's take care of our queen first!"

Brittany Hall stepped forward, and Mrs. Ross led her to a yellow Corvette convertible near the back of the line. Kaylee doubted that anyone had been surprised when Brittany had been named the queen at the conclusion of the pep assembly. Her date, Todd Kelsey, was the starting quarterback and had been named king. Members of the football team did not ride in the Homecoming parade, however. Or even watch the parade. Immediately after the pep assembly, the football coaching staff spirited them away to special, isolated team meetings and a secret-recipe, carbo-load, pre-game meal, so that there would be no distractions and the boys would be appropriately focused and physically ready to play their best game. As a result, any female court members who were paired with football players rode alone in the parade.

One-by-one, Mrs. Ross plucked the chattering girls from the group and deposited them with their drivers. Finally, she signaled for Kaylee to follow. Kaylee hobbled after Mrs. Ross, stopping next to a blue Mustang convertible.

"Mr. Seilor will be your chauffer today!" announced Mrs. Ross, and then she was gone to make her next delivery.

Mr. Seilor reached out, and Kaylee leaned on her crutches to shake his hand.

"I'm Ed."

"Kaylee O'Shay. Thank you for driving. It's a beautiful car." The vehicle gleamed as if made of ocean-blue ice.

Ed smiled, obviously proud of his baby. "Why don't you climb in? I'll help you with those crutches."

Once Kaylee was comfortable, Ed returned to the driver's seat and buckled in. They made small talk—*What's your favorite subject in school? Did you go to the Homecoming dance last year? How did you hurt yourself?* Kaylee kept her answers short and general, particularly in response to the last question. As they talked, members of the Spirit Club came around with posters to affix to the sides of the cars.

"They guaranteed us they could do it in a way that wouldn't harm the paint," said Ed. "They better be right."

Kaylee watched as they attached the poster to the car in front of her.

MARIN KELLY
HOMECOMING COURT

Kaylee decided that this was just about the coolest experience she had ever had. Everyone would see her in a hot car and know her name and know that she had been voted onto court. Then she remembered the feeling of winning first place in PC competition at the Gateway Feis.

Okay, that was cooler. But this is right up there.

Suddenly, Mr. Allen, one of the associate principals, gestured toward the blue Mustang. "You're next in line! Let's go! Parade's starting in two minutes!"

Mr. Seilor turned it over and shifted into gear.

"Wait, your poster!"

One of the girls from Spirit Club sprinted up from behind and attached a poster first to the passenger side, and then to Mr. Seilor's door. Then Mr. Seilor moved ahead and the parade headed out down Park Street.

From what Kaylee recalled of last year's parade, as well as what she could see from her vantage point in the Mustang, the parade was led by the Grand Marshal—usually some local celebrity chauffered in yet another hot car. This year's Grand Marshall, Kaylee remembered, was Mr. Dahle, the retired Rosemary Senior High athletics director, probably the most well-liked member of the whole community. Then came baton twirlers and the color guard, followed by the high school marching band. Then a few floats, a fire truck, the cars containing the Homecoming court, another fire truck, more floats, and then a final fire truck. Kaylee guessed that she was probably about the fifteenth item on the parade menu.

"Here we go!" said Mr. Seilor as they moved slowly down the street. "Just wave and enjoy the ride, honey."

Kaylee felt a bit self-conscious but waved at the first group she saw, which happened to be a crowd of middle-school boys with painted faces. They just laughed, which, Kaylee told herself, was about what she might have expected from middle schoolers.

The next group was older folks—middle-aged and then some. The majority waved at her sort of half-heartedly, while a few seemed to be puzzled by her presence.

They probably don't recognize me, Kaylee thought. *A lot of the other girls on court are much more popular and well-known.*

The next group offered a similar mixed response.

Wait until we get near the library. That's where all the high school kids hang out to watch the parade.

The crowds got thicker as they rolled slowly toward the library, but the uncertain or baffled expressions did not diminish. She was almost ready to dismiss it as her imagination, or as the typical sort of reaction all Homecoming court members received—until she caught a glimpse of Mr. Seilor's face. It was clear to Kaylee that he sensed something unusual in the reaction of the spectators. However, he said nothing.

Now the library had come into view, and as the car began passing teens, the reaction did change. However, instead of the raucous, supportive cheering that Kaylee had hoped for, most teens either stared wide-eyed or broke into laughter, pointing and shouting.

She was relieved when she spotted Will and Jackie standing near Kaylee's mother, who had apparently rushed over from the Stitchin' Kitchen after receiving her call.

"Kaylee!" called her mother, smiling wildly, joyfully, waving like she had front-row tickets at a rock concert. "Sweetheart! We're so proud! We—"

Then she stopped, and Kaylee saw a change in her face. A change in Will and Jackie's faces, too. Shock, dismay, embarrassment.

This was enough for Mr. Seilor. He stopped the car, unbuckled, and stepped out. Then he stood facing his vehicle, a grim expression on his face. "Kids," he said dourly. He tore the poster off the driver's side door, crumpled it in his hands.

Now Kaylee unbuckled and let herself awkwardly out the passenger side, getting the first look at the poster that had been hastily attached just moments before the start of the parade:

NOT PRETTY ENOUGH FOR
HOMECOMING COURT

Tears formed at the corners, but she was also angry. Who would do something like this to her? And why?

But then she remembered the voice of the unseen Spirit Club girl who had put the posters on the car:

Wait, your poster!

She had not thought about it at the time. But it had sounded a lot like Heather Chandler's voice. And Heather was a member of Spirit Club. She could have made the posters right after the pep assembly—incensed that Kaylee had been voted onto court, making her an equal with Heather for the first time—and then she could have placed them on the car and still had time to return to her own vehicle.

Kaylee tore off the passenger-side poster.

Then she and Mr. Seilor returned to their seats and slowly drove on.

Nineteen

"What a gorgeous corsage!" exclaimed Mrs. O'Shay.

Kaylee decided that she was right. It was the most beautiful arrangement she had ever seen, and it went perfectly with her dress.

Mr. O'Shay took photographs, cautioned Mike to drive carefully, and hugged Kaylee more tenderly than she could ever recall. Then they were out the door.

The Rosemary Senior High gymnasium had been transformed by the cheerleaders and Spirit Club into something that looked like a cross between Mardi Gras and a fairy castle. They enjoyed the sumptuous, catered meal, endured the ritual presentation of the Homecoming court—and the crowning of King Tyler and Queen Brittany. Then the night was given over to dancing. Kaylee and Mike did their best, but in the end, they spent most of their time near the concessions garden, talking about everything from life at the age of six, to what colleges they were already considering.

He is so much different than who I thought he was three years ago, Kaylee thought several times during the evening.

"So do you still think you're going to be able to dance at a feis in January?" asked Mike as they sipped soft drinks and caught occasional glimpses of dancers in the distance illuminated by the flickering disco ball.

Kaylee informed him that she hoped so.

"That's kind of my target for being able to do full workouts, too," said Mike. "Maybe I'll come watch you dance at a feis."

Kaylee felt flush with pride. "Yeah. That'd be cool."

"I went to a couple with Brittany," said Mike, "but they were boring. But I think it'd be different with you."

"Why do you think that?" asked Kaylee. "I mean, I'm not even as good a dancer as Brittany."

"That's not what she says," Mike retorted.

For a moment, Kaylee could not process this. Had Brittany Hall actually complimented Kaylee's dancing? "What did she say?"

"That she'd never seen anyone who loved dancing as much as you," said Mike. "That if you had started dancing at age five like Brittany, you would have been in Champs long ago."

Kaylee took a sip of her soft drink without noticing what she was doing. "She just randomly said these things to you?"

Mike smirked. "I think she was worried about you. I guess she was thinking that you might catch up to her."

Kaylee hardly knew how to respond to this. Then she sighed. "Well, she's a hundred miles ahead of me now." She gestured toward her immobilized leg.

Mike's smirk blossomed into a wonderful smile. "I don't know. From what I've heard, I might still bet on you."

Kaylee could not suppress a bashful grin. And this was when Mike leaned forward and kissed her.

Kaylee felt a warm rush. They kissed again.

"Get a room, you two!" Jackie, pulling Will by the hand, coasted up to their table. "It's warm out there on the dance floor," she said, fanning herself with her free hand. "But it looks like it's absolutely smokin' over here!"

Kaylee felt herself blush. "Shut up," she said, smiling as she said it.

Will mumbled something about getting drinks and turned to the refreshment table. Mike pulled himself up on his crutches and said he would be back in a minute, which was Guy Code for using the restroom. Jackie found a folding chair and slid it next to Kaylee. "This year's Homecoming dance is so much better than last year's!" she gushed.

"I wouldn't know," said Kaylee, who had not attended the previous year's event. For Jackie, however, it had been her first date with Will.

"Last year, Will was so shy," Jackie continued. "This year, he kisses me after every slow dance!"

"Ew!" said Kaylee, scrunching her face in disgust. "Ew! Ew! You know what I've told you about saying things like that in front of me! Or if I'm in the same building. Or state. Remember? *Brother?*"

"We were thinking of going over to Lauren's house for pizza after the dance," said Jackie. "You and Mike wanna come?"

Lauren was one of the sweetest girls at Rosemary Senior High. Kaylee smiled, recalling how they had met at the talent show tryouts when they were twelve. Then the smile dissolved. "My parents would go nuclear. I'm supposed to come right home after the dance."

"Actually," said Jackie, "Will used my cell phone to ask them if it was okay. They told him he could stay for an hour. It's only two blocks from your house. And Will was supposed to let you know you could go, too."

Kaylee grunted. "I'll bet if I had asked first, the answer would have been no. With Will, it's yes to everything."

As if on cue, Will returned with cold drinks, and Jackie turned her smiles and attention in his direction.

Ew! Kaylee gazed out toward the dance floor and watched the moving bodies under a strobe light. Then she began to catch snippets of conversation from a large group of girls who had settled at a neighboring table. Mostly they gabbed about dresses that they loved or hated, but then the subject turned to the parade.

"Who built the float with the knight?" asked one girl.

"The knight slaying the dragon with a harpoon?" asked another. Rosemary's team nickname was, after all, the Mariners.

"That was the student government float," said a third girl.

"Where'd they get the knight?" asked the first girl. "It was pretty cool. They didn't make it, did they?"

"Brittany got it," said the third.

"Figures," said the second. "She buy it at a costume shop?"

"No," said the third. "She's a student government rep. I guess she talked to some guy she knows who's in student government at Paavo and he borrowed it from Paavo's drama club."

Suddenly, Kaylee felt a chill. Could that have been what she had seen at the Paavo vs. Rosemary football game? Had

Brittany caught up with Riley while he was getting refreshments
and asked him about the armor? And the hug . . . just a friendly
thank-you? Kaylee had never actually talked about it with Riley,
had never given him an opportunity to explain. *Why do I always
seem to be jumping to conclusions where he's concerned?*

"I'm back," said Mike, cutting into her thoughts. "Feel like
dancing?"

They hobbled to the dance floor, swayed back and forth to a
slow song, the faux-stars spilling from the ball spinning lazily
above them. Mike held her, one arm around her waist, another
over the top of her left crutch—both of his own crutches wedged
under his arms. Kaylee smiled into his eyes for a few moments,
and then rested her head on his shoulder. So warm. So strong.
The shoulder of an athlete. The subtle scent of sweat and spicy
deodorant, almost pleasantly intoxicating. Never in her wildest
dreams. The cutest boy at Kennedy Park Middle School, and
she, just a skinny, uncoordinated amalgam of freckles and
auburn curls. Now, the hottest guy at Rosemary Senior High.
Nicer than she had ever imagined. And Kaylee O'Shay in his
arms.

The song ended. Kaylee raised her head from Mike's
shoulder, and he kissed her, a kiss so warm and strong that, for a
moment, she forgot where she was. Then the lights came on and
Mrs. Ross's voice boomed from the speakers in the gym ceiling.

"Thank you for coming, everyone! This was definitely the
best Rosemary Homecoming dance ever!"

"She says that every year!" said Jackie, and Kaylee realized
that Will and her best friend had been dancing only a few feet
away.

Kaylee squinted up at Mike as her eyes adjusted to the lights.
"Hey, do you want to stop at my friend, Lauren's, for pizza?"

The notion seemed to surprise Mike. "If that's what you
want to do."

The drive to Lauren's took ten minutes, six of which were
spent trying to get out of the crowded parking lot at Rosemary
Senior High. A dozen teens laughed and shared dance stories in
the kitchen as Lauren's parents happily pulled pizzas from the
oven and filled paper cups with soft drinks.

Once again—as it had been in the overheard conversations at the dance—the hot topic seemed to be ugly dresses.

Kaylee introduced Mike. Everyone, of course, knew of him through his reputation as an athlete. And the girls knew of him just because girls always know about boys like Michael Black. Mike, however, was unfamiliar with most of the kids in the room, and Kaylee could tell he was growing bored. Finally, she pulled him into the living room, which was just around the corner from the kitchen, but quieter because they were alone.

"Sorry this isn't much fun," she said.

"I'm okay," he replied, smiling. "Did you want to do something after this?"

Kaylee looked at the floor. "My parents are pretty strict. I only have permission to come *here*. And only for an hour."

Mike took her hands, kissed her lightly.

"You don't have to stay," said Kaylee. "Jackie can give me a ride when she takes Will home."

Mike smiled. "What? And miss my kiss goodnight?"

Kaylee eyed him coyly. "Why would you have to miss it?" Maneuvering awkwardly with their crutches, they stepped outside onto the front step of Lauren's house and shut the door behind them. It was several minutes before Kaylee returned from the front step.

Jackie noticed immediately that her friend was now alone and Kaylee explained.

"Well, you're going to be the talk of the school on Monday," said Jackie. "Being Michael Black's girlfriend carries automatic celebrity status."

Kaylee emitted a little gasp. "I'm not really his girlfriend. We just went to the dance."

Jackie shook her head sagely. "Girl, everyone saw you out there on the dance floor. You went to the moon!"

The others in the kitchen whooped and hooted. Kaylee blushed. She tried to downplay things. "Oh, I'll be the talk of the school, all right. They'll be talking about the sign on my car during the parade and what a big joke I am."

"Brittany Hall," said Jackie bitterly. "She's probably so jealous about Michael that she can hardly brew a proper witch's potion."

"I think it was Heather," said Kaylee.

"Probably both," said Jackie. "One gets the bad idea, the other does the dirty work. Dumb and dumber." She then recounted several classic tales of Brittany-and-Heather cruelties.

Lauren's parents interrupted the gruesome litany with another pizza, and Jackie pulled Kaylee aside. "You know, it's time someone gave Heather what's coming to her."

Kaylee made a sour face. "I don't know if we're clever enough to find where her coffin rests during the day and drive a stake through her heart."

"No," admitted Jackie, "but good old-fashioned vandalism is often a pretty satisfying substitute for cleverness."

"Vandalism?"

Jackie held up her hand in hold-that-thought fashion. She disappeared for several minutes before returning with her coat, although she was obviously using it to conceal something and carrying it in her arms like a baby.

"Let's go!"

Kaylee looked around. "What about Will?"

"He's playing video games in the den with Lauren's brother. I might as well be on another planet."

They exited by the front door and walked as briskly as crutches would allow to Jackie's car. Once inside, Jackie started the engine and opened the jacket to reveal her treasures. Kaylee's eyes widened.

"Toilet paper?" She counted ten rolls.

"I'll drop off some replacement rolls tomorrow," promised Jackie.

"I hope no one eats any bad pizza tonight," said Kaylee. "What's this other stuff?"

"Shaving cream," said Jackie, holding up a can, "and soap. You write on car windows with a bar of soap, and it's nasty to get off!"

Kaylee nodded, beginning to understand. "Where are we going?"

"One of your favorite places," Jackie explained. "I heard rumors that there's a big after-dance drunk-fest over at Brittany Hall's. While they're all out in back getting hammered around the fire pit, we'll trash their cars."

"But my curfew—"

"This won't take long," said Jackie. "It's vandalism, not art."

Kaylee sighed. "This isn't exactly how I thought my Homecoming evening would end. Running around in the dark in a formal dress with a roll of toilet paper."

"It's probably more common than you think," said Jackie as she pulled the car onto the street. In five minutes, they arrived in Oakton Heights, the neighborhood for Rosemary's well-heeled. Jackie parked a block away. Kaylee threw on the sweater that she had brought, for the early-autumn night air was somewhat chilly. She stuffed several rolls of toilet paper under the sweater and carried a jar of petroleum jelly that Jackie had also liberated from the bathroom cabinet at Lauren's house.

"Rub it on a windshield and it's almost impossible to get off!" said Jackie.

At least a dozen cars sat in the Hall driveway or along the street, disappearing into the dark beneath huge, overhanging oaks.

"Let's just do Brittany and Heather's cars," suggested Kaylee. The fact that both girls had been driven to the dance by their dates complicated the matter a bit. However, Brittany's white sports car sat in the driveway, and this was their first target. Jackie wrapped it in toilet paper, since it was difficult for Kaylee to bend down to toss the roll under the chassis. Kaylee covered the windshield with shaving cream and smeared petroleum jelly on the rearview mirrors.

Then they found the car belonging to Heather's date and repeated the process. In the end, two rolls of toilet paper remained, and the girls strung white streamers through the branches of trees in the Hall's front yard, Kaylee bouncing on one foot as she tossed.

"I wish we could stick around and watch," whispered Jackie as they prepared to leave. "But it'll probably be four in the morning before those idiots crawl out to their cars."

Kaylee hobbled as far back as she could while remaining in the shadows of the yard, trying to get a panoramic view of their mayhem. Yes, it was childish. In the end, it would only increase the animosity between the girls—for eventually, Brittany and

Heather would find out who did it. But the thought of Heather stomping around the front yard, cursing some unknown enemy at four in the morning was simply too delicious.

Kaylee turned toward the road, glanced at the string of cars under the leafy canopy, and set the tips of her crutches onto the sidewalk to head in the opposite direction and to Jackie's car. Then she turned back. Of course it was dark, and she might have been mistaken. She edged toward the fourth car in the line, which had a familiar look to it.

"What's wrong?" asked Jackie, jogging to her friend, noticing her tense expression.

Kaylee gestured with a crutch. "This looks like Mike's car."

Jackie shrugged. "Half the people in Rosemary own Fords." Then she sighed. "Okay, so what if it is? There's no rule that says you can't go to another party after you say goodnight to your date."

This was true, admitted Kaylee. But something about the act made her feel uneasy. "He could have told me he was going to stop by at this party. I wouldn't have minded. Much."

"Maybe he didn't remember until he got in his car," suggested Jackie.

Kaylee swung around, stared at the house. "When we were talking about Brittany and the partying, it was like *this* was part of his old life, something he didn't do anymore."

"He's probably not doing anything," said Jackie. "He probably just stopped by to be social."

A slight breeze rustled the dry leaves above them and Kaylee balanced on her crutches, hugging herself. What Jackie was saying made sense. Just because Mike had taken Kaylee to Homecoming did not mean he had to stop hanging out with his old friends.

"But he should have told me. Maybe I would have come with him."

Jackie rolled her eyes. "You want to sneak back there, don't you? Spy on them?"

"I just want to take a look," said Kaylee, heading off across the lawn toward the side of the house.

Jackie caught up. "I don't like this idea. And you know how I hate being the voice of reason, which means this is a *very* bad idea."

"It'll just take a second. I know exactly where the fire pit is." These statements, of course, did absolutely nothing to mollify Jackie.

Coming around the right side of Brittany's house offered more cover than the left, Kaylee observed. The bad news was that the brush scraped against her skin and tugged and poked her dress. She pressed on, trying not to rustle the underbrush too loudly. Now they were parallel to the path leading from Brittany's backyard to the fire pit. Kaylee could already hear the crackling of the flames, smell the burning wood. There was no music, however. In the past, Brittany had strung a long cord from the house. Perhaps they had not wanted to take a chance on disturbing the neighbors. She remembered the chase through the woods and her narrow escape three years ago.

Now the fire circle came into view. Firelight glinted off a litter of beer cans in the dirt. People stood around the fire pit, talking in low voices.

Something's not right.

They edged closer, moving laboriously as Kaylee attempted to balance on her one good foot and keep the crutches from becoming tangled in brush. Then a hand on her shoulder stopped her.

"Look!" hissed Jackie.

Kaylee now saw why the music had been turned off, why the voices had not been blaring at their usual party pitch. The police were there. Several teens sat on logs or in chairs. Some stared into the fire. Others had faces buried in hands. One policeman was busy writing on a thick clipboard. Two were examining a young man in rumpled dress pants, burgundy-colored shirt and dark tie who stared glassily ahead. A third seemed to be taking down information from those who were sitting.

"Busted!" whispered Jackie.

"The police must have parked on a side street and taken the paths through the woods," said Kaylee. "That's how they did it before."

Kaylee did not see Mike. She saw Heather, though, her face etched deeply in anger. And Brittany stood near the end of the group, her normally confident expression now defeated, her eyes red. Kaylee wondered if she had been crying.

"I know they're jerks," whispered Kaylee, "but I feel bad. Can you imagine how awful it would be to get arrested?"

A sudden rustle sounded directly behind Kaylee. Neither she nor Jackie had time to move, and in an instant, a police officer towered over the two girls.

"Lou!" shouted the cop. "We've got two more!"

Twenty

She did not want to come out of her room. But Kaylee watched the digital clock, knowing that in four minutes, it would be 8 a.m. and the buzzer would sound, and quite possibly the worst day of her life would begin.

"You lied to us!" her mother had said the previous night after Tom O'Shay had picked up the girls from Brittany's house. "You missed curfew, you snuck off to a beer party, you vandalized people's property . . . and you ruined your pretty dress!"

Kaylee felt awful about the dress. Skulking through the woods the previous night had scratched the fabric, pulled threads and frayed the edges. She felt awful about letting down her parents, too. They had both arrived at the Hall residence within minutes of Kaylee's call from Jackie's cell.

Worried, concerned, embarrassed.

The Kizobus had arrived a short time later.

After the police officer had flushed them from the woods, Kaylee had wondered whether she would be handcuffed and taken to the police station. She quickly realized how difficult it would be for the police to transport fifteen teenagers. Instead, those who had consumed alcohol had been issued citations for underage drinking. Several had been given field sobriety tests. Only two had ultimately been taken to Paavo Community Hospital for blood tests. Kaylee and Jackie had escaped this fate after it had been established that they had only recently arrived at the party.

This had softened the edges of her parents' anger somewhat. But there had still been the vandalism. The police had awakened Mr. Hall—Mrs. Hall could not be roused except to utter a string of obscenities before passing out again. "She likes to have a little wine before bed," Mr. Hall had explained. Jackie had whispered, "I hear she starts sipping it about ten hours before bed!"

When the police had escorted them around to the front of the house to view the vandalism, Heather had been the first to comment, her eyes bugging out as she caught sight of her date's car. She was also the loudest. Most of her monologue had been devoted to the delivery of various common vulgarities, although she had thrown in numerous promises of retaliation and physical violence before the police had convinced her that it was in her best interest to zip it.

Mr. Hall had stared at Brittany's car for almost a full minute. The police seemed to be waiting for him to make some sort of statement. Kaylee's feet began to automatically move in place, working through the hard shoe dance steps, her recent nervous habit. The wait took long enough so that Heather could not remain quiet.

"Roger spent hours getting his car all clean and ready for tonight!" Heather's date, Roger, had been one of the two that had refused a field test and had been taken to the hospital. "I'm going to make sure he presses charges against you losers! If I had it to do over, I'd write something a lot worse on the sign on your car! Something like LAME PATHETIC FREAK!"

Mr. Hall had looked up from Brittany's car. "You put that cruel sign on her car in the parade?"

Heather said nothing, but she stopped talking and stared dark lasers at Kaylee.

Mr. Hall turned to the police, and what he said next surprised Kaylee and Jackie. "It's just toilet paper. I don't think we need to issue these two a citation."

"Well I want them to get a ticket!" cried Heather angrily.

"No you don't!" Mr. Hall had snapped. "They didn't key your car! They didn't smash windows! Or smash raw eggs on the finish! Everything they did can be cleaned up! And it will be!" Then he had turned to Kaylee and Jackie. "You girls can come here at nine tomorrow morning and clean up this mess. Then we'll call it even. That sound fair?"

Jackie had moaned. "But I was planning on sleeping in!" Then she recovered herself. "Yes sir."

Mr. Hall had then faced Heather again, although he stood so that his own daughter was also a part of the conversation. "And these two didn't organize this party, either," he said, referring to Kaylee and Jackie. "And they didn't ruin the Homecoming parade for one of the court members." He turned his attention directly to Heather. "So what *you* want isn't particularly important to anyone."

Kaylee had been too embarrassed to speak with Mike after the police had pulled her from the bushes. What must he have thought? On the other hand, she still felt hurt that he had come to the party without her. As the police talked to the O'Shay and Kizobu parents on the front lawn, Mike had edged over to where Kaylee stood.

"Why were you in the woods?" he had asked.

"Because I'm stupid," Kaylee had replied humorlessly.

Silence for a moment. Then Mike had said, "I didn't think you'd want to come. Didn't think your parents would let you."

Kaylee stared at her parents, in conference with Rosemary's Finest. "Whatever."

"I wasn't drinking if that's what you're thinking. Just a few sips. Just being social."

Then her parents had returned and there had been the awful ride home followed by the awful lecture at the kitchen table followed by a sleepless hour in her room, staring at the ceiling even though it was too dark to see it.

And that, regrettably, had been merely four hours and fifty-nine minutes ago, Kaylee observed.

Then the alarm buzzed angrily.

Make that five hours.

Her mother was nowhere to be seen when Kaylee shuffled into the kitchen for cereal. On Sunday mornings, she occasionally drove to the Stitchin' Kitchen to pay bills and complete other work even though the store did not open until noon. In some respects, Kaylee was glad of this, for she did not wish to continue the firestorm of the previous night. After rinsing her cereal bowl she changed into jeans and a sweatshirt, brushed her teeth and met her father as she returned to the kitchen, sagging dispiritedly between her crutches. Without much conversation, Tom O'Shay steered his daughter to the garage, and in minutes, they were trundling along toward Oakton Heights.

The weather was sunny and breezy, cool but not frigid, the sort of autumn day that Kaylee normally would have enjoyed. Today, however, she stared out at the passing homes and their gorgeous red, yellow and brown trees, feeling as if she could never be happy again.

Halfway to Brittany's house, Kaylee suddenly asked, "So how long am I grounded for?"

Tom O'Shay glanced quickly at his daughter before returning his eyes to the road. "Grounded?"

"Yeah," continued Kaylee. "For getting caught by the police at Brittany's party. Two months? Six months?" She hoped it would not be longer. But getting busted by the cops and having your parents come to get you in the middle of the night? Kaylee was certain that was pretty much a capital offense.

"You're not," said her father.

At first, she wondered if she had heard him right. When Tom O'Shay saw his daughter's confused expression, he explained.

"You didn't go to a drinking party, Kaylee. The police figured that out. Your mom and I understand it, too."

"Then," continued Kaylee, "how long am I grounded for toilet-papering the Halls'?"

"You're not," repeated her father. "Mr. Hall asked the police not to write a citation—and I hope, by the way, that you take the opportunity to thank him. Your punishment for the vandalism is cleaning up what you did."

Kaylee considered her relative good fortune. These consequences seemed amazingly fair and reasonable when compared with her usual punishments. "You mean I'm not being grounded at all?"

"Not exactly," said Tom O'Shay. "You did miss curfew. And you did leave the place you were supposed to be without telling us or asking permission. And this was after we had already allowed you to stay out later."

She looked at the floor of the car. "Sorry."

"Two weeks," said Tom O'Shay.

Kaylee's head popped up, her eyes wide. "That's it?"

Her father raised an eyebrow while shooting her another glance. "You want more?"

Kaylee shook her head.

"Sweetheart, we know you've been through a lot," said her father. "The accident, not being able to dance, the whole court case. And then Heather puts that sign on the car." He shook his head. "I can't believe she would do something like that. She was always such a cooperative and pleasant person when I used to coach her on the Green Storm."

Kaylee rolled her eyes. "Dad! She was just sucking up! She always been a . . . well, think of something soulless, pure evil and possibly reptilian."

Mr. O'Shay frowned. "Regardless, we know how awful you must have felt. And that certainly doesn't justify revenge. But on the other hand, it wouldn't justify making your punishment any worse, either."

Kaylee felt a tiny bit better, as if a pinprick of autumn sunshine and the thinnest wisp of cool air had penetrated to the depths of her soul.

Jackie and Mr. Kizobu were already waiting when they arrived. "Just use Jackie's phone to call when you're done," said Mr. O'Shay. Then the two men drove off, leaving Jackie and Kaylee in the charge of Mr. Hall. He smiled, showed them the rakes, rags and garbage bags that they would need, and then, mercifully, left them alone.

For the first ten minutes, the two girls said little. Then, becoming more comfortable with their surroundings and certain that they were not being watched over, they recounted to each other the highlights and lowlights of their personal encounters with their parents the previous evening.

"My mom says I have to learn to turn the other cheek," said Jackie. "But no matter which way I turn, Heather is still a jerk."

They started by unwrapping the two cars, one of which was still parked at the curb. About two-thirds of the toilet paper pulled away easily and could be stuffed into trash bags. The other third was still wet from dew and shredded into pasty clumps and strips that continued to cling to the exterior of the vehicles. Once they had finished with the cars, Jackie grabbed the rake and began pulling ribbons of toilet paper out of the trees. Kaylee could not help with this because of her crutches, and so she took a rag and began working on cleaning the windows and side-view mirrors.

The petroleum jelly on the mirrors presented difficulties. It had to be wiped off with paper toweling, yet a thin film of grease remained. More paper towels, and then she sprayed glass cleaner that Mr. Hall had left behind. As Kaylee scrubbed the driver's side mirror, she became vaguely aware that she was being watched. She looked up and saw Brittany Hall, dressed in a fashionable navy-blue warm-up suit, her blonde hair perfect, staring at the prisoners from twenty feet away. Their eyes met and then Kaylee focused on the mirror, continuing to rub.

What's she doing here? Kaylee wondered. If she had wanted to watch Kaylee and Jackie work, she might just as easily have done this from a window in her house. Brittany's face betrayed no emotion, so it did not seem that she had come to make fun of the two girls. It seemed there was really nothing to be gained by Brittany's presence. Brittany knew why Kaylee and Jackie had been skulking in the bushes, so an interrogation was unnecessary. Was she going to yell at them? That seemed a senseless notion, since Kaylee and Jackie were already undoing their damage.

Kaylee hobbled toward the front of the car and began wiping the shriveled, soapy shaving cream scum from the windshield.

Suddenly, Brittany spoke up. "How come you didn't grease the windshield?"

Kaylee looked up from her work. "Windshield?"

"Yeah," said Brittany, "you greased the side mirrors with petroleum jelly, but you just put shaving cream on the windshield. Shaving cream comes off just by running the wipers."

Kaylee thought the answer to this question was obvious, but she supplied it anyway. "Jackie said it makes a mess and you can't get it off. I didn't want anyone to get hurt if they tried to drive."

Brittany nodded, watched for a few moments more and then disappeared inside the house.

Twenty-one

Snow fell outside the little church, but inside, the windows were fogged and covered in droplets of condensation, and so the weather conditions might easily have remained a mystery. Even if the windows had offered a crystal-clear view of the afternoon, the winter scene would have gone unnoticed, so intently was Kaylee O'Shay focused upon her practice.

"Up on your toes!" barked Miss Helen. "Quicker!"

Kaylee winced, willing her body to obey.

Dr. Jung had performed Kaylee's surgery in August. The second week in October—only a week after the Homecoming dance—Kaylee had taken her first tentative steps, then had begun a grueling regimen of additional physical therapy.

"That's it! One and two and step and point!" Miss Helen clapped in time to the music.

She had begun a light weight-lifting routine and had started jogging tiny distances. "Build up gradually," Robert had advised. She was really beginning to hate Robert.

Her first jog had been unpleasant.

"It hurts," Kaylee had reported to her mother after returning to the house within ten minutes. "It still hurts! I thought the surgery was supposed to help!"

"Sweetheart, it's only been a couple months since your operation," said Mrs. O'Shay. "You've got to give it some time!"

Give it some time. Take your time. It'll feel better over time. She was really starting to hate it when people said things like that, too.

October had dissolved into cold rains and the end of a two-win football season for the Rosemary Mariners. She and Mike had gone out for pizza or burgers after most of the games, excepting the ones played while Kaylee was grounded. "If you don't want me to go to those kinds of parties, then I won't," he had told her the week after Homecoming and the Brittany Hall bash. "I'm not exactly an alcoholic, you know. And you're more important to me than that stuff."

Kaylee remembered how she had felt warm all over, hearing those words.

"Point the toes!" called Miss Helen, pulling her once again into December. "Don't relax when you get tired."

Why don't you try it, you old cow! Kaylee thought to herself. Then she remembered that the Old Cow had finished second in the entire world in Irish dance. Of course, that had been more than four decades ago. Still, it seemed hard to imagine that Miss Helen had once been that slender young girl she had seen in the old photograph at Golden Academy.

"All right," said Miss Helen, shutting off the music. "Let's take a break and then we will go again."

She sunk to the wooden floor, resting her back against the tope plaster, swigging from her water bottle. Shutting her eyes, she let her mind drift again to more pleasant moments.

Like the night after the Waterville game—one of Rosemary's rare wins. Mike had driven her home, and they had sat in his car in the O'Shay driveway, talking, for almost an hour. Kaylee smiled to herself. All right, they had not just talked. Thinking about it almost brought back the thrill that she felt when Mike kissed her, his arms around her, their warmth, the fogging windows of the car. And then Mr. O'Shay had flipped on the porch light and Kaylee had said goodnight.

"Put on your hard shoes now," said Miss Helen, and Kaylee's eyes blinked open. Had Miss Helen ever had a boyfriend? Probably not, Kaylee decided. Although she had not always been old and the size of a vending machine, her abrasive personality would have certainly chased away any potential suitors.

Kaylee pried off her ghillies and dug in her bag for the hard shoes. While her soft shoe dances were still awkward and painful, her hard shoe steps established a new low. Kaylee could tolerate the pain for perhaps three-quarters of her hornpipe, and then she had to stop.

"Perhaps you need to try and put the pain out of your mind," said Miss Helen. "By focusing on it so much, you may feel it more."

"I'm trying," grunted Kaylee.

"All dancers go through pain," continued Miss Helen. "To some degree. I used to coach a very good dancer who would say, 'Focus on the prize, not the pain.' It was her way of saying that it seems to hurt less when you're not thinking about it."

Kaylee stared at Miss Helen. "Which dancer used to say that?"

Miss Helen turned away. "Lizzie Martin."

Pain.

Didn't people grow used to pain? She thought that she had read this somewhere. After awhile, it becomes second nature, almost like background noise, like a freeway that runs past your backyard, still unpleasant but something one expects and can live with. She kept waiting for her pain to become part of the background, but it continued to stand at center stage, confronting her constantly.

Pain.

She remembered November, how after a month she could still run only about a mile before the pain became too much.

"More time." Too many people to count had said it.

In late November, the first basketball game of the season. Rosemary beat Cream City Academy. The porch light had come on after only four minutes. She had waved him out of the driveway, watched his taillights disappear down Cranberry Street, and then her mother had called her in to the telephone.

It had been Riley.

"Just felt like calling. What are you doing?"

She explained that she had just gotten home from the Rosemary basketball game.

"I suppose you were at the Paavo game tonight," Kaylee had said.

There had been a pause. "Kaylee, don't you know what day this is?"

Kaylee had sighed, too tired for puzzles. "The Saturday after Thanksgiving—" Then it hit her. She felt ashamed for not remembering, for it illustrated just how far removed from the competitive realm of dance she had become. "You're at Oireachtas!"

She had heard a faint chuckle on the other end. "I recalled."

"Oh, Riley!" In that moment, she would have given anything to have been there with him, standing in the grand hall where results were announced, watching him stride onto the stage for his award. In her mind's eye, she had imagined herself throwing her arms around him after the ceremony.

"Not high enough to go to Worlds," he added.

"But that's still so great!" It had been such a long time since a smile had so completely transformed her face, since she had felt herself so utterly transported by joy. "When are you coming home?"

"Not until Tuesday," he had said, the giddiness now creeping into his own voice. "I thought maybe we could get together later next week, you know, and maybe celebrate."

Kaylee had hesitated. "Celebrate?"

"Yeah," said Riley, his voice somewhat more guarded. "You know, maybe go to a movie. Get something to eat. I dunno."

"Maybe something," said Kaylee, the magic draining from the conversation. "Maybe something to eat."

There had been a silence. Then: "You're still going out with him, aren't you?"

Kaylee had nodded morosely, and then had realized he could not see this. "Yes. But we can still do something."

They had talked for a few more minutes, trading awkward comments, and then it had been over.

You are so stupid! Kaylee told herself afterwards, burrowing her face into her pillow. *Why did you say maybe? Why didn't you simply say, Sure! Anything! Let's celebrate our brains out! You ruined his big night at Oireachtas, and you ruined . . . everything!*

Pain.

Then the following Monday in school, the feeling that people were staring at her as she walked toward the table where she and Jackie always met.

"You haven't heard?" her friend had hissed. "It's all over school!"

Kaylee had continued to feel the eyes burning into her back, and she knew that whatever it was that she had not heard somehow concerned her.

"Mike was arrested on Friday night!" Jackie had reported breathlessly.

Kaylee's heart had begun to thump loudly. "He was with me on Friday. We went to the basketball game."

Jackie had seemed reluctant to speak. "After he dropped you off, he bought beer with a fake ID. Then he went to a party at Heather's. That's where the cops busted them. I guess he resisted. Tried to run."

Kaylee had been unable to speak for a moment.

"I'm sorry," Jackie had said, and had given her friend a hug.

"He told me he was done with that," Kaylee had muttered. "He told me that I meant more to him than . . ."

Pain.

She remembered having her father drive her to Mike's house that evening, how she had rung the doorbell, how she had placed his neatly-folded football jersey—the one she had worn during the Homecoming parade—into his hands, and how she had then walked silently away, not showing him a single tear.

"Let's stop the daydreaming now and see if we can get through that hornpipe today!" said Miss Helen.

Kaylee stood up, and before she knew what she was doing, she blurted, "Did you ever have a boyfriend?"

The only indication that the question might have surprised Miss Helen was that it took her a moment to answer.

"Is Miss Kaylee having boy problems?"

Kaylee sighed. "Boy disasters is more like it!"

Miss Helen nodded quietly, her expression still sphinx-like. "There were a few."

A few?

"Were boys just as stupid back then?"

This caused a slight curl at the corner of Miss Helen's mouth. "I don't know if they were stupid, unless by stupid you mean that they sometimes could break your heart."

Kaylee experienced one of those rare moments where she actually felt a twinge of sympathy for her old teacher.

"But you have probably broken a few, too," Miss Helen continued.

Kaylee thought of Riley, but then she pushed the image away. "Did you ever break anyone's heart?"

Miss Helen seemed to consider this a moment, and then she sighed. "I don't know. I am probably not the best one to ask about boy questions. So many years. But we all have our hearts broken at some point."

Miss Helen seemed like she might continue, and Kaylee wondered whether she might talk about Lizzie Martin and the heartbreak that her abrupt departure from dance had caused. However, her old teacher chose a different course.

"Many years ago, I was engaged."

"To be married?" asked Kaylee, and then realized the stupidity of her question.

Miss Helen smiled wanly. "That is what it usually implies, yes. Johnny McDonnell. A dancer. But he died in a car accident. And that was that."

"I'm sorry," said Kaylee, and she was.

"Well," continued Miss Helen, "it was a long time ago. And there is nothing we can do about the past. But like I said, we all have our little heartaches. Perhaps yours can still be mended."

For a moment, silence enveloped them, and then Miss Helen walked to the music box. "We had better see if we can mend that hornpipe of yours."

Kaylee stepped to the center of the narrow practice area.

"I think I perhaps I owe you a bit of an apology," said Miss Helen as she bent to the machine.

"An apology?"

"Now you know why I did not visit you in the hospital," said Miss Helen. "Last year."

Kaylee understood. She could hardly imagine what painful memories such a visit might have generated.

The music began, but Kaylee called out, "I have another question."

Miss Helen stopped the music, looked around the church's interior with some humor. "This place is hearing its share of confessions today."

"Why did you agree to coach me again? Back in the spring. First you said no, but then you changed your mind. Why?"

Kaylee saw the same odd, fleeting look in Miss Helen's eyes that she had seen before in reference to this question, like a swimmer suddenly caught in a dangerous current. Then it passed as the old woman seemed to gather her resolve.

"Boys are not the only things that can break a heart. I know how it is with you and Irish dance. This is the only way to make it whole for you."

Kaylee nodded, and Miss Helen started the music again. She pointed her toe as Miss Helen clapped and counted in time to the music. "One and two and ready and . . ."

Kaylee's feet began their raucous choreography, a deafening, intricate cadence. Her mind knew the steps, knew them as if they had been written into her soul since birth.

But the pain.

First dull, then blossoming, like a flame fed by gasoline, stabbing, insistent.

Give it time. Her mother's voice.

But she could feel her form beginning to slip. In less than a month, the Snow Feis would be held in Milwaukee. The feis at which Kaylee had planned to begin her comeback. But she knew now, as the pain made itself evident on her face, that she would not be ready in time.

She wondered if she ever would.

Twenty-two

Some things never change, thought Kaylee as she tossed her sleeping bag behind the sofa in Caitlin's vast, comfortable rec room. The Christmas break sleepover had been a tradition dating to Kaylee's first year in Irish dance. Kaylee had hosted it a few times, and Meghan and April once each. This year, Caitlin had invited Jordi and Hannah as well.

"Do you think the Hubbards will have enough room?" Mrs. O'Shay had asked Kaylee.

Kaylee had rolled her eyes. "Yeah . . . unless Caitlin gets carried away and invites another fifty people!"

As Kaylee listened to Meghan recite the list of presents she had received for Christmas, she heard a tumble of footsteps on the carpeted stair. Jordi and Hannah bounced down, their heads twisting to take it all in.

"This must be like the biggest house ever!" said Hannah, her eyes riveted on the fireplace.

Jordi nodded. "I'll bet the presents under Caitlin's tree were a lot bigger than the presents under my tree!"

Kaylee showed the two where to stow their bags. Then Caitlin came down the stairs, carefully carrying three large boxed pizzas.

"One pepperoni, one veggie, and one just cheese!" she announced, setting them on a long countertop. "And we've got breadsticks, too!"

As they devoured the pizzas, the six talked about atrocities that had occurred at school during the first semester, offered their opinions about which feiseanna could not be missed in the new year, and shared tales of their favorite Christmas gifts.

Every present received the requisite oohs and ahs from the group until it was Caitlin's turn.

"I got a car!" she said, unable to stifle a broad smile.

No one said anything for a moment. Then Hannah spoke up. "A real one? The kind you can drive?"

Jordi just shook her head. "No, Einstein, the kind you can fly to the moon!"

Then they scrambled up the stairs to the garage where Caitlin proudly displayed the white coupe.

As they returned to the rec room, Jordi shook her head again. "Caitlin's presents *are* a lot bigger than the presents under my tree!"

Kaylee felt happy for her friend, but also a little deflated. Most of her friends in the junior class already had their licenses.

"Let the movie marathon begin!" called Caitlin, revealing a handful of choices.

They started with a comedy: Boy meets Girl. Boy is kind of a reject. Boy makes enemy of Big Jerk. Jerk tries to keep Boy from achieving his dream. Boy does a lot of dumb stuff that ultimately helps him to prevail against Jerk. And of course, Boy gets Girl and lives happily ever after.

That's the first time I've seen that movie, Kaylee thought, *but it feels like I've seen it a hundred times.*

They moved on to an animated musical—a classic! The girls sang along to all of the songs.

The third was a scary movie about a creepy, teenager-eating evil presence that lived in the shadows at a private school. By the end of the film, they were all huddled together on a single sleeping bag in the middle of the floor.

"That was awesome!" said Jordi.

April, on the other hand, seemed as if she might never sleep again.

"I'm hungry!" moaned Meghan.

Caitlin poked at the empty boxes. "You guys finished all the pizza hours ago. I think we've got cookies upstairs. And I could make sandwiches."

"Do you have any nachos?" asked Jordi. "I'm really in the mood for nachos!"

"Ooh, me too!" chimed in April. "With salsa."

A chant went up for nachos.

"Sh!" warned Caitlin. "My parents are asleep! Besides, we don't have any nachos."

"Let's go get some," suggested Meghan.

Caitlin frowned. "It's after midnight."

"There's a convenience store half a mile from here that's open 24-7," said Meghan. "Caitlin can take us for a ride in her new car!"

They all started jabbering at once, but Caitlin appeared horrified.

"I can only have one other person in the car with me! Besides, my parents would never let me take it out this late."

April offered a wry smile. "Who says you have to tell them?"

They all laughed.

"I'm just messing with you," Meghan said to Caitlin. "We can walk."

"But my parents—"

"We'll be quiet,' said Meghan. "They'll never know."

Caitlin's resolve seemed to falter. "It's December! It's cold! There's snow on the ground!"

"And that's the channel six weather report!" said Meghan, adopting a deep, television announcer voice.

"It's not like we're going to the South Pole," stated April.

"I need nachos!" called Jordi.

Caitlin sighed. "I am so going to get grounded!"

The girls pulled on jeans and sweat pants over their jams, donned their jackets and gloves and carefully let themselves out the sliding glass door leading to Caitlin's backyard. Then they crept around the side of the house.

"My shoes are getting full of snow!"

"Sh!"

Streetlights threw wide, lemon-colored circles onto the snowy streets every couple of hundred feet.

"Isn't this exciting?" asked April.

"Like scuba diving with sharks," replied Caitlin.

"Don't get a nosebleed!" giggled Hannah.

Kaylee sympathized with Caitlin, who clearly was not enjoying the expedition. Kaylee had been grounded enough that she was not anxious to experience the punishment again—or have it foisted upon her friend. However, she was even more concerned that the Hubbard parents might wake and worry when they discovered that all six girls attending their daughter's sleepover had vanished. Any moment she expected to hear the sounds of police sirens as authorities began combing the city for the lost girls.

And then, in a surprisingly short time, the tree-lined streets of Caitlin's neighborhood gave way to a main road. The convenience store stood in front of them. *I know this road*, thought Kaylee. *Another half mile and you come to the college where they shoot off the fireworks. And a little past that is the dance studio.* It occurred to her that after seven years of coming to Trean Gaoth Academy for her dancing, she had gotten to know Paavo pretty well. A dark sedan glided past the convenience store.

That looks like Riley's car!

But it was not. A closer look indicated that it had a white pinstripe that Riley's car lacked. And the man driving the dark sedan appeared to be eighty.

She often did that when she was in Paavo. Riley lived here, too, but in the other direction. Any dark blue sedan made her heart beat a little faster on the chance that it would be him.

And as they approached the convenience store, another dark car slowed to pull into the lot. Kaylee's heart raced. A boy driving, a girl seated next to him . . . the girl, blonde and laughing . . .

Oh, no! Kaylee thought. *Not Riley and Brittany. Not now!*

But as the car coasted next to the pumps and was illuminated by the overhead lights, she saw that it was dark green, not dark blue. And as the boy got out, she saw that he was stocky and had rampant acne. The girl, she now observed, had a wide face and eyes like a fish.

They bought two bags of chips, a jar of salsa and one of a spicy variety of ranch dip.

"Let's eat them while we walk!" said Meghan as they began the return trip.

"No!" said Caitlin. "We'd have to take off our gloves and our fingers will freeze!"

Suddenly, Jordi turned to Kaylee. "You walked!" When Kaylee did not immediately comprehend, she added, "You walked all the way to the store!"

"It only hurts when I dance,' explained Kaylee. "Or run. Any kind of bouncing exercise."

"But I thought that surgery you had in August was supposed to fix that," said Hannah.

Kaylee could not believe she was going to say it. "It takes time, I guess."

"Aren't you going to dance at Snow Feis?" asked April.

Kaylee shook her head. "Don't think I'll be ready. But I've been working hard. I'm back at classes at Trean Gaoth and Miss Helen is giving me private lessons."

Suddenly she remembered what Miss Helen had said about being engaged. It seemed a rather delicious bit of gossip, just the sort of thing appropriate for a sleepover, especially if those attending were Irish dancers.

On the other hand, Miss Helen may not have intended the detail to be confidential. How would she feel if she knew that Kaylee had blabbed it everywhere?

But what was the harm? It wasn't a secret like being an ax murderer or working undercover for a foreign government. Lots of people got engaged.

"Miss Helen told me she once had a fiancé."

April, Meghan and Caitlin made the appropriate surprised noises as they walked.

"Why didn't they marry?" asked Caitlin.

Kaylee explained the car crash.

"Lucky for him!" chuckled Meghan. "She's mega-frumpy."

For some reason this angered Kaylee slightly, made her wish that she had never said anything.

"When she was our age, she looked a lot different," Kaylee retorted. "There's a picture of her at Golden Academy." She turned to address Jordi and Hannah as they walked. "It's hanging on your hall of fame wall."

Both Golden Academy dancers squinted in concentration. After a moment, Jordi asked, "Helen Cole, right?"

Kaylee smiled. "That's her! She was second in the world!"

Now Hannah nodded, too. "The teachers sometimes talk about the dancers on the wall. You know, to inspire us. They said what we should remember about Helen Cole is that she worked harder than anybody else."

Deep inside, Kaylee felt something like pride with regard to her old teacher.

"Dedicated," added Jordi. "They kept using that word."

"Ape-like," said Meghan. "I keep using *that* word."

Kaylee felt her anger surge again.

"I almost forgot she was your teacher," said Hannah. "They said it was too bad what happened to her later."

"Her fiancé dying in the accident?" asked Caitlin.

Hannah nodded. "Only the way I heard it, I thought they were married. You know, because of their daughter."

Kaylee skidded to a halt on the snowy walk. "Daughter?"

No one spoke for a moment. Mouths hung open. The snow pressed silence in upon them. Then Hannah continued.

"I don't remember her name."

"Alexandra!" Jordi offered suddenly. "I just remembered!"

Hannah nodded. "Alexandra. She was four."

"Miss Helen had a daughter!" whispered April.

"What happened to her?" asked Kaylee. "The daughter?"

"She died in the accident along with her fiancé or husband or whatever he was," said Hannah.

They were silent again for a moment, and then Kaylee wheeled on the group. "No one says anything about this!"

Meghan shook her head. "Come on! This is too good!"

"No!" barked Kaylee. "It's too personal. It has to be our secret."

"How come you're suddenly so protective of that old rhinoceros?" asked Meghan.

Kaylee did not answer. She had resumed walking back toward Caitlin's house.

A daughter. And she had died—what?—forty years ago?

Of course this explained why Miss Helen had not visited at the hospital. It might explain why Miss Helen never married afterwards. Perhaps it even explained why Miss Helen had poured herself so relentlessly into her teaching, why she pushed everyone so hard—especially Kaylee. *Do I remind her of her daughter?* If so that might explain why she had agreed to coach Kaylee again. And why the Lizzie Martin betrayal had hit her so hard.

A daughter!

As she shuffled through the snow toward Caitlin's and the promise of nachos and sleep, she wondered what other secrets Miss Helen possessed.

Twenty-three

"You're here! You're really here!"

April had squealed the words and then had given Kaylee a big hug as she settled her bags into the camp area of Milwaukee's Snow Feis.

Being at a feis again as a competitor felt completely familiar as well as terrifyingly alien. It had been seventeen months since she had carried her dress bag to the check-in table, picked up her number, and spread a blanket onto the floor alongside other dancers. Prior to that, she had done it dozens of times. Nothing to it.

Then why did she feel like a skydiver making her first jump after barely surviving a tangled chute?

Kaylee set up her three-legged stool. "I'm only going to dance my soft shoe," she told April. "I'm still not strong enough to do the hornpipe."

"I hope you have a great day!" smiled April, who hurried off. Then Kaylee realized that, despite the hundreds of people milling about, she felt quite alone. Caitlin was missing. That was the reason for her aloneness, of course. They had been coming to feiseanna together for more than five years. Who would she cheer on? Who would she share a nacho boat with?

A picture of Riley flashed into her mind. She willed it out again.

Her father would arrive later. He had dropped her off and then driven to a building supply store to buy assorted doodads needed to repair the constantly-running toilet, the drafty front window and the loose hinges on the kitchen-to-the-garage door. "Only a matter of time before every square inch of that pile of sticks is made out of replacement parts," her father had said.

Settling onto her stool, Kaylee consulted the time schedule and then pulled out her wig casserole, a tight-lidded plastic dish in which she kept her curly Irish locks. She popped the top, pulled out the mass of copper spirals, fluffed them with a bounce and slipped them over her own hair, which she had pinned up at home. A dozen bobby pins later, Kaylee's scalp screamed as if she wore a crown of barbed wire.

At least it's not going to come off while I'm dancing. She had seen that happen a couple of times, and in both instances, the girl whose wig had hit the floor had exited in tears.

Next, Kaylee began to apply her makeup, setting up a small, portable mirror to assist her. Shadow, liner, rouge, lip gloss and the daintiest sprinkle of glitter across her cheeks. As she looked at the girl in the mirror, she could almost imagine that the last seventeen months had never occurred.

If only.

Socks were next. She pulled a clean pair from her bag, slipped them on partway up her calves. Then she rolled on sock glue before pulling them tight.

She checked the time again. It was a little early, but it was her first feis in almost a year and a half, she was antsy, and she didn't care. Kaylee unzipped her garment bag and pulled out her blue dress. She longed to wear the green dress that her grandmother had made for her, but she would save that for a special occasion—not a feis where she was competing in only a single dance.

The final touch was her tiara.

Kaylee found a restroom containing a mirror that captured almost all of her.

Not bad.

She hurried over to stage one. The age group before her was still performing the soft shoe. Then the dancers would have to perform their hard shoe routines. She had a little time, and so she flitted from stage to stage.

"Good luck Jordi! Good luck Hannah!"

"You look beautiful, April!"

"You're going to have a great day, Meghan!"

She loved her dance friends dearly. But somehow, there had been a special connection with Caitlin. She wondered if a similar bond would grow now between her and one of these other girls. They all competed at different times. Jordi and Hannah were a year younger. Meghan had not yet qualified for Preliminary Champion, and April was in Champs.

When she returned to her own stage, she found that half of the girls in the younger group still had hard shoe steps to perform, and so she set about stretching and mentally preparing herself for competition. She walked back to her camp, retrieved her water bottle, took several gulps, and returned to stage one, where her age group was now checking in with the stage monitor.

Then she waited, stretched some more.

She felt anxious, unready, yet eager—much like she had felt at her first feis years ago.

Twenty-eight girls comprised her group. Kaylee would be in the fifth pair to dance. As she watched the first two pairs, her self-doubt increased. *They're so good. Could I really dance like that once?*

Then, somewhere between forever and a split second, she stood on the stage beside a girl in a pink-and-gold dress, smiling, facing the stern countenances of the three judges.

Did I really used to enjoy this?

The musician, a fiddler, began the slip jig music. Kaylee waited, pointed, and glided into her routine.

Skimming across the stage, leaping, up on toes. And smiling. Almost like it had been a year and a half ago, except the fatigue came more quickly, and the burning pain, first subtle and then more insistent. Yet, she pressed on, conscious of her arms, her posture, the height of her kicks.

And then she bowed to the judges and musician.

She was back. Well, partway back, as if she had been stranded on an island and now she could see the shores of the civilized world from her raft. In order to walk on that beach, however, she needed to master the hard shoe, which loomed ahead of her like a rocky shoal.

As she exited the stage, she saw her father clapping from behind the last row of spectator chairs.

"You looked good, sweetheart," he said. "I got here in time to see it all."

Kaylee panted a "Thanks" and realized how out of breath she felt. She gulped some air and after a moment added, "I wish you had seen me when I was really good." *It figures,* she thought. *The one time he gets to see me dance is when I'm broken and out-of-shape.*

She kept her dress on and watched the hard shoe routines of the other girls in her group. Then she flitted from stage to stage, trying to catch at least one dance of each of her friends. Tom O'Shay settled into a folding chair with a newspaper sports page he had acquired from someplace in the hotel. A part of Kaylee wanted to wear the solo dress for as long as she could. So many months had elapsed since she had worn it last, and being in it made her feel like a dancer again. And she wanted to wear it to the awards, just in case—by some miracle—she had placed in her slip jig. Caitlin had once observed that the awards ceremony in PC and Champs was a lot like people waiting to see if their lottery numbers had won them the $100 million prize. Even though the chances were small for some of the dancers, they stood there in the crowd, squeezing their eyes shut as results were announced, muttering "Please, please, please!"

Kaylee did not win one of the medals for a top-three finish in her slip jig. And she already knew that she had finished last—twenty-eighth out of twenty-eight—in the overall standings, since she had not completed both a hard shoe and soft shoe routine. But when she picked up her individual results print-out, she was mildly surprised.

Thirteenth.

On the one hand, she was a long way from where she had been. At the Gateway Feis seventeen months earlier, she had finished second in her soft shoe and first in her hard shoe. The judges had ranked her first overall. Today, she could not dance a complete hard shoe routine, and twelve girls had beaten her in soft shoe.

But she had beaten fifteen. Better than half.

And more important, she had danced in a feis, something that she had once thought might never happen. Kaylee remembered how close she had come to giving up early the previous summer.

Thirteenth this feis. Maybe tenth the next.

"We can go now," she informed her father, although this really meant another half hour of reading the sports pages while Kaylee laboriously transformed herself from Celtic dance warrior back into disheveled, freckle-faced teenager in sweat pants and t-shirt.

"Can we stop at the Stitchin' Kitchen?" asked Kaylee as they drove from Milwaukee. "I know mom will want to hear about everything."

"Sure," said her father. "I'll drop you off and you can ride home with her. I already know how you did, and there's a broken toilet calling my name."

They arrived in Rosemary half an hour later, cruised into the downtown area and pulled onto the side street in front of the Stitchin' Kitchen. Tom O'Shay gave his daughter a hug.

"See you later, sweetheart."

Kaylee bounded out of the car, which pulled away from the slushy curb. A shock greeted her as she turned to face the store. In the front window, her mother normally posted signs that advertised special deals. Today's sign was quite different.

BUSINESS FOR SALE

Twenty-four

"It'll be fun," Jackie had said, attempting to persuade Kaylee to go to the Valentine's dance at the Rosemary Senior High gymnasium on Saturday night.

Fun.

Nothing about the previous week had been fun.

Sunday: The argument with her mother.

They had argued over her mother's decision to sell the Stitchin' Kitchen. Mrs. O'Shay was not selling the actual building, which she rented. She hoped for a buyer who could buy the inventory of fabrics and patterns, the espresso machine, the shelves and sewing machines, and who would either assume the lease in the same building, or move it all to a new location.

Of course, Kaylee's position was the *You can't sell the Stitchin' Kitchen! It's your dream* position, while her mother held the *I gave it my best shot, honey, but with college coming up for you and then Will, I need a more dependable income* ground. This had elicited the *So it's my fault you're selling the store? Fine, then, I won't go to college* retort, followed by the *That's not what I meant! You've got to understand that this makes the most sense financially* plea.

And it had gone on for some time, until what either one said was no longer important; they simply continued to argue to avoid being mistaken for a corpse on the battlefield. The one comfort Kaylee took from the conflict was that buyers for quilt shops were not exactly littering the city streets. It might take months. A year or more.

But one could never be sure.

Monday: The one-mile run.

Kaylee recalled how, at the age of thirteen, she had run three, four, even five miles effortlessly. Well, perhaps not effortlessly, but without the aches and stabbing pains that accompanied her current efforts.

Rosemary Senior High had no indoor track, unlike some of the bigger schools. Some people ran at the Rosemary Fitness Center, but that had only treadmills, and besides, the O'Shays had no money for a membership. Consequently, when Kaylee wished to jog, she took to the streets. In February, this meant choosing one's route carefully, avoiding ice and slush, looking for shoveled sidewalks and streets that had been scraped clean or heavily sanded by the plow crews. It also meant getting bundled up in sweats, mittens and stocking cap. It hardly seemed worth the effort since her limit was about a mile.

Until Monday.

I'm going to push to a mile and a half.

The pain had begun, subtly, shortly after she started. It had progressed in the familiar manner, growing in intensity. By the mile mark, she was sweating more as a consequence of the discomfort than from the quantity of burned calories. Yet, she pushed on. Another minute. Two. Three. Four. And as she arrived back on Cranberry Street, she knew from the time on her watch that she had hit a mile and a half.

Instead of making her happy, however, Kaylee had felt angry to the point of tears. As she burst through the front door, she tore off her stocking cap and mittens, firing them across the living room as she barreled through.

"I thought that operation was supposed to help! It's been six months and it still hurts! I can't do anything like I used to! I'm a stupid cripple!"

Then she had exploded into tears and bolted into her room, slamming the door. She observed that her mother had not said, "You've got to give it more time." At this point, Mrs. O'Shay knew enough to keep that phrase out of play.

Wednesday: Dance practice with Miss Helen.

"The next feis, your goal should be a top-ten placement in your soft shoe," Miss Helen had said. "And to finish your hornpipe. Place is not important."

Six months ago, achieving such goals in a feis might have excited Kaylee. She would have seen them as starting rungs on a ladder that would eventually lead her to the top box on the podium. Now, however, she saw the goal as painful and barely possible. And even if she achieved it, what was the point? How much higher up the ladder could she really climb if her pain remained the same?

She had moved listlessly through her practice regimen at the tiny church. At one point, Miss Helen had switched off the music and had stared at her for a long moment in silence.

"What's wrong?" Miss Helen had asked.

Kaylee had said nothing.

Another long silence had grown between them.

"Have you given up?"

Kaylee had looked at the floor before answering quietly. "I don't know."

Thursday: Dance at Trean Gaoth Academy.

Or rather, the dance practice that never happened. For the first time that Kaylee could remember, she had ditched dance practice . . . just *because*.

"Aren't you going?" Mrs. O'Shay had asked.

"I don't feel well," Kaylee had replied.

And she had stayed in her room.

Friday: Pop quiz in English.

"When a teacher gives a pop quiz," Jackie had said, never shy at offering Kaylee her opinion, "it's like if the football coach tells the team they're going to be playing a tough opponent on Friday night, but then when they show up for practice on Wednesday, the tough team is already there waiting to play! You're almost guaranteeing intimidation and failure! Shouldn't a teacher's goal be just the opposite?"

Which brought them to

Saturday: The Valentine's Day Dance.

Jackie normally would have gone to the dance with Will, but Kaylee's brother and Mr. O'Shay had traveled to Madison for an indoor soccer tournament.

"Half the girls there won't be with a date," Jackie had argued. "We'll do a lot of dancing. It'll be fun."

Like getting wisdom teeth removed, Kaylee had thought.

The dance was scheduled to start at eight, and the two friends arrived about ten minutes early.

"The parking lot is packed!" observed Kaylee as they exited Jackie's car more than a hundred yards from the school.

"There's a girls' basketball game tonight," Jackie explained. "From six to eight. A lot of people will probably be coming straight from the game to the dance."

"I'm glad you didn't talk me into going to the game, too," said Kaylee, zipping her jacket higher against the cold. "After the week I've had, I need something fun. Watching Brittany and Heather hog the ball and smile at the boys in the crowd is just slightly less fun than watching the school nurse mop up vomit."

Jackie whirled toward her friend. "You didn't hear? Brittany was kicked off the team. Heather, too."

Kaylee's eyes widened. "But they're the stars!"

"Not anymore," said Jackie, resuming her forward progress. "When they got those tickets for drinking at the Homecoming party, they got suspended for a couple of games and got put on athletic probation. But then they got busted again last week. So they're done for the rest of the season."

This news took a moment for Kaylee to reconcile. She certainly felt no affection for either girl, but she had to admit that, in the past, the two had seemed to find a way to coast along untouched by consequences. The fact that they had now been dealt such a strong blow was a reality check. Perhaps, Kaylee theorized, they really were human after all and not some invincible demon-wenches.

"Let's go through the janitor's entrance," said Jackie, quickening the pace as they neared the building. "It'll be shorter and I'm freezing."

"It's almost eight o'clock," said Kaylee. "It'll be locked."

"A janitor has to be here whenever there's a basketball game," said Jackie. "He has to slide the bleachers shut, raise the hoops, sweep up. He's got all the special keys."

They rounded the corner of the building and came to a small parking lot behind the gymnasium, usually used by the janitors, the principal's secretary, Mrs. Cobb—an elderly math teacher who liked to sneak out to her vehicle to smoke between classes—and coaches when there were games. Tonight the lot contained four cars. Kaylee assumed one belonged to the janitor. A second—an easy-to-spot red Camaro—belonged to Mrs. Miller, the girls' basketball coach. A third was probably Miller's assistant, Mr. Hardy.

The lot was dark and the first three cars appeared empty, but a driver sat behind the wheel of the fourth. The passenger-side door stood open, and a shadowy figure knelt near the Camaro.

"Heather, you idiot! Let's go!"

Even if she had not heard the voice, Kaylee would have recognized Brittany's white sports car, its headlights and motor off, the only illumination coming from the vehicle's interior light and a dim service bulb over the janitor's entrance. Kaylee stopped, but Jackie edged forward intrigued, and an instant later, Kaylee followed.

"Heather!" Brittany hissed out the passenger door. "The game'll be over any minute!"

Then Kaylee and Jackie heard another hissing sound. *They're letting the air out of Coach Miller's tires,* thought Kaylee. She took a couple steps forward, almost involuntarily, and as she did, she noticed that the vandalism extended beyond mere flattened tires. Deep scratch marks had been carved the entire length of the red Camaro. All of the windows appeared to have been struck with a heavy object, resulting in ugly, concentric spider webs of ruined glass, and the instrument of destruction, a hammer, lay on the asphalt behind Heather. Next to the hammer rested a can of spray paint, and as Kaylee squinted toward the Camaro, she now saw that a vulgarity had been painted onto its side.

Brittany's voice sounded again. "Come on!"

"Just a second!" cried Heather, her voice a mad fusion of anger and glee. The hiss from the front tire grew more faint, and Kaylee could see the hood dip slightly. "Wonder how they're doing tonight? Think Miller misses my twelve points per game?" Then Heather removed the screwdriver with which she had been depressing the valve stem and jammed the tip if it into the side of the now pliant tire, which emitted a sharp gasp and settled still further. Heather thrust the screwdriver into the sidewall in several additional locations to render it beyond repair. "Or your ten? Any coach who's stupid enough to get rid of twenty-two points per game doesn't deserve a nice car."

Jackie stepped forward now, unable to stop herself. "Are you *that* stupid? You did this to yourself! Coach Miller didn't have any choice but to suspend you!"

The voice startled Heather so badly that she dropped the screwdriver, the first time that Kaylee had ever seen her intimidated. Then, as she realized who had spoken, Heather's composure returned and a cruel smile crossed her lips.

"Walk away, Fortune Cookie!"

"Don't call her that!" shouted Kaylee.

Brittany watched intently for a moment from her car and then started the engine. "Come on, Heather!"

Heather took a step toward Jackie, the smile disappearing. Nothing but hatred remained. "I said, *Walk away, Fortune Cookie!* Now! Along with your loser friend! And you're not going to say anything!"

As Kaylee stepped up, she noticed that Jackie's expression looked every bit as malevolent as Heather's.

"You think we're going to let you get away with this?" Jackie thrust a finger toward the wrecked Camaro.

"You should talk!" growled Heather. "I seem to remember you two pukes have plenty of experience in vandalizing cars!"

"But we really didn't hurt them!" Kaylee piped up. "And we cleaned them up!"

"Only because my dad made you!" said Brittany's voice from inside the other car.

"This is seriously twisted and messed-up!" said Jackie. "Just like you two narcissistic parasites!"

Heather glared. "Narci—"

"Sorry," said Jackie, her tone thick with a horrific satisfaction. "I forgot about your D-minus average on vocabulary tests. Let me keep it simple: I'll say anything I want whenever I want to say it! I'm just imagining how good it would feel to know that you were doing a thousand hours of community service. Or thinking of you cuffed, arrested, fingerprinted. Or maybe even expelled! I think that's my favorite scenario!"

At this, Heather lunged toward Jackie. Brittany's voice rang out: "Heather!"

"You're dead, Fortune Cookie!"

"Leave her alone!" cried Kaylee, rushing forward, half a step in front of her friend.

With her right arm, Heather brushed Kaylee aside. At the same moment, Jackie hurtled forward, tackling Heather around the thighs and sending her backwards into the Camaro. The middle of Heather's back connected with the Camaro's side mirror and she bellowed in pain, collapsing onto her side.

"This is the greatest moment of my life!" Jackie hissed to Kaylee, backing away from the Camaro. "I just took down Heather Chandler, the school's best athlete!"

But there was no time for celebrating. Heather had shaken off the pain and resumed her feet, and she rolled toward Jackie like an Old Testament storm.

Jackie was half Heather's size and had surprised her once. Kaylee realized her friend would not be so lucky a second time. She saw the murder in Heather's eyes.

"No!" cried Kaylee, rushing forward to try and pin Heather's arms to her sides. But Heather's arms were quicker.

Kaylee felt nothing at first. After a moment, she realized that she was on the ground. And then the pain in her head came like the rush of foul water.

Twenty-five

The Fox Cities Feis in Appleton was brand new, the first weekend in March. Jordi's mother had offered to drive Kaylee, and of course, Hannah was also along.

"How did you get such a black eye?" Jordi's mother had asked.

"Fell off my bike about two weeks ago. Hit a patch of ice."

Jordi's mother had given it the sort of concerned, pouty look that mothers are wont to give such injuries. "Two weeks? It must have been absolutely dreadful if you can still see it now."

The blackened eye had improved markedly. All that remained were a few discolored patches—pastel shades of yellow, green, light blue. At first, she had looked like a raccoon.

That night had gone so horribly wrong.

Many of the details had been supplied by Jackie. The first one she had guessed, although she could not really remember it. Heather had clobbered her.

"Then she started to come for me," Jackie had told her, "and I thought I was going to have to tackle her again."

But then the door to the janitor's entrance had opened, and the janitor had called out, "Who's out there?" Heather had dived into Brittany's car and they had sped off.

They arrived at the fieldhouse where the feis would be held. A lobby area had been earmarked for camping, and they set up in front of a trophy case. Kaylee had put on her wig at home. "I'm going to need extra time for makeup today," she told Jordi and Hannah as she retrieved her mirror. "Lots of makeup."

The janitor had helped Kaylee wash up in the custodians' lavatory. Then he used his radio to page the athletic trainer, who had been just about ready to leave. Sally, the trainer, had diagnosed a minor concussion. "Probably level one," she had said. "Doesn't look like your cheekbone is broken, but you might want to have your parents take you to the ER in Paavo and get it checked out." She had Kaylee apply ice and then exited.

A few minutes later, the assistant principal, Mr. Powell, who had been helping to supervise the rowdy student section of the bleachers during the game, arrived at the custodians' office. He stared at the two girls, silent and grim-faced for a moment, and then jabbed a thumb over his shoulder.

"Somebody trashed Coach Miller's car pretty badly. You two have an awful lot of explaining to do!"

Kaylee applied the coverup carefully around the eye, although only a small amount of tenderness remained. At first, the eye had been so swollen that Kaylee had refused to go to school for three days. When she did return, she offered up the bike riding excuse.

Now she proceeded through the ritual of preparation, but this feis differed from the one at which she had danced in January. Today she was with Jordi and Hannah, and so she smiled frequently. Watching them help each other with makeup and sock glue was like watching a comedy act.

When Mr. Powell had left the two girls alone for a few moments in the custodians' office, Kaylee had made her friend promise not to tell what had really happened.

"Say we don't know who did it," whispered Kaylee.

"What?" Jackie had exclaimed.

Kaylee had hushed her. "Just do it! You owe me!" She pointed to her eye.

What had followed had been a mess. Lots of raised voices, first from Coach Miller, who they heard from the parking lot during the intervals when the janitor opened the outside door. They resumed when the O'Shays and Kizobus arrived. There were the raised voices of concern over Kaylee's well-being and the horrible appearance of her face. There were raised voices of disbelief when they were informed that their daughters had wrecked a coach's very expensive Camaro. There were raised voices of anger by almost everyone.

Mr. O'Shay: "What is it with you two lately? You girls were never like this before!"

Jackie: "We didn't do it!"

Mr. Powell: "Oh, sure!"

Police Officer Sloane: "Then who did?"

Silence.

Of course, the police, who had been called by Coach Miller, had figured out fairly quickly that Kaylee and Jackie were probably not the responsible parties.

"They didn't have any spray paint in their possession," Officer Sloane had said. "And nothing sharp enough to have made those holes in the tires."

"They probably stashed them somewhere," Mr. Powell had said.

This had prompted a raised eyebrow from Officer Sloane. "So you're saying they painted the car, stabbed the tires, and then went somewhere on foot to stash the stuff, and after that, came back so that one of them could knock herself out next to the car."

Mr. Powell grumbled. "It could have happened."

Officer Sloane had turned to the janitor. "Hugh, you said a car drove away when you opened the door?"

"Yeah," said the janitor. "But it was too dark for me to even tell you the color." Then Hugh had turned to Tom O'Shay, who worked as a custodian at the middle school. "Heck, Tom, I didn't realize this was your little gal."

"Yeah," Mr. O'Shay had said dryly. "She's all mine."

Kaylee slipped on the blue dress, patted herself smooth and exhaled. Her first dance would be her soft shoe. Okay, that would not be so bad, she reasoned. She had done the soft shoe at the Snow Feis. Piece of cake.

Today, however, she would be attempting her hard shoe as well.

"It's going to be awful," she had told her mother before leaving the house that morning. "If I have to stop halfway through because it hurts, I'll be mega-embarrassed! This is so frustrating!" And then, before her mother could say anything, she added, "It's been seven months! Seven months! Football players break legs and are back in the game in seven weeks!"

Mrs. O'Shay had hugged her daughter. "Maybe your healing is complete. Maybe this is the best we can expect. Which means you have to live with the pain—or stop dancing."

Kaylee started to protest, but her mother held her tighter.

"Or," continued Mrs. O'Shay, "maybe it's a question of mind over matter."

"What does that mean?" asked Kaylee.

"It means," explained Mrs. O'Shay, "that you're so aware of the pain that it seems bigger than it is. Maybe you need to get your mind on other things when you run and dance. You know what they say: Focus on the prize, not the pain."

Kaylee laughed and pulled away.

"What's so funny?" asked Mrs. O'Shay.

She was going to tell her mother what a funny coincidence it was, how Miss Helen had told her that was what Lizzie Martin used to say. But then she remembered that her mother never seemed to enjoy conversations that involved Lizzie. Again she wondered what had happened between them back in their college days that had driven them apart.

"That's what Miss Helen said," replied Kaylee. "Kinda funny, y'know, both of you saying the same."

Mrs. O'Shay had nodded. "Kind of funny."

The soft shoe seemed to go well—or, more accurately, as well as Kaylee might have expected. Some pain. A few spots where she knew she had not stayed up on her toes. About the same as at the Snow Feis, she guessed.

As each of the thirty-one girls in her group finished their soft shoe routine, ghillies were exchanged for hard shoes. They gulped water from plastic bottles, tried a couple of quick stretches, and checked in for the second dance.

I hope I can do the whole hornpipe, thought Kaylee. *I won't get another chance until June.*

That's how long her parents had grounded her for this time. The only reason they had allowed her to compete in the Fox Cities Feis was because she had already been registered.

"We've never had these kinds of problems with you, Kaylee!" her mother had said when they arrived home the night of the Valentine's dance that she never actually attended. "Nothing involving the police. And now, twice in one year!"

"But I didn't do anything to that car!" Kaylee had protested.

"No," Mr. O'Shay had agreed, "and it's lucky for you that the police seem to understand that, too. But I think you know who *did* trash that car. And by not telling, you're letting someone get away with a crime."

She had known she could never make her parents understand. If they pointed the finger at Heather and Brittany, it would make things so much worse. It would be war. Especially if Jackie had guessed right and Brittany and Heather were expelled.

But there was something else. Kaylee could not quite explain it to herself. Perhaps it was because Brittany was a dancer. Or that she was friends with Riley.

The music stopped. Kaylee and a girl in a gold and purple dress walked to the back of the stage and stood stiffly while the three judges made notes about the previous two dancers.

Then the fiddler drew his bow across his instrument, and it was time to dance the hornpipe.

Cut bang and bang-bang and jump-jump, and 1-2-3 up and up and bang and bang-bang . . .

It felt nothing like two years ago when she had been a percussive whirlwind, moving across the stage with grace and power. The pain started after only a few steps, its throbbing pulse growing on the beat of the music until it shot through her right leg like nails. She felt the sweat breaking out on her forehead, tried to smile through clenched teeth.

Keep going!

She passed the halfway point. Kaylee could feel her form deteriorating—arms bending, shoulders hunching, toes no longer pointed out, steps no longer generating much sound.

Keep going!

And then it was done. She bowed to the judge, the musician, exited the stage.

She wanted to feel good about the dance. After all, it was the first time she had completed both a soft and hard shoe dance at a feis in almost nineteen months. But Kaylee could not quite get to that point. If it had taken her nineteen months to stumble through a grotesque caricature of a hornpipe, how did she expect to dance well enough at the Oireachtas—which was only another seven months away—to qualify for Worlds?

She pushed the thought out of her mind. One thing at a time.

Jordi and Hannah had returned to the camp area. Kaylee slipped out of her dress, donned sweat pants and followed them to stage four where they were about to dance their slip jig. Then the girls took a lunch break, visiting the food vendors on the far side of the fieldhouse. Kaylee nibbled on a slice of pizza while Jordi and Hannah prattled on about anything that flitted into their minds.

And then she saw him.

Riley sat two tables away, hunched over a paper trough of nacho chips and cheese sauce—which he shared with a slim, pretty girl wearing a dark wig.

"I'd better check on awards," she told Jordi and Hannah, pushing away from the table, tossing the unfinished pizza slice in the first trash receptacle she passed. Kaylee crossed the fieldhouse, trying to let the strange combination of music and voices fill her mind, to push out the image of the dark-haired girl. At the camp, she pulled on her dress and headed for the site where PC and Champs awards were announced. Yellow rope draped between portable standards kept onlookers a comfortable distance from boxes marked one, two and three where the award winners would stand. Since most groups had more than three award winners, the others would fan out on either side.

Kaylee could not help but remember the Gateway Feis when she had stood on the top box. That would not happen today. Her name would not be called for an award. But individual results sheets would be distributed after the presentation of trophies, and she was anxious to see where she had placed overall among the thirty-one girls.

As she stood in the growing throng, her feet nervously tapping out her hornpipe steps, Kaylee found a familiar face, although not a welcome one. Brittany Hall hovered about twenty feet away, just behind the yellow rope, smiling, beaming with confidence.

The exact opposite of how Kaylee felt.

Brittany had danced in Champs, and according to the posted list, her group would be announced immediately after Kaylee's. She watched Brittany laughing with friends, smiling. *She knows she's going to win.*

Then a woman moved to the microphone and announced Kaylee's PC competition. "We're awarding sixteen places. In sixteenth place, from the Holly School, Diane Weillor."

She worked her way down the list, finally announcing the champion, a girl Kaylee did not recognize. They bowed in unison and then the top three in the hard shoe and soft shoe dances were announced.

"Thank you girls," said the woman with the microphone. "You can now come up for individual results."

Kaylee ducked under the yellow rope and pressed forward with the other dancers. She showed her number and grabbed the offered print-out containing the three judges' scores.

In Preliminary Champion competition, each judge gave a dancer a numerical score based on how well the dance had been executed. The judge also had the option of including comments—which happened about half the time. The dancer's score would then be ranked against all of the others who had done that dance.

Kaylee looked first at her soft shoe scores. The first judge had ranked her 17th. The second had ranked her 11th. The third had ranked her 13th. She felt a sudden sense of dread. She had hoped to be 10th or higher in soft shoe. What must her hard shoe scores be? When she found them on the page, her heart fell:

30th, 31st and 31st.

She had expected as much, but seeing it on paper brought the tears anyway. And there was her overall place: 30th out of 31.

She had to get out of there. Kaylee pushed through the crowd, her last image of the awards area a smiling Brittany Hall, chin up, straining forward as the awards ceremony for her Champs age group began. Kaylee picked up her pace, turning first to the right—but that was the camping area. She did not want her friends or a lot of strangers to see her like this. Straight ahead was a double door with frosted glass upper panels. She pushed through these and found herself in a narrow passage that slanted down somewhat. She realized that it was probably a tunnel through which students passed from one building to another during inclement weather. Kaylee ran the short distance down, then back up to another double set of doors and pushed through them.

She found herself quite alone in a small campus chapel: a dozen rows of wooden pews, separated by a center aisle; vaulted ceiling with exposed wooden beams; four stained-glass windows on each side; assorted statuary and paintings of Biblical events; and a wood-and-tile table at the front upon which a lighted candle sat, although the chapel was well-lit from electric sconces along the walls.

Oh, this is just great! She had intended to let out all of her emotion—cry, scream, curse, pound on things. But it did not seem right to do that in a church. Except, perhaps, for the crying part.

She let the tears come, an amazing torrent that surprised even Kaylee. Her deep, rasping gasps echoed off the plaster walls. *Who am I fooling? I'll never be good enough by Oireachtas to qualify for Worlds.* She remembered her place in today's feis. Thirtieth out of thirty-one. With only six months of qualifying remaining, Kaylee could not even imagine that she would dance well enough to make it to Oireachtas.

Which meant . . .

It was really over. She would be a high school senior when the next Oireachtas occurred. After that, she would be off to college, and her competitive days would be finished. If she did not qualify for Worlds at the Oireachtas seven months from now, she would NEVER dance in Ireland.

Kaylee's sobs diminished. She walked to the front of the chapel, stood staring at the lone candle burning on the table next to an open Bible. For six years, a fire had burned inside of her, a fire that blazed from her heart to Ireland, fueled by her passion and the strength of her dreams. But the fire had not been strong enough to withstand the tears of the real world. She wet her fingertips by sweeping them across her moist cheeks, reached out to extinguish the flame between her thumb and forefinger.

And then she jumped back, startled, as the double doors she had passed through minutes earlier burst open again. This dancer seemed not to care whether the place was a chapel or a construction site, and her vulgar remonstrations grew louder by the second. She pounded a fist against the wall, kicked a wooden doorstop across the room, grabbed a hymnal from a pocket on the back of a pew and hurled it behind the last row of pews.

Then she saw Kaylee.

Brittany Hall!

"What are you doing here, O'Shrimp?"

Kaylee took a step back from the still-burning candle, smoothed her front, tried to summon her dignity. "Having a bad day."

Brittany regarded her silently for a moment, then picked up another hymnal, seemed to think better of it, and replaced it in its pocket.

"What happened?" asked Kaylee.

Brittany's eyes flashed angrily. "None of your business."

"Did the Great Brittany Hall finish second?" taunted Kaylee.

"Shut up!"

"I suppose you threw your runner-up trophy in the trash!"

Brittany glared. "I didn't place!"

This left Kaylee momentarily speechless and Brittany continued.

"There were twenty-six girls. They placed thirteen. I was fifteenth. This is the first feis in two years where I haven't placed! Stupid judges!"

Kaylee took a step toward Brittany. "Yeah, well don't cry too much. It's one bad feis. I'm still looking for one good one. I was thirtieth."

Brittany's eyes widened. "Thirtieth?"

"Out of thirty-one," added Kaylee.

Brittany shook her head. "How can a person place that low? You used to be pretty good!"

"It's the leg they operated on," said Kaylee. "It still hurts when I dance hard shoe. Two of the judges ranked me last place!"

"Last!" exclaimed Brittany. "Let me see!"

"What?" cried Kaylee. "So you can laugh at me?"

"Yeah, maybe," said Brittany, stepping forward. "I just can't believe it's that bad."

Kaylee stood tentatively, pointed, began the first few steps of her hornpipe. "It's okay for the first few bars, and then—" She grimaced. "The pain starts."

Brittany nodded. "Yeah, that's pretty awful."

Kaylee's temper flared. "At least I have an excuse! You've never had anything bad happen to you, and you still bombed today!"

Brittany's eyes narrowed. "Never had anything bad happen to me? You don't know anything about me!"

"I know you've had something against me ever since we met!" cried Kaylee, unable to hold back anything now.

"You're nuts!" exclaimed Brittany.

"Am I?" asked Kaylee, nervously shuffling her feet, feeling the sweat form on her palms. She had never confronted Brittany like this before—and now, there was no one to stop them, or to protect her. "You and Heather abused me every day in soccer practice when I was on the Green Storm!"

Brittany snorted a derisive laugh. "Get over it! We were kids! It's what kids do! And it doesn't help when your daddy's the coach! Anyway, that was years ago!"

"What about the solo dress you burned?" asked Kaylee, moving nervously, her feet habitually repeating dance steps.

"I sold you that dress for less than a tenth of what it was worth!" growled Brittany, taking another step toward her. "Heather was the one who held it too close to the campfire!"

Kaylee's feet moved faster. She licked her lips nervously. "My eye still hurts from that night behind the gym!"

Brittany's gaze faltered. "That wasn't supposed to be about you. And in case you didn't notice, Heather was the one who trashed Miller's car. She told me to drive back there and stop. I thought she was just going to spray something on the window. When I saw what she was really up to, I tried to get her to leave."

As Kaylee replayed the events of that evening in her mind, she realized that this might indeed have been the case. She remembered Brittany's plea: *Heather, you idiot! Let's go!*

"Heather can get a little out of control at times," added Brittany.

"You think?" Kaylee hopped and tapped in place almost subconsciously.

Brittany emitted a little grunt. "You should talk, Little Miss Psychopath! You think anyone who says more than three words to your boyfriend is trying to steal him away!"

Kaylee felt her face redden. "He's not my boyfriend!" She felt her pace quicken as her feet repeated the step over and over.

Brittany snorted again. "Tell *him* that."

"What's that supposed to mean?" asked Kaylee.

Brittany shook her head and the ghost of a humorless smile played at the corner of her mouth. "You really are clueless, aren't you? And I'll bet you never even gave a thought to how it made me feel when you were dating Mike."

Kaylee blinked. "I thought you were okay with it."

Brittany took another step forward. Kaylee's feet continued their anxious, repetitive movements.

"I was okay for the most part. It was when you broke up with him that I felt . . . angry. Jealous, I guess. "

Kaylee gasped. "Jealous? Of me?"

Brittany's gaze dropped to the floor. "You always seemed to have everything going for you. Your dad was your coach and he didn't have to work 24/7 so he could be there with you. Your mom wasn't a drunk. Everybody knew what a hard worker you were and that you were going to be in Champs soon. And guys like Mike and Riley thought you were cool. And then you dumped Mike. That really made me feel good."

"So what?" asked Kaylee. "So we both broke up with the same guy!'

"No!" said Brittany, shaking her head bitterly. "Mike dumped *me!*"

Kaylee's eyes traveled to the floor. Feet moving, moving. "How can you be jealous of me? Ever since the accident, I've been—"

"Oh yes," interrupted Brittany savagely, "you've been playing that for all it's worth! Now everybody feels sorry for you!"

"Playing?" Kaylee wanted to tear Brittany's expensive dress to shreds. "You don't know how this feels!"

"I know what I see."

"But I can't dance!" cried Kaylee, and now tears streamed down her face again. "Especially hard shoes! The pain is so bad, I can't make it two minutes without looking like some kind of pathetic freak!"

"Really?" said Brittany with a grunt of laughter. "Well that's funny, because you've been dancing here the whole time we've been talking!"

Kaylee stopped moving. How long had she and Brittany been shouting at each other? Five minutes? Six? Ten? Kaylee had been dancing in her hard shoes the whole time. A typical hard shoe set lasted about two minutes. Why could she do it now, but not at practice or during a competition?

Focus on the prize, not the pain.

That was what her mother and Miss Helen had said. But what if it wasn't just focusing on the prize? What if it was simply focusing on something other than how you felt?

"I wasn't thinking about the pain," said Kaylee uncertainly. "And I danced!"

"It didn't hurt?" asked Brittany, suddenly inquisitive, her own anger fading.

Kaylee's eyes darted from her feet to Brittany and back. "A little. Not like usual."

"And it's never been like that before?"

"Not since the accident," said Kaylee. "Every time I danced or ran, I'd think about it. How soon's the pain going to start? That was always what I'd be wondering."

Neither girl said a word for a bit. Then Brittany said, "You'll be able to dance your hornpipe."

Kaylee's eyes widened. "We don't know that."

"But," countered Brittany, "it's possible."

And for the first time in nineteen months, Kaylee felt like it truly might be possible. Focus on the competition. Focus on the steps. Focus on the prize. Anything except the pain.

Kaylee suddenly felt herself shaking, and an instant later, the tears came again. They were not tears of frustration this time, nor were they tears of joy. They were the tears accumulated behind nineteen months of disappointment, tears of hope. She slumped onto her knees, covering her face with her hands, sobbing as if finally seeing her rescuer after lying broken along the roadside for so long.

And after a minute, Brittany dropped to her knees beside Kaylee, wrapped her arms around her shoulders and held Kaylee as she cried.

Twenty-six

Three days after her seventeenth birthday, on a sunny morning that meant summer vacation waited only two weeks ahead, a time when most teens felt a sense of joyful anticipation, Kaylee O'Shay sat grim-faced and tense, facing the worst fear of her life.

"Park behind the blue car," said the stone-faced woman in the passenger seat, tipping the top of her clipboard in the general direction of the curb.

Parallel parking, the part she hated most. Kaylee gripped the steering wheel more tightly, her hands so moist with sweat that she half expected them to slip off, sending them into an out-of-control spin, through the guardrail and over the two hundred-foot cliff to their deaths on the jagged rocks below. But there was no cliff. Unfortunately, there was only the blue car.

Kaylee eased alongside of it the way she had been taught in driver's education class, activating her right blinker. Then she swiveled her shoulders and began the task of angling the car into the amazingly tiny space which, in fact, seemed to have shrunk to half of its size since she had begun the maneuver. She gritted her teeth, backed slowly. Docking the space shuttle at the International Space Station, bringing the Queen Elizabeth into harbor, landing the Hindenburg . . . all of these things had to be easier than squeezing behind this blue car, she thought.

But then, it was done. She let out her breath, which she realized she had been holding since she had turned on the blinker.

"All right," said the evaluator, "head back to the testing station."

Kaylee signaled, checked her blind spot, and pulled into traffic as the unsmiling woman beside her scribbled more notes onto her clipboard.

Is it over? Did I pass? You'd think she'd tell me if I passed.

A minute later, Kaylee pulled into the testing station parking lot.

"Park it there," said the woman, pointing again with the clipboard.   "Congratulations," she said, her tone more appropriate for informing someone that she had discovered a small boil on her elbow. "You passed."

Kaylee turned off the car. Passed? "That means I get my license?"

"Yes, dear," said the woman, neither pleased nor annoyed by the question.

And now Kaylee smiled.

Inside the building, she suffered through the taking of the photo, the wait to have it laminated, and finally, she stood with her very own driver's license in her hands.

"You even took a pretty picture," said her father, admiring the document over her shoulder.   "Remember, that's a probationary license."

Kaylee knew. It meant she could only have one other person in the car with her, she could not drive after midnight and any violation would count double against her. It also meant freedom. No longer would she have to depend on her parents or Jackie to take her places.

"Can I drive to school on Monday?" asked Kaylee as they exited the building and headed for the car.

"How am I going to get to work?" asked Mr. O'Shay. "You'd have to get up an hour early to take me."

Kaylee frowned. "The Madison Feis is coming up in two weeks. Can I drive there?"

Her father eyed her doubtfully as they climbed into the vehicle, Kaylee in the driver's seat. "That's more than an hour away. A pretty long drive for someone who's only had her license a couple weeks."

Her frown deepened. "What's the use of having my license if I can't ever drive anywhere?" Then an idea popped into her head. "When we get home, can I take Jackie out for ice cream to celebrate?"

Mr. O'Shay sighed. "Sure."

Kaylee hugged him and turned the key in the ignition.

"Life was sure a lot simpler when you were little," her father continued. "I can hardly believe that you're going to be a senior this fall!"

Kaylee smiled, pulled the car onto the street. She looked forward to her senior year—the social events, finally getting to take some of the electives she had always wanted, being able to drive, visiting colleges. But the year's approach also frightened her. It wasn't just the becoming-an-adult-and-leaving-home thing. The Oireachtas was fewer than six months away. Qualifying for it would end in about four months. Kaylee had not danced at a feis since March.

What if she did not qualify for Oireachtas? That was her last chance to make it to Worlds, which were held in February. Then her senior year would end and she would be off to college and her competitive Irish dance career would be over. Over without ever having danced in Ireland. It had been all she had dreamed of since that day as a ten-year-old when she had taken her first lesson. If she failed to qualify for Worlds, it would not matter whether Rosemary crushed Paavo in the Homecoming game, whether psychology class was really as much fun as everyone said, or whether she had the prettiest dress at the prom. Senior year would be a tragedy.

"Have you given any more thought to what you might want to study in college?" asked Mr. O'Shay.

"Maybe teaching," said Kaylee. "Social studies would be cool. Or maybe I'll get an art degree."

Mr. O'Shay chuckled. "Get ready to starve."

"Aunt Kat didn't starve," said Kaylee. "People liked her stuff. But I also thought maybe a business degree. Someday I could open up my own store."

"Get ready to starve," repeated Mr. O'Shay. "It's not easy, owning your own business. You've seen how hard your mom works."

Ever since Bethany O'Shay had opened the Stitchin' Kitchen, it seemed that she had put in an enormous number of hours at the store each week. The FOR SALE sign was still in the window, but Kaylee had overheard her parents talking recently about two parties who might be interested in buying it. If that happened, it would be yet another big change.

"What kind of store?" asked her father.

"I haven't figured out that part yet," said Kaylee.

Mr. O'Shay laughed. "You've still got plenty of time to figure out what you want to do." Then his face grew more serious. "Unfortunately, you don't have plenty of money in the bank to pay for this college education."

"I've got the money Aunt Kat put in that special fund," noted Kaylee.

"That'll help a lot," agreed Mr. O'Shay, "but you'll still need money for clothes, books, laundry, that kind of stuff."

"And entertainment expenses," added Kaylee. "Movies, restaurants, going to clubs—"

"Oh, there won't be any time for that," countered Mr. O'Shay. "You'll be doing too much studying."

"I hope it's a coed dorm!"

"I don't think they have coed dorms at convents."

They both laughed

It was going to be a good summer, Kaylee decided.

She repeated this notion to Jackie half an hour later when she picked her up to drive her to the ice cream shop.

"All right, O'Shay!" cried Jackie, knocking fists with her friend. "You've got wheels!"

Then the conversation had turned to the much anticipated summer vacation. "I've already arranged to return to my job at Grant Farms taking care of Trooper and the rest of the horses, so making money for the extra expenses at college is taken care of. And dancing is going better!"

By focusing on something other than the pain, Kaylee found that, at times, she hardly noticed it. Some images worked better than others to hold her attention. Concentrating on her dance steps worked a bit. Thinking of Caitlin or Jackie—even better. And, of course, there was Riley. But what seemed to work best was imagining herself on a stage in Ireland at the World Championships.

"I hope it works when I step onto the stage at the Madison Feis," said Kaylee as they pulled into the parking lot of the shop. Madison was one of three feiseanna for which Kaylee was registered during the summer. She would also dance at the Rockford Feis in July and the Gateway Feis in Kenosha in August. She had to qualify at one of the three, or there would be no Oireachtas and no chance to qualify for Worlds.

But her hard shoe was starting to look better. She had begun running again—albeit short distances. She was making it all the way through her classes at Trean Gaoth Academy. Miss Helen was even yelling at her again, just like old times. "There's no way I'm going to miss qualifying for Oireachtas," she told Jackie as the two girls scanned the billboard menu above the counter. Then she sighed.

I hope.

Twenty-seven

Kaylee finished brushing the horses—she always saved Trooper for last.

"You're a good boy, aren't you?" she said, brushing a hand across Trooper's shining, black mane. The deep brown horse nuzzled her playfully, and then Kaylee headed out to the farmhouse. The house stood at the right-hand side of the driveway turnaround, yellow with white shutters and green window boxes. A cedar rail fence stood in front, and a stone walkway passed through an opening in the fence on the way to the front door. Kaylee knocked once and then stepped inside, traversing a short hallway and entering the kitchen, where Mrs. Grant stood busy at the stove.

"Cookies for Amber to take back with her," said Mrs. Grant, pulling a sheet from the oven. Her daughter, Amber, was home from college in Minnesota for the Fourth of July. "Are you going over to Paavo for the big fireworks show tomorrow?"

Kaylee shrugged. "I don't know. It's pretty much the same every year."

"Well, we're going," said Mrs. Grant. "Where else is there to go on the Fourth of July?"

Kaylee was silent for a moment. Then she replied, "I wish I were at Nationals."

Mrs. Grant spoke while using a spatula to transfer the finished cookies to the cooling rack. "For Irish dance?"

Kaylee nodded. "I probably would have qualified for Nationals last year if not for the accident. Now I probably never will."

"Nationals," said Mrs. Grant, thinking it over. "Is that different than Oh-rock-tess?"

"Nationals is all of North America," explained Kaylee. "You can qualify by placing high at Oireachtas, which is just the Midwest."

Mrs. Grant began spooning dough lumps onto the baking sheet, shaking her head. "Oh yes. Oireachtas is the one in the fall, the one you're working on."

"I've still got two chances," said Kaylee. The Madison Feis had marked an improvement over her previous outing in March, but not enough. There had been thirty-four girls in her group at Madison. Kaylee had placed eighteenth—one place away from an award and making it to the Oireachtas.

"Next time for sure," Jordi had said, giving Kaylee a hug after the awards were announced.

Kaylee hoped so. She was running out of next times.

"I have no doubt that you'll make it to your Oireachtas," said Mrs. Grant. "You seem completely healed. I'd never guess you were hurt so badly. How's that boy doing? The one who was with you that day in the car."

"Riley?" Kaylee felt herself blushing, but she tried to appear nonchalant to Mrs. Grant. "Oh, he's good. In fact, he's dancing at Nationals on the Fourth."

"Ah," said Mrs. Grant with a knowing smile. She turned and slipped the reloaded cookie sheet into the oven. "No wonder you'd rather be there instead of at the Paavo fireworks."

"It's not like that," said Kaylee, avoiding eye contact, getting a glass from the cupboard and filling her cup at the kitchen sink.

"So he's not interested?" suggested Mrs. Grant.

"No, he's . . . I don't know. He talks to me online sometimes. But I can't use the computer very often at my house. And he stopped by once, but I wasn't home and he had to talk to my mom. And he sent me a Valentine's card."

"So you're not interested in *him*, then?"

"I, no . . . I don't know." Kaylee floundered for the right words. "I think he likes someone else."

Mrs. Grant nodded, began running warm water into the sink. "How long has he been seeing this other girl?"

"I don't really know if he's seeing her," said Kaylee. "I just saw him eating nachos with her at a feis."

"Eating nachos?"

Kaylee nodded. "Back in March."

"That's all they were doing?" asked Mrs. Grant, squeezing dish soap under the running faucet.

Kaylee nodded less enthusiastically.

"And you only saw them once, four months ago?" asked Mrs. Grant.

This time Kaylee did not nod.

Mrs. Grant wiped her hands on her apron, went to the refrigerator. "I've got a couple of carrots here that you might want to give to your pals in the barn before you go. And a sugar cube for your special friend."

Kaylee took the proffered items, thanked Mrs. Grant and made her way back to the barn. She fed each horse a piece of carrot, and then slipped Trooper the sugar cube. He gobbled it down, and then rubbed his nose against her shoulder. She stroked his mane and allowed her head to come to rest against his.

What had Mrs. Grant been trying to say? That maybe she had jumped to the wrong conclusion when she had seen Riley sharing the nachos with the dark-haired girl? That Riley still liked her? That maybe she was avoiding him?

She remembered the conversation with Brittany in the chapel at the Fox Cities Feis:

He's not my boyfriend!

Tell him *that.*

What had she meant? Tell *him* that?

She stayed in the barn for awhile, resting her head against Trooper, who despite his otherwise stubborn and uncooperative nature, did not seem to mind. She thought of Ireland. She thought of Nationals, and how nice it would be if she were there right now.

Even if she were not dancing.

Then she walked back to the house, changed into her shorts and running shoes, and began the three-mile run home.

Twenty-eight

"I've got a good feeling about today," said Kaylee as she settled her bags in the camping area next to April and Meghan.

She had ridden to Rockford with April's family. April was one of the nicest girls she knew, and while it was not quite the same as being at a feis with Caitlin, Kaylee enjoyed April's company.

Kaylee also felt good because her workouts had been going so well. She had increased her running mileage to four miles a day, had been attending dance classes four days a week, had resumed weight training and had even watched *Isle of Green Fire* the night before the feis.

And then, at the registration table, she had run into Riley.

"Hi."

"Hi."

They had chatted for a moment, and then he had offered to buy her lunch after they both danced.

"Sure," she had said. "That would be nice."

"You're certainly in a good mood,' April's mother had said as Kaylee finished applying her makeup.

Yes she was.

Once she had pulled on her dress, Kaylee worked her way to stage one, checked in and closed her eyes, visualizing her hard shoe routine. Soft shoes would be danced second in today's competition.

I'm ready to dance now! Kaylee told herself.

The age group before Kaylee's seemed to take forever, but then it was time.

Kaylee marched onto stage and stood next to a girl in a brown, black and gold dress. The judges dismissed the previous two, and the music began again.

I can do this!

She focused on her steps, on the joy of dance, on Ireland. And, of course, on Riley. The pain gradually built, but to a minor, dull ache like a bruise. She drank in the crowd faces, the sound of the accordion struggling to be heard against the cheering, the chatter and the mix of feis sounds. Kaylee felt a foreign energy, something that had been missing for a long time.

Two years.

Her feet move across the stage with power and precision, a percussion symphony.

And far too quickly, it was over. What had seemed like a marathon just months ago had turned into a sprint. She could almost feel the wind in her face as she bowed to the judge, then to the musician.

"You looked awesome!" said April, hugging Kaylee as she found her stool and began changing into her soft shoe. "I hope *I* look as good today in Champs!"

Kaylee beamed.

"I'm psyched!" she told April. "I think I really nailed the hard shoe! And my soft shoe is my stronger dance!"

All I need is a halfway decent soft shoe, and I'm going to Oireachtas!

She could hardly stand the wait, but soon, all of the twenty-six girls in her group had completed their hard shoe dances and were lining up for the soft shoe.

And then Kaylee again stood at center stage with the girl in the brown-black-gold dress, smiling, pointing. The music began. Kaylee pointed, leaped, moved across the stage, focusing on Ireland, her movements graceful and athletic, the muscles flexing again as they had two years earlier. She moved to the near left corner, pivoted, skimmed to the center, turned, leaped.

I'm going to do it! I'm really going to do it!

And then, she kicked up, but when she came down, something was wrong. Had she kicked too high? Had her foot slipped? She had no clear notion of what had happened, only that she fell, coming down heavily on her backside. She winced, gritted her teeth, stifled a cry. The music played on, and she tried to get up, slipped, and then realized that it was over.

Not the dance. But her chance at qualifying. As the other girl finished her routine, Kaylee picked herself off the stage and plunged into the crowd.

She cried because she was mortified, and also because she had been defeated. She had been so close to qualifying—yet, one moment of awful luck had doomed her.

Arriving at the camp, she tore off her shoes, hurriedly shed her dress and folded it into the garment bag, pulled on sweats and a t-shirt and ran to a quiet hallway where she let the tears come.

Then she realized that she was not alone.

Riley stood across the passageway, watching her with sad eyes. *He must have been watching me dance*, she thought. *And then he followed me out here after it happened.*

"I'm sorry," he said.

"What are you sorry about?" asked Kaylee. "You didn't make me fall."

"I just mean that I wish it hadn't happened."

"Me too," said Kaylee bitterly. "I wish a lot of things hadn't happened."

They were silent for a moment. Then:

"Is there anything I can do?" asked Riley.

Kaylee turned away, covered her face. "Leave me alone."

"Maybe you'd feel better if we got a Coke or something."

"I want to be alone!" cried Kaylee.

Riley took a step toward her. "You're upset."

She turned back, looked at him angrily. "Don't you understand? I would have qualified for Oireachtas today if I hadn't fallen! And now I've only got one more chance! But it's probably not a big deal for someone like you! You've already made it!"

"I do understand, I—"

"I want to be by myself," said Kaylee, less forcefully as if her batteries were rapidly draining. She turned and faced the wall, staying in that position for several minutes. When she turned around again, wiping her wet cheeks with the back of her hand, Riley was gone.

At first she was relieved. Her disappointment was so acute that she could not imagine having to share her emotions with anyone.

Then relief was gradually replaced by guilt and anger at herself. *He wanted to help and I chased him away again!*

But he would understand. Right? She was running out of chances to qualify for Oireachtas. Perhaps she was also running out of chances with Riley.

Or had she already run out?

Twenty-nine

Second, third and fifth.

Kaylee had stared at the results sheet from the Rockford Feis, had stared at it some more, had tried several different methods of staring at it: in disbelief, in consternation, in shock, in anger. Then she had taken a break for three minutes before staring at it again, and then intermittently throughout the rest of the day—and at less frequent intervals since.

Second, third and fifth.

The three judges had ranked her thus on her hard shoe performance at Rockford. So she had been right. She had nailed it.

But because she had left the stage after her fall in the soft shoe, her rankings there were a disaster.

"If you had gotten up and finished, they might have ranked you high enough to place," Caitlin had suggested when Kaylee called to vent. "But if you leave the stage . . ."

Of course, this had made Kaylee even more angry and frustrated.

Now she was down to one more chance. Today was the Kenosha Gateway Feis. There were actually other feiseanna held between the Gateway Feis and the qualifying cut-off, but many of them had already reached their competitor limit. And money was also an issue. Registering for feiseanna was not cheap, and until Mrs. O'Shay sold the Stitchin' Kitchen, there was no extra money for extra feiseanna.

She had almost sold the business in July. One of the two buyers had seemed ready to sign the papers, but then had backed out at the last minute. The other, according to Mrs. O'Shay, "says she's still interested, but hasn't made a specific offer."

And so the business continued to limp along, struggling even more mightily since the college had dropped the sewing classes that Mrs. O'Shay had taught out of the store. "A cost-saving measure," she had explained. Another victim of the tough economy.

And so the Kenosha Gateway Feis loomed large.

But Kaylee was also hopeful. Because of her performance at the Rockford Feis, she knew her hard shoes were ready. And her soft shoe routine had been good enough for months. All she had to do was smile, dance well, and she would be on her way to Columbus, the site of this year's Midwest Oireachtas.

The first step toward Ireland.

She was also hopeful because the Gateway Feis two years ago had marked her first win in Preliminary Champion competition. At the time, she had been certain her second win waited mere weeks in the future, and that would have vaulted her into the Champion category. If Kaylee were a Champs dancer, she would not have to worry about qualifying for Oireachtas. Champs dancers were automatically invited to enter. PC dancers had to qualify. But at the Oireachtas, both PC and Champs dancers competed together for the awards—one giant pool of enormously talented dancers.

Kaylee had been up since five. According to the Gateway Feis syllabus, her competition would not start until about 11 a.m. However, she could not sleep. Her mother had left the house at seven-thirty to open the Stitchin' Kitchen. The ladies who came to sew and buy fabric enjoyed their morning cup of coffee. Will and Kaylee's father had exited the house half an hour before that, off to Oshkosh for a soccer clinic. That meant Kaylee was all alone in the house. But she was ready to be picked up at nine by April and her mother.

She checked and rechecked her bags. Dress, shoes, socks, glue, makeup, wig, tiara, stool, bandages . . . everything seemed to be in order.

Kaylee put on her dance music, went through the steps.

I'm ready.

Even Miss Helen had commented in recent days that she seemed to be almost back to her old form. The thought made her smile.

She checked the clock. Eight-forty-five. The phone rang.

Probably April, making sure I'll be ready when they arrive.
However, when she picked up, it was Mrs. Grant's voice that she
heard.

"I'm not scheduled to work today," Kaylee reminded her
employer. "I've got a feis."

"I know," said Mrs. Grant. "It's something else. Trooper is
down."

Kaylee felt as if her heart had leaped into her throat.
Trooper was more than an animal to be cared for. He was like a
friend.

She responded shakily. "What's wrong? Is he going to be
okay?"

"He's very bad, honey," said Mrs. Grant, her own voice full
of emotion. "We've called the vet. I'm afraid we're going to
have to put him down."

Kaylee gasped. "No!"

"He's suffering, dear," said Mrs. Grant, and Kaylee could
tell from her tone how hard this was for her. "If you want to say
goodbye, you'll have to come now."

This was worse than any nightmare. If she hung up, ignored
the call and went to the feis, Trooper—her favorite, her friend
ever since her first day working at Grant Farm—would die
without seeing her, without a goodbye, a final pat of his great,
chestnut head. Would he think of her in his last moments?
Wonder why she had not come? Were horses even capable of
such thoughts? Even if Trooper could not think these things,
Kaylee could, and she knew that if she did not go, it would haunt
her forever.

On the other hand, missing her chance to qualify for
Oireachtas would be equally horrifying. Yet, perhaps there was
a way. April was a Champs dancer, and so she would not dance
until after the noon hour break at the feis. Kaylee was the one
who needed to be there by eleven. However, feiseanna often ran
behind schedule. She had frequently been slated to dance at ten
or ten-thirty, only to have the event drag on, have the judges
break for lunch, and then finally reach her competition at one or
two in the afternoon.

She did the mental math. It would take ten to fifteen minutes to bike to Grant Farms. Her father and Will had one car, and her mother had the other at the Stitchin' Kitchen. She considered biking to her mother's shop and persuading her to let her use the car, but by the time she did that and explained everything, it would probably take longer than just using her bicycle. Plus, she would have to take time to return the car to her mother afterwards. She had no recourse but to use the bike.

She composed a quick note to April and her mother, explaining the situation, telling them to come inside, the door is unlocked, grab her dress and gear bag, and then meet her at Grant Farm. She drew a map on the back and taped this to the front door.

Then she hopped on her bike and raced. The three miles seemed to take forever, and when she veered into the Grant Farm drive, her tires slid and the bike went down, scraping raw her right elbow, knee and a spot on her cheek. Kaylee picked herself up and pedaled on, tossing the bike in the grass in front of the farmhouse. The vet truck with its white trailer was parked in the turnaround.

I can't be too late!

Kaylee raced down the embankment, through the latched fence and into the barn. Trooper lay on his side in his stall, the vet and Amber kneeling near him, Mr. And Mrs. Grant standing off to the side.

"He's not—" The words caught in her throat.

"No, honey," said Mr. Grant, his face drawn and forlorn. "Not yet."

"What happened, dear?" asked Mrs. Grant, reaching out instinctively as she spotted Kaylee's cuts.

"I'm okay," Kaylee assured her and edged closer to the stall. Amber, slid over and let Kaylee kneel next to Trooper's head. The great animal's tired eyes followed her and he seemed to gain a flicker of strength, but this lasted only an instant and he gave out a great sigh, as if the effort of summoning the moment of joy had been overwhelming. She stroked his head, his mane, leaned close, resting her cheek against him.

"I'm here, Trooper," she whispered. In reply, Trooper gave only the slightest movement, but it was enough. *He knows. He's glad I'm here.*

"I'll give you a few minutes," said the vet, a man about her father's age with a kind face. "Then we've got to say goodbye."

She knelt there, remembering the way he had raced around the corral while the other horses had shuffled out in such an orderly fashion, how he had seemed to possess a sense of humor as he stole carrots, how the little rebel had always returned to her for brushing and affection.

"I'll miss you, Troop. You're a good horse. You've got so much spirit. I'll never forget you."

She repeated these things in the dim barn for an indeterminate amount of time. Then Mr. Grant said, "All right," and she felt as if the world had dropped away beneath her. Kaylee kissed Trooper's forehead, and then Amber placed an arm around her shoulders and the two girls walked slowly out of the barn and into the corral. They stood there in the soft mud, holding onto each other, finally letting their tears come, both of them. Kaylee had only known Amber casually before. The older girl had taught Kaylee how to care for the horses three years ago, and Kaylee had asked her how college was going during her occasional trips home. Now she could see that Amber loved Trooper as much as she did.

They stood so long that Kaylee seemed to run out of tears, and then Mr. Grant came out of the door. "Well," he said slowly, "he was a good horse."

Amber hugged her father.

Then he turned to Kaylee. "Do you need a ride home?"

Now Kaylee remembered the feis. "I've got someone coming," she said, mumbled an awkward goodbye, and hurried out the latched gate. At the top of the hill she saw April Lee waving grimly from the passenger window of her car.

"We got your note. Are you okay, honey?" asked April's mother as Kaylee climbed into the backseat.

Kaylee nodded, although she was far from okay. April gave Kaylee's hand a squeeze.

"I'll get you there as quickly as I can," said April's mother. "I'm sure it'll be all right. These things rarely start on time."

"What time is it?" asked Kaylee. She had completely lost any sense of how many minutes had passed since she had entered the barn.

"Ten-fifteen," replied Mrs. Lee.

Please let the feis be running slowly.

Her bags rested on the seat beside her, and Kaylee began the process of getting ready as they drove. April retrieved some moist, disposable wipes from a storage compartment and Kaylee used these to swab the scrapes on her face, elbow and knee.

Oh, I'm going to look just great! Please let the judges focus on my dancing!

She pinned up her hair, pinned on her wig, worked on her makeup to the best of her ability. She pulled on socks, glued them, and then bounced nervously in her seat as they closed in on Kenosha.

They pulled into the hotel parking lot at 10:58.

"I'll drop you girls off at the door!" said April's mother.

The two tumbled out of the car, lugging their dress bags with them. They hurried through the revolving door into the lobby and were confronted by a large placard.

GATEWAY FEIS – WELCOME
REGISTRATION IN WEST HALLWAY

Kaylee checked her watch. 11:02.

"I think last year it was this way!" called Kaylee, and they sped off to the right. They passed a gift shop, an exercise spa, and then headed down a long hallway that turned to the left. There they found the registration table.

11:05.

The good news was that there were no other girls in line. Most of the dancers checked in early in the morning at feiseanna. The bad news was that the woman sitting behind the small box of registration materials for last names beginning with J and ending in R was talking with the lady sitting behind letters A through I. She went on and on about how awful her neighbor had treated her cat. Kaylee could not tell whether the woman did not notice her standing there, or whether she was operating under the assumption that this conversation was somehow more important than a frantic dancer's desire to get to her stage before it was too late. She checked her watch again.

11:08.

Finally Kaylee said, "Ma'am, can I get my number?"

She said it politely, but the woman eyed her as if she had just dared to interrupt the reading of some sacred scroll."

"Last name?"

"O'Shay!" blurted Kaylee, a bit too loudly. "Kaylee O'Shay."

With an audible sigh, the woman thumbed painstakingly through her box, finally withdrawing the competition number and a data card.

"Ribbon's at the end of the table,' said the woman, pointing vaguely, and then she resumed her cat narrative.

Kaylee needed no ribbon, as her dress had a clip sewn to the front. She thanked the woman, picked up her bags and checked the time again.

11:12.

Time never moves this fast in math class!

The two girls hurried to the great ballroom, glanced around for a place to camp.

"It's nothing but people!" said April, gesturing toward the roped-off area where blankets and lawn chairs reposed. NO CAMPING signs were affixed to the walls at ten-meter intervals around the rest of the room. They tiptoed through the human sea, looking for an open square.

This is insane.

11:15.

"Let's just go to my stage!" called Kaylee, checking her data card. "I'll dress there!"

April nodded and the two made their way out of the camping area to stage one. Kaylee dropped her bag beside a row of folding chairs, stripped off her sweats and t-shirt, unzipped the garment bag. She pulled out the blue dress, slipped it on. April helped with the cape. She clipped the number on the front, pawed her shoes from her bag.

"Which first?"

April looked at the card. "Soft!"

Figures. Soft shoes took longer to lace. As she finished the task, Kaylee wondered whether she had set a record.

"Go!" cried April. "They're just lining up!" Kaylee bolted for the stage and stepped behind a young-looking girl in a red dress. The dancers edged forward until it was Kaylee's turn to check in with the stage monitor.

"Kaylee O'Shay," she said, breathing a relieved sigh, as the woman moved to check her off on the clipboard she carried. Then the stage monitor frowned.

"You're not on the list."

Kaylee froze. "I've got to be. I've got a number. This is stage one!"

The middle-aged woman eyed her warily, but with motherly concern. "Under fifteen?"

Kaylee shook her head. "Under seventeen."

The woman nodded as if she now understood and pointed to the large dance schedule posted beside the stage. A smaller notice had been taped up near it:

COMPETITION PC617 MOVED TO STAGE 7

"They announced it over the public address system about half an hour ago," said the woman kindly.

"I wasn't here half an hour ago!" wailed Kaylee. "Where's stage seven?"

"Out the door and to the left," instructed the woman. "The Lighthouse Ballroom."

11:24.

Kaylee turned, weaved through the crowd, past April.

"Where—"

She kept going, not waiting for her friend to finish the question. She raced through the great room, nearly upsetting a stroller carrying infant twins in the process.

"Sorry!" she called, but did not stop. On she raced, out the doorway and to the left, her progress slowed by the growing crowds, surging toward the food vendors. She reached the end of the hall and the Lighthouse Ballroom, ducked inside and surveyed the scene. While similar to the previous room, the Lighthouse Ballroom was smaller and held only three stages. Stage seven was, of course, the last of these.

Kaylee hurried to the side of the stage where dancers were lining up.

11:27.

"Excuse me," she said breathlessly to the square-jawed woman monitoring the stage. "I'm here for PC617. Kaylee O'Shay."

The woman seemed surprised, then frowned. "You missed soft shoe. We're lining up for hard shoe now."

Kaylee looked. Sure enough, all the girls in line wore their hard shoes. "How did they finish so quickly? It was supposed to start at eleven!"

The square-jawed woman shrugged. "Small group today. Only thirteen."

"Oh, please!" said Kaylee desperately. "Can't you let me dance my soft shoe? Can't you talk to the judges?"

The woman's expression seemed to soften at this, and she turned, walked to the judge at the nearest table. She spoke for a few moments, and Kaylee saw one judge, an older woman, peer around the stage monitor to get a look at her. The judge moved her hands expressively as she replied, although Kaylee could hear none of it, lost as everything usually was in the cacophony of a feis. Then the square-jawed woman returned.

"Well, I've got *some* good news," she said.

Kaylee's heart leaped.

"You can dance your hard shoe with the girls here," she said. "The judges are fine with that. But they say the soft shoe is over. It's your responsibility to get here on time."

Kaylee stared out at the stage for a moment, then her gaze dropped to the floor and she turned.

"Do you want to change into your hard shoes?" called the stage monitor. "Young lady?"

Kaylee continued through the room, not turning back. She did not stop until she had reached the hallway where she sat down, her back against the wall.

It was over.

There would be no Oireachtas.

No Ireland.

And Trooper was dead.

She sat there saying nothing, unable to even cry.

Thirty

They sat on the living room sofa, Bethany O'Shay's arm around her daughter. "I'm so sorry, sweetheart," said Mrs. O'Shay. "For Trooper, for everything."

Kaylee said nothing for awhile. She felt numb. She had felt that way ever since the moment earlier in the day when she had realized that her dream would never come true.

The kitchen door opened and Will and Mr. O'Shay barged noisily in, talking about soccer and adventures that had occurred on their trip to the clinic. It took only a few minutes for them to appreciate the nature of Kaylee's situation.

"Sorry, sweetheart," Mr. O'Shay said, and then he and Will quietly busied themselves making sandwiches in the kitchen.

"Mom," said Kaylee hollowly, "can't I go to another feis? It's not like I tried to miss my dance today."

They had been over this before. Several times. Mrs. O'Shay knew they would go over the same argument several more.

"All of the feiseanna that you could use for qualifying are closed," said Mrs. O'Shay. "And we just don't have the money. Not until I sell the store."

"Will got to go to a soccer clinic!" protested Kaylee.

"It was a free clinic," noted Mr. O'Shay. "The coaches donated their time to help kids prepare for the start of the high school season next week."

Kaylee sat silently again, her eyes focused on her knees.

"But you could find money for an emergency," Kaylee pleaded.

Will stepped into the living room, leaned against the doorway munching on a sandwich. Kaylee had always marveled at how much cereal he consumed. Now that he was going to be a high school junior, she was amazed at how tall he had grown, how his shoulders had broadened. He was still dating Jackie after two years. He would probably be one of the leading scorers on the high school soccer team this fall. Somehow, he seemed to coast through life. Why was it so hard for her, she wondered?

"What's the big deal about going to another feis?" he asked, his speech muffled a bit by sandwich.

"I need to dance at a feis to qualify for Oireachtas," said Kaylee stoically. "If I don't dance at Oireachtas, I can't go to Worlds."

Will chewed, swallowed. "Can't you just go next year?"

Kaylee had trouble holding her voice steady. "Next year I'll be in college. This was my last chance."

Will took another bite, seemed to be thinking. "This is, like, the thing you've wanted to do forever."

Kaylee said nothing for a moment, then nodded.

"Sometimes the guys at soccer practice complain when we run hard or do drills over and over," said Will. "And I always tell them what wimps they are, that my sister works ten times as hard as any of them."

Kaylee wanted to hug him. She also wanted to cry.

"It's not fair that you don't get to go to Worlds," he continued. "You train harder than anybody I know. I think you love dance more than I love soccer." Then he smiled. "I *know* you do."

Will finished the rest of the sandwich in a giant gulp. The food seemed to give him an idea.

"If all you need is money, I can pay for your feis."

Kaylee sat up a little straighter.

"Where are you going to get the money?" asked Mr. O'Shay.

Will twirled his fingers vaguely toward the stairs that led up to his room. "I can sell a couple of my old video games. The ones I don't use anymore. I've got plenty of them. I'll put an ad online."

Now Kaylee lifted off the back of the couch, her eyes widening. "You'd do that for me?"

"Hey, I don't play some of them anymore, so it's no biggie."

Kaylee turned hopefully toward her mother, whose expression reflected doubt. "Will, that's a very sweet offer. But

Kaylee, it's not just money, remember? If it were, your father and I would scrape together the entry fee somehow. It's like I told you before. The registration deadlines for most of the feiseanna have passed. They're closed. Back at the beginning of the summer, we didn't realize that we'd need to register you for anything after the Gateway Feis."

"But you haven't checked them all to make sure they're closed," Kaylee pleaded.

Mrs. O'Shay stared into her daughter's face and then pulled her into a hug. "I'll go online right now and check, sweetheart, but I don't think we're going to have any luck."

She rose from the sofa and moved to the family computer. After a few minutes, she pulled up the calendar of feiseanna for the fall. Kaylee peered over her shoulder.

"Chicago, closed. Rochester, closed. Aurora, closed."

"That one's open!" Kaylee cried suddenly, pointing.

"That one's in Florida, honey," said Mrs. O'Shay. "That'd require plane fare, lodging. Will isn't going to get that much money for his games. It's got to be close enough to drive to."

Then she narrowed her gaze on the screen. "Here's one that's still open in South Bend, Indiana. First weekend in September. But it won't work."

"Why not?" asked Kaylee.

"I can't drive you," explained Mrs. O'Shay. "I have to work. And your father has already agreed to chaperone the soccer overnighter to Verona with the high school, so he can't drive you either."

"I've got my driver's license," argued Kaylee.

"You've only been driving a few months," said Mr. O'Shay. "We're not going to let you drive all the way to South Bend by yourself. That's five hours. And it's through Chicago. Traffic is awful, even on a good day!"

Mrs. O'Shay tapped away at the keyboard. "Here's the time schedule for the Fighting Irish Feis—"

"Fighting Irish?"

"It's held at Notre Dame University," said Mrs. O'Shay. "If you went there, your age group would dance at ten in the morning."

"So?"

"Remember, there's no money for a hotel room," said Mrs. O'Shay. "Even if one of us could drive you, it just won't work."

Kaylee stared at the screen.

"Caitlin can come with me," she said suddenly, her eyes bright with the electricity of an idea. "She's had her license for more than a year. We can trade off driving. Remember, I can drive if there's one other person in the car. We'll leave at five in the morning."

"You'd need time to get ready," said Mrs. O'Shay.

"Okay, four in the morning."

"And you need to build in extra time in case the Chicago traffic is bad," noted Mr. O'Shay.

"Three."

The O'Shay parents stared at her. Will had left and now returned to the doorway with another sandwich.

"Absolutely not," said Mr. O'Shay.

"Out of the question," said Mrs. O'Shay. "It's too dangerous for two seventeen-year-old girls to be by themselves on a trip like that."

Kaylee's gaze now moved back and forth between her two parents. "You're wrong."

Mr. O'Shay shook his head in the dad way. "When you're a parent, you sometimes have to make tough decisions to keep your children safe."

"Safe?" cried Kaylee. "Will plays one of the most dangerous sports on the planet! A lot more dangerous than driving through Chicago!"

"Kaylee," pleaded Mrs. O'Shay, "we just don't want to see you get hurt."

"You don't want to see me get hurt?" Kaylee could hardly believe her ears. "Trooper died today. I missed the most important feis of my life. The last two years were nothing but pain. I couldn't even crawl at first! I had to learn to walk! And then when I tried to do the thing I loved most, I felt like somebody was pounding my leg with a hammer!" She paused, closed her eyes, opened them again and continued. "I've already been hurt! But there's still one thing that could hurt me even more!"

She stared at them in silence. Then Mr. O'Shay looked at the floor, shaking his head. Mrs. O'Shay simply adopted a pleading look. Will finished the second sandwich.

Kaylee turned, walked resolutely to the front door, opened it, but turned back at the last moment. "You know, one year from now, Caitlin and I will be going off to college. We won't have any parents around to hold our hands. It might even be someplace farther away than South Bend." Then she burst into the dusk of Cranberry Street. She sat on the front step, crossed her arms on her knees and rested her chin atop them.

Goodbye, Trooper.

It seemed to Kaylee that life was just one goodbye after another.

Goodbye Aunt Kat.

Goodbye Grandma.

I never even got to wear the beautiful green dress she made me!

The sunset contained the perfect mixture of clouds and dusty blends of primary colors. Kaylee did not notice it.

A car turned down the street, slowed, stopped in front of the O'Shay house. A familiar car.

Riley stepped out. Kaylee tried not to show her surprise.

"Hey."

"Hey."

He walked across the lawn to within a few feet of where she sat.

"What are you doing here?" she asked.

His eyes seemed to bore into her, trying to find some softness. "I heard about Trooper."

Kaylee felt her eyes become moist, but she fought the feeling. "Who told you that?"

"I think one of your friends who was at the feis told Jordi and Hannah," said Riley.

"Probably April."

"You know how those two are," said Riley with a smile. "If they know it, a hundred people are going to know it. I heard you missed your soft shoe, too. Pretty cruddy day."

"Well, thanks," said Kaylee, nodding, attempting to keep her voice from wavering. "This was just what I needed: Someone to come over and remind me of all the details of the worst day of my life."

"That's not why I came over here."

Kaylee knew he was trying to comfort her, but she could not help herself. She felt as if she had suffered the worst defeat imaginable, and it hurt. "I don't need your pity."

Riley shook his head. "I don't know why you're like this. You keep avoiding me, trying to push me away. Do you think you're the only one who ever gets hurt?"

Kaylee said nothing.

"I don't know what I'm doing here," he said, throwing up his hands. "But I'm tired of never knowing how you feel."

He turned and headed back across the lawn.

Goodbye, Trooper.

Goodbye Aunt Kat.

Goodbye Grandma.

Goodbye to my dance dreams.

And now, goodbye to Riley.

Kaylee stood suddenly, ran to Riley, pulled an arm so that he faced her. She stared at him angrily, raised her right hand and cried, "You know what?" But she did not give him a chance to respond, throwing her arms around his neck and pulling him into a kiss every bit as passionate and exciting as their first kiss two years ago at the football game. Then she kissed him again, and his arms tightened around her. By the third kiss, she had almost forgotten the pain of the past two years.

She opened her eyes. "What a beautiful sunset," she whispered, peering over Riley's shoulder.

As she spoke, the front door opened. Her father stepped out. "Let's talk about South Bend."

Then he saw his daughter, her arms around Riley's neck. Kaylee thought he might be upset, but instead, a faint smile appeared on Tom O'Shay's face.

"I guess you really don't need me to hold your hand anymore," he said, and then motioned Riley and Kaylee into the house.

Thirty-one

She stood in front of the gigantic banner. *I can't believe I'm really here.*

Not that the road had been easy.

Riley squeezed her hand. As always, any gesture of intimacy, no matter how small, seemed to trigger a reaction from one or both of Kaylee's parents, as if to let the two of them know that they were under observation.

"Let's get a picture of you both under the Oireachtas banner," said Mr. O'Shay, holding his camera a few inches below his face as he moved for the perfect vantage point.

Kaylee and Riley turned, smiled, were hit by the flash.

"That's a keeper," said Mr. O'Shay.

Since the Midwest Oireachtas was held over the Thanksgiving holiday, Mr. O'Shay was off from his job at Kennedy Park Elementary, and so he had driven the family to Columbus. Mrs. O'Shay had proclaimed that, after everything her daughter had gone through to get here, she was not going to miss the event, and so had closed the store for the long weekend in order to come.

"It's already a sinking ship," she had shrugged sadly. Still no buyer. Number two had bowed out.

Will had been dragged to Columbus, too.

"Why can't I stay home by myself? It's not like I'm a baby! I'm sixteen!"

Mr. O'Shay had grunted a laugh in response. "Better if you *were* a baby! A sixteen-year-old is more likely to get into serious trouble at home alone than a six-year-old."

They stood in the lobby of the host hotel where one of the giant Oireachtas banners hung. Similar banners served as backdrops for each stage. The O'Shays were not staying at the host hotel, however. Kaylee's father had found rooms online at one-third the cost, although they were in a hotel that required them to walk half a mile to the venue. "We're lucky we can afford to come at all," he told Kaylee when she complained about being "away from all the fun." Will had expanded his video game sales, and Mrs. Grant had given Kaylee a nice end-of-the-season employee bonus for her work on the farm. Even though they had to pinch pennies, Kaylee was excited, for it was the first time she could remember that they were all together at a dance competition.

The most important Irish dance competition of her life.

Riley's mother had ridden with him to Columbus and they were registered at the host hotel. Linda Horne had met the O'Shays previously, but this was the first time the parents had really been able to catch their breaths and talk.

"It's all so exciting!" said Mrs. Horne, snapping pictures of her own. Unlike her son's dark hair, Mrs. Horne's was long and almost white-blonde. And where Riley was lean and tall, Mrs. Horne was shorter than Kaylee and thickly built. "Riley's father was the tall one," she explained. Kaylee knew that Mr. Horne had died when Riley was six. "He would have enjoyed this."

"Can I rent video games on the TV in our room?" asked Will.

"Ask me later," said Mr. O'Shay.

"Let's get a picture of you and Kaylee over near the Christmas tree!" Mrs. Horne said to Riley. They moved in front of the enormous, beautifully decorated spruce. It did not yet feel like Christmas to Kaylee, but she knew the stores had already been decorated in candy canes and tinsel for weeks.

"Kaylee's so beautiful!" said Mrs. Horne after snapping the shot. "How long has she been in Champs?"

Kaylee explained that she was still in Preliminary Champion.

"She had a devil of a time just qualifying for the Oireachtas," explained Mr. O'Shay, who then went on to narrate the highlights of the last-chance trip to South Bend.

"Kaylee and Caitlin were going to leave at three in the morning."

"Caitlin slept over," interjected Kaylee. "And then we decided to leave at two, just to be on the safe side."

"Neither had ever driven through Chicago before," continued Mr. O'Shay. "We made them promise to call us every hour on Caitlin's cell phone."

Kaylee made a face. "Worry warts."

"And with good reason," said Mr. O'Shay. "Although apparently the traffic through Chicago at three in the morning wasn't that bad."

"It was after Chicago that were had problems," said Kaylee. "We got a flat tire."

"In Gary," noted her father, cringing.

"Caitlin was driving," said Kaylee. "We pulled off the freeway and it was all factories and a couple of closed-up stores. Nothing was going on at four in the morning. We were freaking. We both started to cry. We didn't know whether to call my dad and wait for him to come and fix it or try to do it ourselves. We figured out we'd be way late if dad came to fix it, so we decided not to call. But we were scared. It was a spooky-looking place, like in the movies where people get robbed and shot."

"Neither of them had ever changed a tire," said Mr. O'Shay. "Had no idea how to do it."

"We opened the trunk, starting looking at the tools and the spare tire, and we both just started bawling," said Kaylee.

"Then a car drives up," said Mr. O'Shay.

"A taxi," said Kaylee. "It parks behind us and this tall guy gets out and asks if we are lost. He sounds Jamaican or something, and at first we can hardly understand him. But then he looks at the car and realizes what our problem is."

"And he changes the tire for them!" said Tom O'Shay.

"His name was Roberto," said Kaylee. "He has two kids and he's been driving a cab for six years."

"They tried to give him some money after, but he wouldn't take it," said Mr. O'Shay.

"So Caitlin and I did an Irish dance for him and he clapped. Then he wished us luck and told us how to get back on the freeway."

"But they still got lost and used up another half hour. Wasn't really their fault. There was a lot of construction and the signs were confusing."

"But we made it to South Bend, and that's when we realized that we had changed time zones! It was really an hour later than we thought it was!"

"That's my fault," said Mr. O'Shay. "I should have remembered the time change. Oh well . . ."

"So now I'm like, 'Oh no! I'm going to miss my dance again! I'm going to miss my dance again!' And I'm just throwing on my stuff as we get into the building. Tears are running down my face as I'm getting my registration materials. I'm thinking how stupid I am, how this whole five-hour trip is going to be for nothing."

"But the good news," said Mr. O'Shay, was that the feis was running behind schedule.

"I danced!" said Kaylee, hopping up and down excitedly. "I placed third! My second-highest place ever in PC!"

"What an adventure!" said Mrs. Horne.

"And then on the way home we were so exhausted because we had been up since two and we actually hadn't gotten to sleep until ten-thirty the night before, so we were operating on less than four hours of sleep," added Kaylee. "So on the south side of Chicago on the way back, we stopped at a travel oasis, bought a couple of soft pretzels and fell asleep in the car for two hours."

"They got home at one in the morning," said Mr. O'Shay. "That's where I first heard about the flat tire story."

Kaylee smiled, gave her father a tiny kiss on the cheek. "So for my first long trip without parents, I think it went pretty well."

Kaylee began to recognize other faces in the lobby, some just checking in, others passing through on their way to check out the vendors or the stages in the adjacent convention center.

"You made it, safe and sound!" said Annie, her teacher at Trean Gaoth Academy, giving Kaylee an enormous hug. "Oh, you really deserve a good Oireachtas! Good luck, honey!"

Tara, an assistant at Trean Gaoth, hugged her as well. Kaylee found herself missing Miss Helen. Since she was no longer employed at the school, she no longer came to competitions. "The school used to pay my way," Miss Helen said in the week before Kaylee had left. "But now I'm retired and my income is only so-so. But you do not need me there. You are dancing better than ever. Better even than before the accident!"

Kaylee decided that she had never received a nicer compliment.

April passed through the lobby with her mother and the two girls hugged while the parents talked about rooms, dance schedules and which restaurants should be avoided.

"This is weird," said April. "We'll actually be competing against each other on Saturday!"

"Good luck!" called Kaylee as April and her mother disappeared across the lobby.

While perusing the vendors in the convention center, the group literally ran into Jordi and Hannah who bounded out of a practice room and almost collided with them.

"We're on a ceili team!" announced Hannah. "It's so exciting!"

Kaylee had been to Oireachtas once before, three years earlier, as a member of a ceili team. She remembered the excitement of competing with seven friends and almost envied Jordi and Hannah. Being a member of a ceili team helped to absorb some of the largeness of the event.

"When are you dancing?" asked Jordi.

Kaylee told her that she would dance just after lunch on Saturday, while Riley was scheduled for right before lunch on the same day.

"We'll come and watch!" said Hannah, and then the two girls ran off.

As they eyed the tables full of Irish jewelry, sweaters, scarves, knick-knacks, candy, as well as Irish dancer t-shirts, sweat pants and accessories, they passed other members of Trean Gaoth Academy. Kaylee greeted these teammates with either a wave or a hug. Riley frequently gave a wave to friends from Golden Academy.

"I haven't seen Brittany yet," said Kaylee suddenly, giving Riley a sideways glance.

He fielded the observation deftly. "She won't be here until tomorrow afternoon. I guess she and her father are flying in."

"Figures," said Kaylee. Then it occurred to her that she would be competing against Brittany, too.

April, Brittany and so many other good dancers from across the Midwest. How could she ever expect to beat half of them, much less finish high enough to qualify for Worlds?

No, she told herself. *Push away the doubt. Focus on the positives On the prize!.*

Then they turned into Ballroom A and stared down the long aisle to the stage where they both would dance on Saturday. They walked forward, and Kaylee climbed onto the raised platform, turning to face the row upon row of padded spectator chairs.

"Just seeing how it's going to feel," she said.

After a few moments, her mother said, "Well, let's go have Thanksgiving dinner!"

"Are you going to a restaurant?" asked Mrs. Horne.

Mrs. O'Shay shook her head. "I packed turkey sandwiches and pumpkin pie in a cooler. It's in our hotel room. It's a bit of a walk, but you're welcome to join us."

Mrs. Horne looked to Riley, then back to Kaylee's mother and smiled. "That would be wonderful! Thank you!"

Kaylee felt happy. For awhile, she had wondered whether she ever would again. But she was at Oireachtas. With Riley. The competition would begin tomorrow and she would dance in two days. The thought made her tingle. It was almost like Christmas.

She hoped she would get what she wanted.

Thirty-two

Friday. Lots of ceili teams. Lots of tiny solo dancers. Lots of excitement.

Kaylee attended some of the awards presentations, too, and imagined herself accepting the winner's cup and sash.

"How many dancers qualify for Worlds?" Will asked.

Kaylee sighed, for it was not a question with an easy answer. "It depends on the number of dancers in a competition. Usually it's ten percent that go to Worlds. But if there are dancers that have already won World or National medals in the competition, an extra qualifying spot is added for each of them."

Will nodded. "So how many dancers are you going against?"

"One hundred and five," said Kaylee. It was the first time she had said it out loud, and it sounded immense.

"So they'll take ten to Worlds?"

"I think there's a few medal winners from Nationals, so the number will probably be about thirteen or fourteen."

Will shrugged. "You're a good dancer. You should be able to do that."

Kaylee smiled. "I wish you were one of the judges!"

And then, just like that, it was Saturday. Riley did not seem nervous at all, but Kaylee thought that she would burst.

"Time moves so slowly when you're waiting for something important!" she told her mother.

She had waked up at six in the morning and had moved around so restlessly that no one else could sleep—except Will, who Kaylee believed could sleep through a train wreck. They had breakfasted, walked to the convention center and then

Kaylee had spent hours fussing and perfecting her makeup as well as going over her steps. At about eleven, her routine ground to a halt as she watched Riley dance.

He looks flawless, she thought. *I hope I dance as well.*

When Riley finished his second dance, he headed immediately to the back of the ballroom where Kaylee stood waiting and gave her a hug. "Now we wait for results!"

Kaylee shook her head. "Now I get even more nervous, because it means I'm up soon!"

Of course, *soon* means *forever* when it is used to indicate an event after the lunch break at an Irish dance competition. And so Kaylee practiced.

And practiced.

And practiced some more.

"It's time," said her mother finally. She kissed Kaylee on the forehead. "Make your dance as beautiful as you are!"

Kaylee opened her garment bag, gazed proudly at the amazing green dress that her grandmother had sewn. I wish you could be here, Grandma. With a deep breath, she lifted it from the bag, turned it, slipped it on. The jewels that had been painstakingly glued to it shimmered in the ballroom lights.

"Wow!" said Riley.

"I think the judges are going to notice you," said Mr. O'Shay, smiling.

Her mother zipped the back, attached the cape, and when she stood back to admire her daughter, she put a hand over her mouth. "Oh, my!" she gasped, her voice full of emotion, and then she looked away, tried to compose herself. When she faced Kaylee again, tears streamed down her cheeks.

"Mom, what's wrong?" asked Kaylee.

Mrs. O'Shay kept her hand over her mouth, shook her head. "It's . . ." She turned away again, wiped her cheeks, turned back and struggled to keep her voice level. "You just look so beautiful!"

It's because grandma made the dress, thought Kaylee, but then she saw her father's face. Although he was not crying, the expression on it differed from the "proud dad" look that she might have expected. *He looks shocked. Like he just saw a ghost!*

A moment later her father's expression softened, he smiled and wrapped her in a hug. "Good luck, honey."

She proceeded to the stage.

You are dancing better than ever. Better even than before the accident!

Miss Helen's words drowned out the distractions of the Oireachtas. She visualized herself on stage, felt her feet moving flawlessly, saw Ireland, and the green fire burned inside of her.

She checked in, but now she knew there would be another wait. Twenty-seven dancers would complete their soft shoe dances before Kaylee. Another seventy-seven would follow her. Then they would start again, this time doing their hard shoe routines. An hour or two or three after they had finished, those who recalled would be announced. Those fifty-three dancers would return to the stage to perform their set dance, another hard shoe number. At the end of the day, the final rankings would be revealed.

Kaylee spotted April and Brittany. April smiled from about thirty feet away—and seemed very nervous. Brittany gave a businesslike nod and returned to her own stretching.

As dancer forty-one took the stage and the music began, Kaylee moved toward the back of the ballroom and continued stretching and practicing her dance moves.

One and two and kick—

A sudden ripping sound horrified her. *My dress!* She felt with her hand, then ran to Mrs. O'Shay, who conducted a hurried inspection.

"Oh, sweetheart, this is quite a tear!" said Mrs. O'Shay. "Your grandmother didn't reinforce this spot where the old material meets the new."

"Old material?" asked Kaylee.

"It can be fixed," continued Mrs. O'Shay, still focused on the tear, "but not here. You've got the blue dress in your bag, don't you?"

Kaylee nodded, but this news took some of the wind out of her sails. She had been saving the green dress for a big moment, a special occasion. She could think of no occasion more appropriate than qualifying for Worlds. Unfortunately, the blue dress would have to do.

She hurried back to where she had left her gear, pulled out the blue dress, carefully placed the green dress inside. In a few minutes, she was ready to go again. *It'll be okay*, she told herself. *Look how well you did at the Fighting Irish Feis in the blue dress.*

But this was not the Fighting Irish Feis. This was the Oireachtas.

She resumed her preparations, and finally, she stood at the side of the raised stage.

I'm dancing solo at Oireachtas! I'm dancing to qualify for Worlds!

At the bell, she walked to center stage, waited. Then, at a signal from the judge, she stepped forward. All eyes were on her now. Music played. She pointed her right toe, smiled, thought of Riley, of her Grandmother, of Aunt Kat.

She thought of Ireland.

"I don't know that I've ever seen you dance better!" said her mother, hugging her mightily after she finished her second dance. She then collected hugs from her father, Jordi and Hannah, Will, Mrs. Horne and Riley.

His was the longest.

"Hopefully it won't be too long before they announce recalls," said Kaylee. She changed out of her dress, bought some yogurt, and then came back to the stage to watch April and Brittany dance.

Both seemed to dance beautifully.

Everyone's so good! How can the judges decide? One little waver, a toe not pointed, a kick not high enough, a slight error in timing, and a dancer might easily plunge forty places in the rankings.

Now more waiting. She and Riley walked through the vendors again. Kaylee had seen all of the merchandise already, and her eyes skimmed the displays without really focusing. Then Riley talked her into a nacho boat, and they found a quiet place behind a planter in a side hallway that offered a respite from the bustle of the competition.

They talked about school for thirty seconds, which was all Kaylee could stand to spend not talking about recalling. "If I don't recall, I don't know what I'll do. It'll be awful, I'll—"

Riley stopped her by leaning in and delivering a nacho-flavored kiss. Then he smiled at her.

"Don't worry."

"But I can't help it," she protested. "Ever since I started dancing, I've wanted to go to Ireland—"

"You're amazing." His words stopped her. "You've worked harder than anybody. And you've accomplished so much. Even if you don't go to Ireland. You might already be a world champion."

"What do you mean?" asked Kaylee.

"I don't think anyone else in the world would have kept going through everything you've had to suffer. I think anyone else would have quit a long time ago. Would have said, 'Oh well, I guess it just wasn't meant to be.' But you kept going."

She hugged him. "I love Irish dance."

Will suddenly appeared around the planter. "There you are! Come on! They're announcing results!"

Kaylee leaped to her feet, grabbed Riley's hand and followed Will down the hallway, around the corner, and into the ballroom where their stage was located.

"You both made it!" cried Mrs. Horne. "You both recalled!"

Riley found her and they hugged again.

Step one had been qualifying for the Oireachtas. Step two was recalling. Mission accomplished. Now it was time for step three: Dance a great set.

"They'll be starting the sets soon," said Mrs. O'Shay. "We'd better get over to the stage."

They moved through the crowd, back toward their camp. Kaylee felt the nervous energy growing again. Then, just where the mob was thickest, a voice rang out above the general hubbub.

"Lizzie Martin!"

Kaylee felt her heart race. Someone had called Lizzie Martin's name. She looked around, but with people moving in a hundred directions, she could not tell who had called out. It had sounded like a woman's voice, an adult. Kaylee's mind raced.

She could think of only one thing the name might mean: Someone in the crowd had actually seen Lizzie.

It made perfect sense. Lizzie Martin had probably come to Columbus to watch the Oireachtas. An old friend, perhaps someone who had danced with her at Golden Academy, had recognized her.

"Mom, did you hear that?" called Kaylee, but her mother kept pushing through the crowd, her eyes straight ahead. Kaylee tried again. "Mom, Lizzie Martin's here!"

"We don't have time for that now," said Mrs. O'Shay, quickening her pace, her eyes still focused on some point in the distance. "We've got to get you ready to dance."

Kaylee twisted around as she followed, although she realized the futility of her action. Lizzie Martin might be only three feet away from her and Kaylee would not know it, for she had never seen her. And even if Kaylee could pick her out of the crowd somehow, her mother might not stop. Something had happened between her mother and Lizzie, something that had destroyed their friendship. Now Mrs. O'Shay seemed to have no interest in resuming the relationship.

They reached the camp, and Kaylee pulled on her dress. She hugged Riley goodbye so that he could go off to his stage, and then Kaylee began warming up all over again. Mrs. O'Shay seemed more anxious than Kaylee had ever seen her before a competition.

She knows how much this means to me.

A short time later, Kaylee checked in for her set dance, waited, practiced.

And then she stood on center stage for her final dance at Oireachtas.

And smiled.

And hoped.

There was something reserved in the way Riley hugged her when his name was announced.

"And qualifying for Worlds . . ."

"You made it!" she shrieked, throwing her arms around Riley's neck as he returned to his seat after accepting his award.

He pulled her close, but not too close, stroking her cheek.

"Let's hold off on the celebrating for a little bit," he said. "Then we can do it together!"

She understood. Mrs. Horne, however, could not be contained, giving her son a great squeeze and kissing him twice on the cheek. Kaylee's father shook Riley's hand. Even Kaylee's mother gave him a hug, although Kaylee noticed that Mrs. O'Shay had donned sunglasses. "Migraine," she explained.

The great ballroom was packed—not a chair empty, and people packed the open space behind the chairs all the way to the back wall.

Then they heard the announcement for Kaylee's group to come forward. Riley kissed her. She felt light as air and skittered to the side of the great stage along with the other fifty-three award winners.

"In fifty-third place, competitor number 52, Amy Mills of Kelliher Academy."

Each dancer came up, received her award and took her spot on stage.

April sidled up to her. "Good luck!" said her friend. "You looked so good!"

"You too!" said Kaylee, wondering what the chances were that she and April would both qualify for Worlds.

"I've never recalled before!" said April, bouncing up and down on her toes. "I'm so nervous!"

"Me too," said Kaylee, listening intently for her number, glad when she failed to hear it.

"A tie for fortieth place, competitor number 11, Alexis Conroy, Mirren Dance School, and competitor number 93, Jamie Smith, Kelsey School of Irish Dance."

April bounced more rapidly. "We're both in the top forty at Oireachtas!"

"In thirty-eighth," said the announcer a few moments later, "competitor number 58, April Lee of Trean Gaoth Academy."

April shrieked, turned a shocked face to Kaylee and then hurried up the steps to take her place with the others as the crowd applauded.

April is in Champs and I finished ahead of her! Kaylee thought, but then it occurred to her that most of the girls here were in Champs. She would have been in Champs herself if not for the accident.

The numbers continued to fall. Kaylee closed her eyes, imagined Ireland, drawing upon every TV show, every photograph, every movie, everything she had ever seen about the Emerald Isle.

Thirtieth place, twenty-fifth . . .

Oh, please! Oh, please!

"In nineteenth place, we have a tie. Competitor number 51, Brittany Hall of Golden Academy!"

The crowd applauded, led by the raucous antics of the large Golden Academy contingent. Kaylee's jaw dropped. I beat Brittany! The last time they had danced on the same stage, Brittany had destroyed her. Brittany had always been light years ahead—so graceful, so strong, so quick. But today, Kaylee had finally—

"Also in nineteenth place, competitor 68, Kaylee O'Shay of Trean Gaoth Academy."

More applause. Kaylee felt stunned, trying to digest this turn of events. Nineteenth place. That was amazingly good. But she had not been paying close attention. Had the announcer said anything about Worlds? She climbed the stairs, crossed the stage, received her award, stood next to Brittany, who smiled at the audience without acknowledging Kaylee's presence.

"And now, ladies and gentlemen," continued the announcer, "the top eighteen places. These dancers qualify for the World Championships in Ireland."

Kaylee stood on the stage, smiling yet not really feeling much like smiling. As the final eighteen dancers bounded up the steps to receive their awards, Kaylee gazed across the sea of faces and felt her heart breaking.

Now it was over.

There were no more second chances, no more obscure qualifying procedures or feiseanna that could help her. She had given it her best shot and had come up one place short. She realized that she should probably feel proud of herself for having come so far. Just a few months ago, she could hardly dance for a minute. Now she was top twenty at Oireachtas.

But knowing that did not help. All she felt was hollow.

She would never dance in Ireland.
Never.

Thirty-three

The hotel room seemed smaller.

Noisier, too. Will lay on his stomach on one of the beds, manipulating the games controller, destroying alien life forms on the television.

"Do you have to be so loud?" Kaylee asked crossly.

Will glanced in her direction, shrugged and returned to the pixilated carnage.

Kaylee listened to the firing of lasers and the explosions of plasma grenades for another thirty seconds, and then lofted another question to the community in general. "Do we have to stay here another night? Can't we just drive home?"

Mrs. O'Shay stepped out of the restroom in pink cotton sweatpants and a I LOVE QUILTING powder-blue t-shirt—her pajamas. "We wouldn't get home until tomorrow morning. Your father would be driving all night with no sleep."

"I could help drive," said Kaylee.

"Room's already paid for," interjected Mr. O'Shay from behind the newspaper he was reading, sitting in a comfy chair near the far window.

Kaylee flopped back onto the bed, stared at the ceiling.

It had surprised her when she had not cried. Missing Worlds by one place—on one hand, she felt proud to have placed among the top twenty dancers in the Midwest. Although her goal had always been the World Championships in Ireland, she knew that she had come an incredible distance in just the past few months.

On the other hand, knowing that she would never dance in Ireland hurt. It hurt a lot. Ever since she had watched *Isle of Green Fire* that first time on TV, she had wanted it. Knowing that she would never see Ireland—at least from the middle of a dance stage—felt like when she had lost her grandmother and Aunt Kat. It was the Never Again feeling that made your insides feel heavy and numb.

Mrs. O'Shay had cried rivers. "We're so proud of you! Oh, I know how much you wanted to go to Ireland!"

And somehow, Kaylee knew her mother understood her pain as acutely as if she had been an Irish dancer herself.

She had borrowed Riley's cell phone to call Caitlin. "Oh, my!" her friend had gasped. "Top twenty! That's amazing!"

Kaylee felt happy for Riley, but she knew that his triumph had been tarnished by the fact that Kaylee would not be going along to Worlds.

"What are you going to do now?" asked Caitlin. "Will you still dance?"

She had asked herself that question right after the awards ceremony. Her ultimate goal was now unreachable. What was the point?

The answer, of course, was love. That was the point.

Kaylee O'Shay loved Irish dance. When she had begun dancing at age ten, she had not danced because she might go to Ireland in seven years. She had danced because it had been fun and beautiful and she had been good at it.

And she had made loyal friends, like Jordi and Hannah, who had given her long hugs after the awards. And April, who had not seemed one bit upset that Kaylee—a PC dancer—had finished ahead of her at Oireachtas.

However, there were always exceptions. Brittany Hall had disappeared quickly after the awards. "She looked angry," Riley had said. "Really angry."

Naturally, thought Kaylee. *It must be driving her nuts that we tied.*

"I'm going to dance at the Snow Feis in January," Kaylee had told Caitlin. "Maybe I'll make Champs. Then I can dance at Nationals in the summer before I go off to college."

It wasn't a bad plan. No, it would not be the same as dancing in Ireland, but it would be another step higher on the mountain. And as Aunt Kat had said, "The view keeps getting better the higher you climb!"

Kaylee sat up on the bed. "If we're not leaving tonight, can we at least rent a movie? It'd be better than watching Will destroy the universe."

Mrs. O'Shay looked at her husband. "She's got a point."

"I'm only destroying the bad guys," said Will. "Mostly."

They were interrupted by a knock on the door. Mr. O'Shay peered over his paper as his wife turned, peered through the peephole, and then opened it.

"Annie! This is a surprise!"

Kaylee sat up straighter, offered a weak smile, wondering why the owner of Trean Gaoth Academy had come to her hotel room at ten in the evening.

"Oh, Kaylee," said Annie, stepping into the room, and then stepping forward to give her young dancer a hug. "I tried to catch up with you right after awards, but you got swallowed up by the crowd. The Hornes told me where you were staying. You were amazing!"

"Thanks," said Kaylee.

"I think it's nothing short of incredible, how you were able to overcome your injuries and do so well at the Oireachtas," continued Annie. "I saw all three of your dances today. I don't think I've ever had a dancer who looked as good. You were the best one out there, in my opinion."

Again Kaylee muttered a thank-you, and added, "I wish you'd been one of the judges."

"I think they made a mistake," said Annie. "But that happens when you have judges. It's not like the long jump, where you use a tape measure to determine the winner. Would you like to see your results?" Annie pulled a print-out from her pocket.

"I completely forgot about those!" cried Kaylee, accepting them eagerly and hurriedly attempting to interpret the numbers and rankings. Her eyes widened. "I did really well! Except . . ."

"Except in two of your dances, one of the three judges scored you way low," said Annie.

"If you really think she got ripped off," said Mr. O'Shay, "can't you file a protest or something?"

Annie shook her head. "I've never heard of one succeeding. In any case, you'd have to have some pretty dramatic evidence of wrong-doing, like a dancer hitting another dancer with a sledge-hammer. I'm afraid the results are final. I know how badly you wanted to dance in Ireland this coming April at Worlds."

Kaylee nodded. She had felt in control all afternoon, even after the awards ceremony. Now, however, she felt like she might succumb to her emotions. "Thanks for bringing over the results."

"And for being so supportive of Kaylee," said Mrs. O'Shay.

"Oh, that's not really why I came," said Annie. "As I said, I know Kaylee wanted to dance in Ireland in April. But since that didn't work out, I was wondering if she might want to dance there in February."

Kaylee's heart skipped a beat. "In Ireland?"

Annie nodded. "You're familiar with the All-Ireland Championships? It's not as big as Worlds, but a lot of the same dancers will be there. Coaches are able to enter dancers who've achieved extraordinary performances throughout the year, and I certainly think you qualify."

A security guard arrived at room 245 three minutes later to report that guests had heard an exceptionally loud and piercing scream, and he inquired as to whether everyone was all right. Inside the room, he saw five people in a mass hug, sort of hopping and quivering and laughing.

He smiled, closed the door and went back to the cup of coffee waiting at his desk.

Thirty-four

The two months since the Oireachtas had gone quickly. Christmas was always over in the blink of an eye, but even so, this year's holiday had offered more than usual for the O'Shays to celebrate.

"I've found a buyer for the store," Mrs. O'Shay had announced on Christmas Eve. Although Kaylee had smiled, for this meant that her parents could begin climbing out of debt, she also lamented the end of her mother's dream.

"Actually," her mother continued, "it's more like a partner."

Kaylee was stunned to learn that Mrs. Hubbard, Caitlin's mother, was buying half-ownership in the business. "She has been looking for a way to keep busy. Mr. Hubbard has always made enough that she didn't need to work. And she enjoys sewing!"

The money would help get the business out of debt, and since Mrs. Hubbard would be working the store part of the time, it would give Mrs. O'Shay more time to spend with her family.

Then in January, Kaylee had danced at the Milwaukee Snow Feis. And she had won her second PC competition.

Now she was in Champs.

Kaylee continued her practice at Trean Gaoth and her workouts in the little church with Miss Helen. Her old teacher worked her even harder. Early on the afternoon of the first Sunday in February, Kaylee suffered through a particularly grueling workout with Miss Helen.

"Up on your toes! That's it!"

I'm leaving in two days! I'm going to Ireland!

She felt tired at the end of the workout, but strong. The usual pain throbbed down her right leg, but during the dancing, when she had focused on Ireland, Kaylee had hardly felt a thing. As she laced on her street shoes, Miss Helen stood over her.

"I wish I could have seen you dance at Oireachtas," said Mss Helen. "Annie said you were wonderful."

"I did okay."

"She said you were the best one there," said Miss Helen. "Annie is not one to give false praise."

Kaylee said nothing, continued to lace her shoes. Miss Helen was not one to give false praise either. Kaylee remembered the years of gruff commands and icy stares from her old teacher.

She was the same today—yet, not the same. Or was it Kaylee who had changed? As people grew older, did they look at relationships with teachers and other authority figures differently?

For a year and a half, Miss Helen had been giving Kaylee private lessons. She had worked Kaylee harder than a marine drill sergeant. But Kaylee welcomed it. Seven years ago, she had resented the old woman's demands and fiercely uncompromising point of view.

"So," continued Miss Helen, "this is our last practice together."

"Until I get back from Ireland," said Kaylee, stuffing her dance shoes into her bag.

Miss Helen shook her head. "I retired two years ago. Then you asked me to help you. Well, you are going to Ireland! You don't need my help anymore."

"But what about Nationals in July?" asked Kaylee, her voice rising anxiously. "You've got to train me for that!"

This brought the merest of smiles to Miss Helen's lips. "Your dream has always been Ireland. It's like a fire that burns inside of you. I know it will be your finest moment as a dancer."

Somehow, Kaylee knew that this was true. She might dance at feiseanna for another five months. Maybe through the summer. But nothing would compare to standing on stage at the All-Irelands, dancing against the best in the world in the home of Irish dance.

"You should be there," said Kaylee. "You should be there to watch me dance."

"I watch you dance every week," said Miss Helen.

"That's different," countered Kaylee, rising to her feet. "You should be there because—"

She stopped. What should she say? To see that Kaylee was not like Lizzie Martin? When Miss Helen saw her on stage in Ireland, would the old woman finally be forced to admit that she was wrong, that Kaylee was not a quitter? Or perhaps Miss Helen had never really felt that way at all.

Maybe it was me. Maybe I was afraid that's how I'd turn out.

She looked at Miss Helen and saw the young girl in the photograph at Golden Academy, standing on an award platform somewhere in Ireland, second in the world.

She saw Miss Helen in love, saw her four-year-old daughter.

Saw the sadness in her eyes, the greatest sadness a mother can ever endure, a sadness that no amount of time could erase.

She saw Lizzie Martin reflected in those eyes, a reflection of both triumph and heartbreak.

And she saw herself, ten years old, shaped by Miss Helen's strong and steady hand, a rough diamond gradually beginning to sparkle. Then in a blink, she lay broken in a hospital bed, and she saw Miss Helen in her home, paralyzed by a grief that had rushed back upon her through the years, unable to come, not because she cared so little, but because she cared so much.

"You should be there because I need you there!" She stared at the old woman for a moment, and then stepped forward, embracing her teacher, Kaylee's head on her shoulder.

Kaylee's voice broke as she continued. "You've helped me more than anyone! I never could have made it to Ireland without you!"

"Yes you would have," said Miss Helen, and for the first time, Kaylee heard her voice falter. "I have never met anyone so driven!"

"You deserve to be there! You're my teacher! My coach!"

"Annie will be with you," said Miss Helen shakily. "I no longer teach for Trean Gaoth, so they do not pay for a ticket for me. And now that I am retired, I can't afford to go on my own."

Kaylee sniffed. "I wish I could give you the money!"

Now Miss Helen's arms came around Kaylee and pulled her into a hug. "You have given me a much greater gift. Your dedication. Your friendship. And your love." Then she relaxed her hug, and leaned away slightly. Kaylee lifted her head and took a step back. Miss Helen looked at the floor, dabbed her eyes with a sleeve, and added, "And you are the best dancer I have ever taught!"

She wondered if this included Lizzie Martin, but one look at the old woman's eyes confirmed that it did.

On her way home from her final lesson with Miss Helen, Kaylee had one more stop to make. She knew it would break her heart, but she could not leave for Ireland without paying a visit to the cemetery in Rosemary.

A thin layer of snow covered the ground, but the headstones were clearly visible. Kaylee stood in front of her aunt's gave, remembering how kind and upbeat she had been, even as she succumbed to her cancer.

"This is for you, Aunt Kat," said Kaylee. "You wanted to take me to Ireland. Now I'm going. You taught me to keep climbing the mountain! I love you!"

There was, of course, no response; only the slight whistle of the afternoon wind.

Kaylee stood for a long time, remembering. Then she turned to look for her grandmother's headstone. She had been to the cemetery only a few times since her grandmother's death. The last time had been right before Christmas, when the snow had been deeper and only the tops of many of the smaller headstones like her grandmother's had been visible. She had also visited the previous Memorial Day, standing back by the car while her mother arranged a wreath of flowers. Before that had been the burial, when the headstone had been covered with the greenish blankets that had been lain around the open grave. This was the first time she had ever seen her grandmother's headstone.

She had been buried next to her second husband, since Grandpa Joey's remains were drifting on the winds somewhere in Ireland. *Mom fixed, the dress, Grandma. The one you made! It's beautiful! Thank you so much! I'm going to wear it at—*

Kaylee lost the thought. Something had caught her eye. At first she was not even sure what had broken her concentration or why it seemed important now.

She looked again.

KITTY MARTIN BIRDSALL

This was something from the distant past, almost from the time before her earliest memories. Everyone had called Grandma Birdsall's first husband Grandpa Joey, and so it had been easy to forget his last name. Yet, a very long time ago, Grandma Birdsall had been Grandma *Martin*. Kaylee had, of course, known this, but it had been filed away in such seldom-used territory of her brain.

When Kaylee considered the lost letter and her quest to find its author over the past several years, the coincidence—that Grandpa Joey's last name was also Martin—was almost funny.

Almost.

Thirty-five

"Twenty minutes!" called Mr. O'Shay. "If we're not backing out of the driveway by then, you're going to miss your plane!"

Kaylee breezed out of her room, garment bag over her shoulder, and plunged out the front door into the chilly morning. She deposited this on the back seat and hurriedly returned to the house.

"I wish we could come to Ireland with you, sweetheart," said Mrs. O'Shay, crossing items off a trip checklist on the kitchen table. "But, well, you know."

Kaylee knew. There had been barely enough money to pay for her ticket.

"But Annie and Tara will be there," Mrs. O'Shay added. "And aren't two other girls from your school going?"

Kaylee nodded and darted through her doorway. April and another younger girl named Alyssa had also been invited to All-Irelands, although they would be on a different flight.

"Where's my ticket? It was right here on my desk!"

"It's on the kitchen table," called Mrs. O'Shay. "You set it out here so you wouldn't forget it." Then she called up the stairs. "Will!"

Mr. O'Shay came into the room. "Everything loaded?"

"There's just Kaylee's suitcase," said Mrs. O'Shay, pointing to the green rectangle near the front door. Then she called up the stairs again. "Will!"

This time, Kaylee heard movement above, and seconds later her brother bounded down.

"Your sister's leaving," said Mrs. O'Shay.

Will shuffled forward, gave Kaylee a hug. "Good luck, little sis."

"You're younger than I am!" exclaimed Kaylee, still trapped in his embrace.

"I said little, not younger," said Will. "Jackie says you're going to win this thing. She says she's more excited than when Angelo Zizzo played in the world championship soccer game last year."

"Wow!" said Kaylee. "I finally rank ahead of Angelo Zizzo!"

Will released her, flashed her the number one sign, and then flew back up the stairs.

"Fifteen minutes!" called Mr. O'Shay, bending to scoop up Kaylee's suitcase. He grunted as he lifted. "Did you pack my bowling ball? And your mother's? This thing weighs a ton!"

Kaylee shrugged. "Just underwear and stuff."

Tom O'Shay winced. "Underwear in the Middle Ages didn't weigh this much! I'm sure this'll be just the thing for my sore back." Then he headed out the door.

"You know what they say," Kaylee called after him, "Focus on the prize, not the pain!" She smiled at her own cleverness. Although it was really her mother's cleverness. Or Miss Helen's. Or Lizzie Martin's.

Out of nowhere, a shiver shot through her, along with the memory of her grandmother's gravestone.

KITTY MARTIN BIRDSALL
But Martin is a common name.

Now the stolen note flashed into her mind.

Hey,

Thanks for inviting me for pizza with you and the gang, but I can't on Friday. Big soccer game. What can I say? It's my life! We'll do the pizza some other time!

Lizzie Martin

Just a letter from Lizzie to her mother.

But what if it wasn't to my mother? When she had discovered the note, she had assumed that Lizzie Martin had written it to Bethany O'Shay. But there was no name at the top, only the word "Hey." Was the note to someone else? If so, what was it doing in a box of her mother's things?

Suddenly she ran for her room.

"Forget something?" called Mrs. O'Shay, but Kaylee did not answer. She opened her desk drawer and pulled out the faux math folder, quickly retrieving Aunt Kat's sketch book, one of Kaylee's dearest possessions. It represented her aunt's immense artistic talent, how the world looked through Kat's eyes, and even a glimpse into the future, for she had sketched a picture of what Kaylee might look like in a gorgeous, green solo dance dress.

Or had it been a glimpse into the past?

The first pages of the sketch book were filled with drawings from Aunt Kat's college days while the later pages offered scenes from feiseanna and life in the year before Kat's death. However, the drawing of Kaylee in the green dress had always seemed out of place at the front of the book, and Kaylee's fingers trembled as she turned to it now. She had always assumed that Kat had found a blank page amongst the college-era sketches. But as she examined the sketch now, she realized that the dress was not something that Kat had created out of her imagination four years ago. *This is my dress!* The style of the neckline, the hem and the sleeves on her own dress were more modern than the dress in the sketch, although every other jewel or bit of embroidery matched perfectly. But that was not possible. Her Aunt Kat had been gone for four years. Her grandmother had only sewn the dress during the past two years.

Or had Grandma Birdsall simply taken an older dress and updated it so it would fit in with today's styles?

She remembered what her mother had said when the dress had ripped at Oireachtas: "Oh, sweetheart, this is quite a tear! Your grandmother didn't reinforce this spot where the old material meets the new."

Kaylee looked again at the drawing. *Aunt Kat drew this more than twenty years ago!* She shivered once more. It had been easy to see why Kaylee had been fooled. The dancer in the sketch looked so much like Kaylee.

So much.

This has got to be wrong, she told herself

Then she remembered the look on her father's face when he had seen her in the green dress at Oireachtas. Like he had seen a ghost.

Perhaps he had.

Kaylee pulled out the photograph of her mother and Aunt Kat standing together on the day of the conference track meet, Aunt Kat in her track uniform, Kaylee's mother in street clothes.

"Oh, your mom didn't run track," Aunt Kat had said years ago.

Kaylee had always assumed that Bethany O'Shay had never been very athletic. As an adult, she seemed to lack the essential coordination and physical prowess that would suggest a history of sports involvement. Then Kaylee thought of her own circumstances. In the year after her accident, would anyone have guessed that she had been an athlete?

Lizzie Martin died a long time ago, her mother had said. But a little on-line detective work by Kaylee and Jackie had revealed that Lizzie had survived, but had been badly injured in a car crash, her soccer career ruined.

Maybe Lizzie Martin did kind of die in that crash, thought Kaylee. Lizzie and Bethany were both forms of Elizabeth. Maybe Lizzie Martin the soccer player became plain old Bethany Martin, whose lack of athletic prowess was the result of her foot injury.

Kaylee felt a bit light-headed, slightly nauseous. She attempted to steady herself. Her mind traveled back to the note. And in an instant, Kaylee felt her feet land on firm ground again.

The note.

It proved that her mother was *not* Lizzie Martin.

If my mother was Lizzie and had written the note to someone else, why would it be in a box of my mother's old papers?

She sighed heavily. This felt better. Lizzie Martin had always been an emotional subject for her, and now it was clear that Kaylee had jumped to an absurd conclusion once again. On the plane to Ireland, she would have plenty of time to think it over, to come up with logical explanations for the dress, the sketchbook . . .

"Ten minutes!" came the shout from her father in the kitchen. "I'll be outside!"

Her *father*.

Hey,

Thanks for inviting me for pizza with you and the gang, but I can't on Friday. Big soccer game. What can I say? It's my life! We'll do the pizza some other time!

Lizzie Martin

All of the insanity came rushing back. The note had been written from her mother to her father. That was why it had been with her mother's things.

And now the floodgate seemed to open.

Her mother, always sitting in her car during dance practices, always avoiding the Trean Gaoth studio where she might encounter Miss Helen, her old teacher.

The disappearance of the letter! Her mother must have taken it to make sure Kaylee never compared the handwriting in the letter to Mrs. O'Shay's handwriting.

And Kaylee thought back to the Oireachtas. *Someone in the crowd recognized my mom!* Someone had shouted to Lizzie Martin, and then Bethany O'Shay had gone undercover. Her head spun as she considered more examples.

Kaylee stood, gripping the closed sketchbook, feeling small and suddenly very vulnerable in her room in the little house on Cranberry Street. Only it did not seem like her home anymore. Something about it was different, as if she were living with strangers.

Kaylee walked slowly into the kitchen as her mother cheerily checked the last item off her list. "I think everything should be packed and ready!" Then she saw her ashen-faced daughter. "Sweetheart, what's wrong?"

Kaylee set the sketchbook on the kitchen table, opened it to the girl in the green dress.

Mrs. O'Shay gazed at the drawing, smiling. "You're going to look even more beau—" She noticed the odd, almost desperate look in her daughter's eyes. "Sweetheart?"

Kaylee was not certain whether to feel angry, betrayed, shocked. When she spoke, her voice sounded lost. "Why didn't you tell me the truth?"

Mrs. O'Shay blinked, uncomprehending. "The truth?" Kaylee said nothing, and Mrs. O'Shay's eyes were drawn back to the sketch. A look of horror now swept across her face. "Oh, honey, you don't understand—"

"You're Lizzie Martin."

Mrs. O'Shay shook her head. "No, it's not—"

"Don't lie to me anymore!"

Bethany O'Shay stared into her daughter's conflicted eyes for a long moment. "I'm sorry. Sweetheart, I'm so very sorry."

It was as if her world had shifted in that brief I'm-sorry moment, black becoming white, all known noise ceasing while everything that had previously been silent filled the air with a freakish cacophony, the law of gravity suddenly irrelevant. Kaylee struggled for words, but ultimately, only one question seemed important.

"Why?"

Her mother sighed. "After my accident in college, I was crushed. It changed my whole life. You know what that's like."

Kaylee nodded, but her expression of tortured amazement remained.

"I was always Lizzie Martin the soccer star," Mrs. O'Shay continued. "And now I couldn't be that anymore. It hurt. Not just physically. So I put it behind me. Your grandmother had always called me Bethany, so I went back to that. It was less painful to look ahead, forget what I could no longer have. I guess that's why your father and I got married and had you so quickly. I needed something new in my life to focus on."

"But why didn't you ever tell me?"

"It was difficult for me to think about that part of my life. If you hadn't been able to return to Irish dance, think of how it might have haunted you. The goals you had left unfulfilled . . . what your life might have been like if things had turned out differently . . . So I kept the past in the past, where it didn't sting so much. But there was another reason I didn't say anything. I didn't want you to have to live up to anything I had done. To compare yourself to me. I wanted you to choose your own way, not push you into living my life. I have to admit, it was a bit of a shocker when you decided you wanted to become an Irish dancer."

"You could have told me after that," said Kaylee. "Once I'd been in dance a year or two."

Her mother's eyes, Kaylee noticed, were as sad as they had seemed right after Grandma Birdsall's death. "I didn't want people to say, 'Oh, there's Lizzie Martin's daughter,' and force you to have to live up to that. Although it looks like you've had no trouble becoming successful on your own."

Kaylee said nothing, and her mother continued. "Then when I found out that Miss Helen worked at Trean Gaoth Academy, that was another reason for me to keep quiet. When *I* quit dance, there were a lot of bad feelings."

"It hurt Miss Helen a lot," interjected Kaylee.

Mrs. O'Shay nodded, and Kaylee noticed that tears had formed at the corners of her eyes. "When you started trying to find Lizzie Martin, I tried to steer you away. By that point in time, I thought you'd be angry. Not because I had lied to you up to that point, which I hadn't. But because I hadn't told you the whole truth. And I knew you'd be upset because of what Lizzie had come to represent to you: A quitter. Someone who had betrayed Miss Helen. Someone who had turned her back on Irish dance, which you loved."

A tear slid down her mother's cheek, but Kaylee made no move toward her. Her mind still spun as the ramifications of this new information hit home.

"All that time I was searching for Lizzie, I really just wanted to know one thing. Why did you quit Irish dance? You could have danced at Worlds? Miss Helen said you could have been a world champion!"

"She's a good woman," said Mrs. O'Shay. "It's not really all that complicated. I did it for the same reason you chose dance over soccer. I liked soccer better."

"That's it?"

Her mother nodded. "But a part of me has always wished that I could have gone to Ireland with Miss Helen. To have stood there on the awards box, making her proud. But you can't change the past, can you?"

"I'm not so sure," said Kaylee. "Mine seems to have changed pretty dramatically in the past ten minutes!"

Mr. O'Shay called from outside. "Time to go!"

Kaylee looked at her mother, who seemed simultaneously like a stranger, and at the same time more familiar than ever. Still, her emotions churned. It was too much to sort through all at once. And so she grabbed her coat, rushed out the door and into the car.

Mr. O'Shay had been warming it up for a few minutes, and so the inside was toasty. He put it in gear and they backed down the driveway.

"Isn't mom coming to the airport with us?" asked Kaylee, startled.

"No, she's got to open the store," said her father. "Didn't she tell you that?"

Kaylee had figured she would have time to let her emotions settle during the trip to the airport, that the requisite tearful goodbye would be played out within a few paces of the metal detectors. She wanted to tell her father to stop the car, to rush back inside the house and give her mother a great hug. But he was already halfway down Cranberry Street.

Thirty-six

Somewhere below, the ocean moved in darkness, alive and mysterious. Kaylee stared out the window of the plane, unable to see it at this hour, thinking of Ireland, of the upcoming competition.

Mostly, though, she thought about her mother.

It seemed silly, a wild tale one might tell to shock the listener. Then everyone could have a good laugh after.

But this had been no story. Her mother was Lizzie Martin.

How hard had it been for her to tell Kaylee the truth? That was one thing that had crept upon Kaylee during the long plane ride. When one is confined for eight hours above the Atlantic, one has plenty of opportunity to think about things—especially the things that trouble her. Or her regrets.

She understood her mother's point of view completely. Still, it angered Kaylee that she had been misled for so long.

How could I have not seen it?

Kaylee wished she could call Jackie, to scream, "I found Lizzie Martin!" Wouldn't Jackie be surprised when she learned the details? And Caitlin?

Surprised? Blown away.

She had no cell phone, however. When she arrived at the airport in Shannon, Tara would meet her, and Kaylee would use her cell phone to check in with her parents. Then she would call again to tell them how she had danced. It would be a week before she was back in the States and could spill her guts to Jackie and Caitlin.

But Riley would be there, arriving a day later. He had qualified for Worlds and had opted to dance at All-Irelands, too.

239 / Rod Vick

"Are you kidding?" he had said to her. "You and me, together in Ireland? How could I pass that up?" The memory made her smile.

She wondered what Riley's reaction to the Lizzie Martin news would be.

Kaylee sighed. *I still can't believe it. Lizzie Martin is my mother.*

How many times had she said, "I'll never be like Lizzie Martin"? Yet, both of them had made tough choices. Lizzie had chosen soccer, Kaylee had chosen Irish dance. Both had been badly injured. But only Kaylee had gone on to fulfill her dream by dancing in Ireland. Lizzie's dreams had been irreparably broken in the car crash.

Or had they?

Did her mother have other dreams? Kaylee thought about it. Maybe she and Will were the fulfillment of her mother's dreams. Or maybe it was the Stitchin' Kitchen.

But she never made it to Ireland.

Kaylee sat quietly for a long time, watching the blue-gray expanse of water far below. Finding Lizzie Martin had been so important. Kaylee had felt certain that Lizzie could help her. *Why did you quit dancing, Lizzie?* Kaylee had imagined the answers she might have gotten. Because of a boyfriend. Or a soccer scholarship. Or dance was too hard. And Kaylee would have known that none of those things would have ever dissuaded her from dancing.

She would have known that she was *different* from Lizzie Martin.

And when Kaylee had been recovering from surgery, she had hoped that Lizzie could offer her the kind of inspiration that can only come from a champion dancer. But she had run into a dead end. And after all those years, Lizzie Martin had been no help to her at all.

Focus on the prize, not the pain.

Or had she?

Hadn't "Lizzie's" words inspired Kaylee to dance again?

And how many times had Lizzie taken her to feiseanna through the years?

Or sat with her late at night, helping her to understand why boys were so stupid?

Or sat by Kaylee's hospital bed?

How many times had Lizzie sat in the Trean Gaoth parking lot while her daughter danced inside, and how difficult must that have been?

And could she ever count the number of times that Lizzie Martin had been there with a bandage, a cookie, a kind word or . . . just to *be* there?

It seemed to Kaylee that Lizzie Martin had been helping her all along.

She looked out again from her dimly-lighted shell high in the sky, into the vast mystery of the world. *Thanks, Lizzie.*

And then she slept.

As the great plane touched down in Dublin, Kaylee felt herself overcome by a great wave of emotion. *I'm in Ireland!* She was not in Ireland for terribly long, however, as she found herself in the air again, bound for Shannon. Although this flight was far shorter, it seemed to take forever, and Kaylee wanted nothing more than to be done with flying for awhile.

Tara met Kaylee at the airport along with Alyssa and April, all of whom had been in Ireland for two days already. "It's so beautiful!" said April after she had administered the requisite number of we're-both-in-Ireland hugs. "You know the pictures they show you in magazines and on TV? It's even better!" Then the quartet headed for the rental car.

On the two-hour drive to the house they had rented, Tara went over the schedule. "Annie and I will have a workout for you girls later today and then again tomorrow, but most of the day will be available for sightseeing." The trip passed quickly as Alyssa and April described the wonders they had already seen, and as Kaylee watched the world outside her window transform from city to gorgeous emerald countryside. Emerald Isle, she decided, was a completely appropriate nickname.

The six-bedroom house Annie had rented for the group rested in a quiet neighborhood only a mile from the brand-new Dunloe Arena where they would be dancing. Kaylee settled into a room she would share with April, and then they stretched their legs by taking a walking tour of some of the local shops. Kaylee discovered her new favorite food when she purchased "chips and gravy" for supper.

In a later conversation with Jackie, Kaylee would describe the next day's sightseeing as "a blur with cliffs." She attributed this to her nervousness and how focused she was on the upcoming competition, plus the fact that her body was still operating on Wisconsin time.

Some people had told her, prior to her trip, that Ireland looked a lot like Wisconsin. More rocks, perhaps. Rolling countryside. Lots of cows, although Wisconsin was up to the challenge there. And that was true. But Wisconsin had nothing to compare with the Dingle Peninsula. The stone forts perched above rocky cliffs . . . the thundering surf crashing against an amazing scatter of rough boulders that jutted from the sea. "They say a volcano exploded a long time ago and scattered these boulders," explained Tara. Kaylee took it all in, amazed, and later fell asleep in the car on the way back to the house.

She woke for the short evening workout and for supper, but then drifted back into what Annie predicted would be a good night's sleep before the big day. She found herself awake again at two in the morning.

My body clock must really be messed up.

No one else in the house seemed to have any trouble. Kaylee moved through the quiet living room, illuminated only by a night light. Tara's phone rested on the coffee table. For just a moment, Kaylee considered "borrowing" it to call Jackie. But even though Tara would probably have agreed—if she had been awake—Kaylee could not persuade herself to use the phone without permission.

Maybe I'll take a walk. Or a run.

She had not had a good run in almost three days, and she decided that she needed to stretch out her muscles after half a day on planes and another half sightseeing. She pulled on her jogging pants and her Trean Gaoth jacket, laced on her running shoes, and quietly let herself out of the front door, slipping into the cool night. Lonely islands of light shined from a few windows in the neighborhood. Kaylee jogged to the street, picked up the pace as she neared the main road, and headed toward Dunloe Arena. After a few hundred feet, she slowed, stopped, unable to take her eyes off the brilliant, starry sky. The clouds had disappeared, allowing the cosmos to wrap itself around her like some majestic shawl. *I'm really in Ireland*, she thought. *But Jackie and Caitlin can look up at these same stars. And my parents. And Miss Helen.* In a way, the stars seemed to connect them to her, even though they were so distant.

"I wish you were here, Lizzie Martin!" she said to the stars.

Kaylee began to run again, and in a few minutes, the lights of the arena came into view. A mile to the complex, a mile back. A good workout. And then maybe she would be able to go back to sleep.

When she pulled even with the main entrance, she stopped and stared at the great building. Then she spotted a man in a security uniform, leaning against one of the glass doors to keep it open, smoking a cigarette.

The smoking reminded her of Miss Helen, and she wished again that her teacher was there.

An idea occurred to her. And since it was after two in the morning, it was cold, and she was out on a run more than five-thousand miles from home, Kaylee could think of no reason to not be bold.

"Excuse me," she said, mounting a couple of the steps and addressing the guard, who eyed her warily. "I'm going to be dancing here tomorrow. Do you think I could take a peek inside?"

The man assessed her quietly, taking a long drag on his cigarette. At length, he seemed to decide that a slightly-built teenager in a jogging suit posed a scant security risk, and since this was Ireland, and thus a bit more laid back when it comes to issues of this sort, he nodded his assent. "Don't be too long," he said, offering a friendly grin. "I'll be leaving around sunrise, you know."

Kaylee assured him she would not be that long and slipped inside. She passed through a second set of doors, crossed a wide hallway and walked through an entryway that took her into the main part of the arena. Thousands of seats rose up in rows from a raised stage where she would dance in only a few hours. At this hour, the cavernous expanse was mostly dark, illuminated by safety lights, exit signs and one small bulb above the stage. She edged down the aisle, step-by-step, until she stood next to the stage.

Kaylee felt like a climber standing only a few feet from the summit of Everest. How long a journey it had been—more than seven years from when she had taken that first step in an old pair of ballet shoes onto the dance floor at Trean Gaoth Academy. How difficult, even impossible it had seemed at times. She thought of the candle that night in the chapel at the Fox Cities Feis.

The fire had almost gone out.

Now the fire in her heart burned more brightly than ever.

She moved to the side of the stage, mounted a stair, but then stepped off again. She wanted to stand on the stage, to feel what it would be like before she actually had to face the judges tomorrow. But should she? Would it be bad luck to do so?

She shook off the notion, started up the steps again, strode out onto the dance surface.

And stood, facing the empty auditorium.

But it was not really empty. Her mother, father, Jackie and Caitlin, Miss Helen, Grandma Birdsall and Aunt Kat—they were all with her.

They were always with her.

Thirty-seven

How different the Dunloe Arena looked in the daylight.

There must be a thousand people watching! thought Kaylee as she stood in the warm-up area near the stage. She had been too nervous for breakfast. She felt tired, too. By the time she had returned from her run and had slipped—unnoticed—back into her room, it had been after three. It had taken more than an hour for her to fall asleep, and then Annie had waked her at five-thirty.

The first couple of girls in her age group had already finished their soft shoe steps. Kaylee estimated that she would be up in another fifteen minutes.

She spotted a familiar face in a yellow, blue and white solo dress. Ariel Blake. She had finished third at Worlds last year. Many of the dancers seemed to have picked her as the favorite to win it all this year. But Kaylee knew there were half a dozen other girls in the crowd who were as good, or nearly so. Every once in awhile she would spot one of these minor celebrities and feel her own confidence ebb.

April would dance near the end of the group today. She and Kaylee had exchanged hugs when they had arrived, but now each had settled into competition mode, doing whatever stretching, performing whatever rituals, summoning whatever mental state was necessary in order to propel them to their best efforts.

Kaylee had spotted Brittany Hall, too. "I heard that she's been here for four days already, getting used to the time change and everything," April had told Kaylee.

"Figures," said Kaylee. "Brittany's father probably had her flown over on Air Force One."

"I guess she really wants to do well," continued April. "I think she's still upset that you tied her at Oireachtas!"

This did not surprise Kaylee. Brittany had not spoken to her in the almost three months since the Oireachtas. Although she rarely saw Brittany in school.

Kaylee scanned the crowd. She had seen Riley for the first time since arriving in Ireland. He had rushed up to her as she headed toward check in.

A good-luck.

A hug.

A very light kiss so as not to upset the delicate balance of makeup.

Then she had been whisked off by Annie and Tara. She scanned the crowd for them now, but finding anyone was difficult, for there were so many people.

Kaylee sighed, continued her stretching. Her stomach did flip-flops.

Less than ten minutes. Then she would set foot on the summit.

The view keeps getting better the higher you climb.

Her thoughts were interrupted by a tap on her shoulder. She turned to face a very blonde dancer in a frilly orange, white and black dress. "Your coach wants to talk to you," said the girl, pointing vaguely behind her.

Kaylee thanked her and began weaving through the dancers, relieved to know that Annie and Tara were indeed nearby. She wondered what last minute words of inspiration they might have.

And then, as she edged past a girl in a purple dress, Kaylee almost screamed, covering her mouth in startle.

Miss Helen stood at the edge of the warm-up area. She wore a calf-length black and green skirt, a blouse and sweater, and she looked beautiful. Her smile lit the auditorium, and Kaylee ran to her, delivering an enormous hug.

"You will ruin your makeup," cautioned Miss Helen.

"I don't care!" said Kaylee, trying to hold back her tears, because she really *did* care. Finally pulling back, Kaylee asked, "How?"

Before Miss Helen could answer, an equally amazing sight greeted her. Coming up behind Miss Helen were her parents.

Kaylee's mouth fell open, and she uttered a second "How?" before smothering her parents with hugs.

"I thought you couldn't afford to come to Ireland?" she said when her power of speech returned.

"We couldn't," said Tom O'Shay.

"Then how?"

Her father chuckled. "You can thank your friend, Brittany."

"Brittany?" Kaylee wondered whether she had heard right.

"Riley gave us the whole story," explained Mrs. O'Shay. "Brittany came over a few days ago, I guess. Flew by herself. Her father couldn't come right away because of his work."

Kaylee recalled how alone she had felt without her parents and friends. What had it been like for Brittany?

"Mr. Hall's company decided it was going to fly him over here on their corporate jet," continued Mr. O'Shay.

"Riley happened to be texting a good luck message to Brittany," said Kaylee's mother. "And he mentioned that you were over here all by yourself, too. But that your father and I weren't going to be able to come."

"So Riley convinced her to ask her dad if you could fly along?" asked Kaylee.

Mrs. O'Shay shook her head. "No. The idea never occurred to Riley. Brittany called her dad on her own, and then he called us. Said there were a few seats available, why not use them?"

Kaylee turned to Miss Helen, her eyes a question.

"Your mother called me and asked if I wanted to come along," said her old teacher. "How could I say no? I have waited so many years to come to Ireland with Lizzie Martin . . . and watch the best dancer I have ever coached!"

Kaylee gasped. "I'd better get back! I don't want to miss my first dance!"

Again she hugged her mother and Miss Helen. Her father bent forward, gave her the tiniest of kisses, and then held her at arm's length, as if examining a rare jewel.

"Sorry I quit soccer, dad," she said softly. "I know that was always your dream for me."

The most tender of smiles spread across his face. "Kaylee, when you were a little girl, kicking the soccer ball around almost before you could walk, I always dreamed that you'd become a

/ Rod Vick

great athlete." He hugged her to his chest. "And now, it's made me so proud to see that you have!"

Kaylee hugged him back. Then, smiling, she turned and weaved through the pulsing human rainbow to where she had been warming up. Four more dancers. It was almost time.

But there was still one more thing to do.

She raised herself up onto her toes, scanned the wigs and silks and Celtic knots, found the familiar figure and set off to cover the short distance. Brittany Hall practiced her steps diligently, but paused as Kaylee approached.

"Thank you!" said Kaylee, searching for the right words, shaking her head in frustration at her inability to find them, and finally repeating, "Thank you!"

Brittany stared back at her for a moment, and then a slight smile crept onto her face. "I love Irish dance. But you love it more. More than anyone I know. It'd stink if your parents couldn't see this."

Kaylee shook her head in disbelief. "That's it?"

Brittany's smile disappeared. "You didn't put petroleum jelly on my windshield."

"What?"

"You didn't want me to get hurt. Even though you don't like me, you still didn't want me to get hurt. And you didn't turn me in that night that Heather trashed Miller's car!"

Kaylee gave Brittany Hall a hug. "Maybe we just kept running into each other under the wrong circumstances. Maybe I'm an idiot. We're in Ireland now. That's a good place for a fresh start!"

Then Kaylee turned back to the stage, took her place near the stairs. A minute later, she stepped up, walked to center stage, faced the five judges. It surprised her that, despite the large number of people in the auditorium, she picked out two:

Miss Helen and Lizzie Martin, their eyes shining.

Kaylee returned the smile as the music began.

Thirty-eight

She could never recall having been late for school before. "Sorry," Kaylee's mother apologized, "but I slept right through my alarm. And you must have forgotten to set yours."

Kaylee had thought she had set it, but after a week in Ireland, it did not surprise her that she had fallen out of her normal school routine.

"Just our luck," added Mrs. O'Shay, "that your father decided to go in to work early today to start getting caught up on everything that had piled up during his absence."

And so Kaylee, Will and Bethany O'Shay rushed around, doing their best to share the small bathroom, finally arriving at the car in a presentable state. Minutes later, Mrs. O'Shay pulled the vehicle into the visitor parking lot in front of Rosemary Senior High.

"I have to let the attendance lady know why you're late," explained Mrs. O'Shay. "Otherwise you'll both get detentions."

"You could have just called," grunted Kaylee.

"Well, I'm here," said her mother, bustling the two children through the glass front doors ahead of her. They hurried to the main office through the eerily empty hallways.

Everyone's in class, noted Kaylee, to whom deserted hallways at arrival time seemed alien.

Through the double doors leading into the main office plunged Mrs. O'Shay, immediately explaining her situation to the woman behind the long reception counter. The woman nodded, motioned Mrs. O'Shay to a room down a short hallway behind the counter.

"Stay here," she ordered, and disappeared.

Moments later, a broad-shouldered, stern-looking man in a scratchy-looking suit emerged from a different office behind the counter. "Just arriving, are we?" asked Mr. Powell, raising an eyebrow. Kaylee remembered him from the night Heather had vandalized Coach Miller's car. "Kaylee O'Shay, am I correct?"

Unfortunately, he seemed to remember her, too.

Mr. Powell pointed to Will. "Young man, if you'll proceed to Mr. Bronkowski's office, third door down?" Kaylee recognized the name of the school's other assistant principal and guessed that he would be handling Will's consequences for being tardy.

With a hopeless glance toward his sister, Will rose, and in a moment, disappeared in the direction Mr. Powell had pointed.

"And you, young lady, if you'll follow me."

"But," Kaylee protested meekly, "my mother is in the attendance off—"

"Yes, yes," said Mr. Powell impatiently. "I'm sure it's a very good excuse. Now please." He extended his hand toward the door, and Kaylee rose and preceded him through it.

"Our alarms didn't go off," she muttered as she walked. Mr. Powell either did not hear, or he chose to ignore this. "I just want to go to class."

"First things first," said Mr. Powell, and Kaylee decided to stop talking, for she had no idea what he meant. Were they on their way to detention study hall? That seemed an odd punishment for a first-time tardy offense. And, in fact, they were heading away from that area.

Half a minute later, they arrived at the gymnasium. GO MARINERS painted in red above the windowless double doors.

"Wait here," said Mr. Powell, and he ducked through the doors.

This is weird, thought Kaylee, and a moment later, it got a bit weirder as Mr. Bronkowski arrived—but instead of Will, he brought with him Brittany Hall. Leaving her beside Kaylee, he also disappeared through the double doors.

"Nice t-shirt!" said Brittany, and Kaylee noticed that both girls had worn their green All-Irelands t-shirts to school. *Well, that's no mystery*, thought Kaylee, reasoning that they had both just returned from one of the most thrilling adventures of their lives. "You were tardy, too?"

Kaylee nodded. "Alarm didn't go off."

"Mine neither! What do you suppose they're going to have us do? Scrub toilets? Or maybe make us targets for the kids playing dodgeball."

Kaylee shook her head worriedly. "This isn't right. This is spooky."

One of the doors popped noisily open, and Mr. Powell barked, "Come on!"

Kaylee swallowed hard and led Brittany into the gymnasium. As they rounded the bleachers, a cheer erupted, and Kaylee suddenly understood why the hallways had been so quiet. All one thousand and three hundred students plus the Rosemary faculty were packed into the bleachers, facing a small dais that had been erected in the center of the gym about twenty feet in front of a wall upon which hung an enormous banner.

The noise was deafening, and as they approached the dais, Kaylee noticed familiar faces in folding chairs set up for special guests:

Her parents. Brittany's parents, too. Miss Annie and Tara and Clarissa Golden. And Miss Helen.

In the crowd, she began to pick out faces of her friends. There was Jackie, right in the front row. And Will next to her, both applauding and cheering. Had Will known about this all along? Then she blinked. Was that Riley and Caitlin next to them? But they attended school in Paavo. Perhaps they had gotten special permission to attend this surprise event.

The clapping and cheering continued as the two girls stood next to the high school principal, Dr. Wells, who seemed to want to say something using a nearby microphone. Even in its amplified state, though, his voice was no match for the roaring crowd, and so Kaylee drank it all in, gave Brittany a hug, turned to admire the banner.

Large green shamrocks flanked the words. She could still scarcely believe it.

WELCOME HOME
ROSEMARY COMPETES WITH THE WORLD'S BEST

BRITTANY HALL 5TH AT ALL-IRELANDS

And then, below that, the most amazing words she would every read:

KAYLEE O'SHAY, ALL-IRELAND CHAMPION

The world was full of surprises, Kaylee O'Shay decided. Occasionally, good ones. And her Aunt Kat had been right.

The view keeps getting better the higher you climb.

Finding Lizzie Martin

A look back at the clues in books one through six

CAUTION: This section immediately contains spoilers that you may not wish to read if you have not read the first six books in the Kaylee O'Shay series.

*

At the end of *The Winds of Ireland*, Miss Helen, Kaylee's demanding dance instructor, makes a startling discovery: Kaylee's own mother is Lizzie Martin, the subject of a long search by Kaylee.

Perhaps some readers figured out Lizzie's identity ahead of time. Others may have been shocked upon reading the last line of book six. In either case, you may have found yourself going back over the previous books in the Kaylee O'Shay series, trying to find all of the hints that would have pointed toward Lizzie's true identity. I'm going to try and list most of them here.

Some of the hints are very slight. Others—in light of what we ultimately learn—seem quite direct.

From *Kaylee's Choice*

In chapter two, we find out Grandma Birdsall was "twice married and twice widowed," and this is why she has moved into the O'Shay house. We also learn that Grandpa Birdsall passed away five years earlier. If Grandpa Birdsall was Grandma Birdsall's *second* husband, that means he was not Bethany O'Shay's father. Hmmm . . . I wonder what Grandma Birdsall's *first* husband's last name was?

In chapter three, when Kaylee asks her mother about taking Irish dance lessons, her mother is "shocked" but then she says she will check into it, responding to her daughter as if she were "in a dream". Perhaps she is recalling her own memories of dance.

A similar moment of glazed remembrance occurs in chapter seven just before Kaylee's mother reveals that she has signed up her daughter for Irish dance lessons. "The water had begun to boil, but Mrs. O'Shay was simply staring at the box of pasta."

In chapter eight, Kaylee's mother takes her to Trean Gaoth Academy for the first time. As they enter the building, they encounter Miss Helen, who is standing outside, smoking a cigarette. "This

253 / Rod Vick

seemed to startle Kaylee's mother, who stopped in her tracks, her eyes suggesting that she might flee to the car." The reader is led to believe that the mother is appalled by the uncouth appearance of Miss Helen. Actually, Mrs. O'Shay is started because she recognizes her old teacher.

In chapter ten, Kaylee dances at home for her mother for the first time. "'Wow!' said her mother, and Kaylee noticed a brightness in her eyes that she had not seen before." Seeing her daughter Irish dance has obviously tripped some emotional trigger—perhaps her own memories of dance.

In chapter thirteen, we learn that, unlike the other mothers, Mrs. O'Shay usually runs errands or sits in her car reading during dance practices. This, of course, is to avoid potentially running into Miss Helen who, if she should recognize Kaylee's mother as Lizzie Martin, might create a very awkward situation. Remember, Miss Helen hates the fact that Lizzie quit dance to pursue soccer. Would she respond angrily if she recognized her former pupil? Would she take it out on Kaylee? It's likely that Mrs. O'Shay simply wants to avoid the potential drama.

From *Green Storm*

In chapter one, Kaylee wakes up from a "seriously twisted and possibly just pure evil" recurring dream she has been having about soccer. Her mother tells her she's probably having the dream because she misses soccer, and she lets it slip that she used to have a similar dream when she was younger. When Kaylee asks her mother what she missed, Mrs. O'Shay is at first flustered, but eventually recovers and tells her daughter that she used to dream about missing teaching after she quit to open the Stitchin' Kitchen, her combination coffee bar/sewing shop. Perhaps Mrs. O'Shay really did have such a dream, but one gets the impression that her current thoughts were on a different dream. In retrospect, we could guess that it was a dream about how Mrs. O'Shay had missed Irish dance after she gave it up for soccer. But, of course, she can't tell this to Kaylee.

However, Kaylee almost catches her in the lie. Mrs. O'Shay had told her daughter, "I used to have a dream like that when I was a little older than you are." After Mrs. O'Shay improvises the teaching dream, Kaylee astutely points out, "You weren't my age when you dreamed that. You were old." Mrs. O'Shay breezily downplays the slip and says, "I just meant that I was younger than I am now." Pretty lame, but Kaylee buys it. And why not? At this point, she has no reason to believe that her mother is lying to her.

In chapter two, Grandma Birdsall introduces us to the memory of her first husband, who everyone refers to as Grandpa Joey. Somewhat out of the ordinary to refer to one's grandfather by his first name, but not unheard of. Of course, this gives us the opportunity to conceal Grandpa Joey's last name. Anybody thinking it might be "Martin"?

In chapter three, Kaylee is talking excitedly with Grandma Birdsall about what her first feis will be like. Grandma seems to understand how the competition works: "But you won't compete against all of them. Only the girls in your age group." That's curious. But she knows this because of her own daughter's dance history.

In chapter four, Kaylee and her mother go on-line where Kaylee gets her first look at how many feiseanna are conducted in different states throughout the year. Mrs. O'Shay is not as surprised as her daughter. Why not? After all, she had done the feis thing when she was Kaylee's age.

From *Fire & Metal*

In chapter four, we once again see Kaylee's mother dodging an encounter with Miss Helen. Mrs. O'Shay's intention is to talk to Annie Delaney to tell her that the O'Shay family will be moving. However, she spots her old teacher having a cigarette outside the main entrance to Trean Gaoth Academy of Irish dance as she arrives for Kaylee's practice. "You go ahead dear," says Mrs. O'Shay, pretending to try and find something in her purse. "I'll be there in a minute." This constant avoidance of Miss Helen should begin to strike the reader as "curious".

Chapter eight is where we really get into the thick of the mystery. After the O'Shays announce that they are moving, Mrs. O'Shay compels Kaylee to help her clean out the office at the Stitchin' Kitchen, Mrs. O'Shay's combination fabric store/coffee shop. Kaylee's mother asks her to sort through cardboard boxes, disposing of junk but keeping photographs and other important papers. Apparently the boxes contain items that have been haphazardly packed away for years—the kinds of boxes that many households have, boxes that we resolve to get around to dealing with someday.

Eventually Kaylee runs across a bundle of letters. These appear to be from her mother's college days. One is a letter from her father, which Kaylee finds remarkable only for its lack of romantic spark. The second letter she reads, however, is from her Aunt Kat, her mother's older sister. In the letter, Kat alludes to her younger sister's impulsiveness, such as when Bethany O'Shay got married after her junior year in college. Aunt Kat's letter suggests that Bethany is now pregnant and considering postponing her student teaching. Kat implores Bethany to complete her teaching. "I'm just afraid that if you don't do the teaching now, you'll get busy with motherhood and never get your diploma. Don't give up on your dream this time, Beth."

This statement puzzles Kaylee: "But what did Aunt Kat mean: *Don't give up on your dream this time?* What dream did her mother abandon? And was it because of Kaylee?"

In retrospect, we have an idea. Kat is probably referring to her sister's decision to quit Irish dance when she could have been one of the world's best.

But the next letter Kaylee finds is the real bombshell.

Hey,

Thanks for inviting me for pizza with you and the gang, but I can't on Friday. Big soccer game. What can I say? It's my life! We'll do the pizza some other time.

Lizzie Martin

Kaylee is amazed! A letter from Lizzie Martin to her own mother! They had apparently been friends in college. Kaylee has already developed a minor obsession over Lizzie. She is fascinated by Lizzie Martin because she seems to provide the motivation for much of Miss Helen's anger. But Kaylee is also obsessed with finding out why Lizzie would give up a promising dance career to play soccer. We suspect that Kaylee either sees something of herself in Lizzie, or suspects that Miss Helen sees something in Kaylee that reminds her of Lizzie.

In book six, of course, we learn that Kaylee has misinterpreted the letter. It is not a letter from Lizzie Martin to Bethany O'Shay, it is a letter from Lizzie Martin—her own mother—to Tom O'Shay.

Kaylee believes the letter explains why Miss Helen is so tough on her. She suspects that, somehow, Miss Helen knows that Lizzie and Mrs. O'Shay were friends, and so she is taking it out on Kaylee. Ultimately we learn that Miss Helen has no idea that there is a Lizzie Martin connection to the O'Shay family. She is tough on Kaylee because that's her personality.

In chapter nine, when Kaylee mentions to her father that she has found a letter from Lizzie Martin, he says, "That's a name I hadn't heard in a long time." Kaylee then asks if he thinks that's why Miss Helen doesn't like her. Mr. O'Shay says, "I really doubt that Miss Helen has made the connection." This seems to confirm to Kaylee that the Lizzie Martin in the letter is the same Lizzie Martin who was once an Irish dancer. Mr. O'Shay, however, means that he doubts Miss Helen has figured out that Mrs. O'Shay and Lizzie Martin are one in the same. In retrospect, we can imagine that Kaylee's father told Mrs. O'Shay about this conversation at a later time, and then Mrs. O'Shay probably advised him to leave it at that, to not spill the beans.

In chapter fifteen, Kaylee confesses to her mother that she found a letter from Lizzie Martin.

"Everyone says (Lizzie) was an amazing dancer," said Kaylee. "Was she? Did you ever watch her dance?"

Kaylee's question makes it apparent to her mother that Kaylee does not understand who Lizzie really is. Of course, Mrs. O'Shay does not reveal the truth to us, either. However, she answers Kaylee's questions truthfully, without revealing too much, and only later do we appreciate the appropriateness of her responses.

"I watched her dance," said Mrs. O'Shay.

"Was she amazing?" Kaylee asked breathlessly.

Her mother nodded slowly. "I don't think I appreciated her gift at that time."

"Miss Helen says she could have been one of the best in the world!"

Mrs. O'Shay's jaw muscles seemed to tighten. "I'm sure Miss Helen would know more about that than I would."

Kaylee also asks about Lizzie walking out on Irish dance, a recurring concern, and a motivation for Kaylee to pursue a meeting with her.

From *Christmas in Ireland*

In chapter three, Kaylee and her mother are having a conversation about choices that Bethany O'Shay and her sister, Kaylee's Aunt Kat, made when they were younger. Kaylee asks her mother what bad choices she made. After thinking about it for a moment, Mrs. O'Shay responds with, "None of your business." Is this because she is perhaps thinking about her decision to give up Irish dance?

In chapter seven, Kaylee dances at a feis, and Aunt Kat gets to watch her for the first time. Afterwards, Kat says, "You were wonderful, athletic, beautiful. Of course, that doesn't surprise me at all. After all, you are your mother's child." The "athletic" comment confuses Kaylee. In response to this, Kaylee's mother gives Aunt Kat a horrified look. Why? Aunt Kat is obviously referencing Bethany O'Shay's own dance history, though Kaylee doesn't get it.

In chapter twenty-one, Kat gives Kaylee her sketch book. Kat has had the book since college and has filled it with dozens of drawings. She has recently begun adding sketches of Irish dancers at feiseanna to the blank pages remaining in the book. However, Kaylee finds a drawing of an Irish dancer in a green dress at the front of the sketch book. The dancer looks like her, and Kaylee wrongly assumes that Kat has tried to approximate what Kaylee would look like dressed in the green solo costume she has always wanted. However, it is actually a sketch of Kat's sister, Bethany O'Shay, in her own solo dress years earlier.

From *The Secret Ceili*

In chapter seven, Kaylee discovers that someone has stolen the letter from Lizzie Martin to her mother. However, she can see no motivation for anyone to have done this. As we look back, knowing that the letter was actually written by Kaylee's mother, we can infer a motive: Mrs. O'Shay probably wanted to get the letter away from her daughter so that she did not eventually compare handwriting and discover that her mother had written it.

In chapter nine, Jackie and Kaylee resolve to track down Lizzie Martin. Since they believe she went to college with Mrs. O'Shay, Kaylee calls her father's old soccer coach at Northland College. Coach Warren at first seems eager to talk to the daughter of Tom O'Shay, one of his former star players, and he is equally happy to talk about Lizzie Martin—until Kaylee asks if he knows where she might be now. Then he abruptly ends the conversation, advising Kaylee that "this is a question you'll need to take up with your parents." The response puzzles both Jackie and Kaylee, but neither makes the connection. Coach Warren knows that Tom O'Shay married Lizzie Martin. When Tom's daughter calls asking where to find Lizzie, he knows that something is amiss, but probably feels it is not his place to fill in the blanks for Tom and Lizzie's daughter.

In chapter ten, Kaylee asks her grandmother for information about Lizzie. Like Coach Warren, Grandma Birdsall advises Kaylee to talk to her mother. Grandma Birdsall, of course, knows that her daughter has not been completely honest with Kaylee about Lizzie Martin's identity, but like the coach, she probably feels it is Bethany O'Shay's responsibility to reveal the truth—at the appropriate time.

Also in chapter ten, Kaylee approaches her mother about Lizzie. Bethany O'Shay tells Kaylee that Lizzie died in a car accident before Kaylee was born. Metaphorically speaking, this is true. When the accident ended Lizzie's soccer career, Bethany O'Shay distanced herself from that identity and its painful memories. "Oh, you don't know how I cried," confesses Mrs. O'Shay, describing her reaction to Lizzie's "death".   And since we now know the changes that the accident inflicted on her, we suspect that she really did cry rivers.

From *Winds of Ireland*
In chapter five, Jackie shows Kaylee evidence that Lizzie Martin did not die in the car accident. This will become important later.

In chapter nine, Jackie and Kaylee return to the Northland College web site and visit the alumni message board. Here they post questions about Lizzie Martin, hoping that an alumnus from the Lizzie era will see them and respond. Several people do, although their responses are full of misunderstandings, false information and half-truths—a consequence of relying on memories that are almost two decades old. Ultimately, one reply suggests that Lizzie was dating a Roger Hartenstein, that he was going to medical school after graduation, and that the two planned to live in Wisconsin after marrying. And indeed, this was the plan, for Kaylee's mother had dated Roger Hartenstein in college.   What the two girls—and apparently some of Lizzie's former college teammates—don't realize is that Lizzie and Roger broke up before graduation. And, of course, Lizzie went on to marry Tom O'Shay. This sends Jackie and Kaylee off in the wrong direction, chasing "Mrs. Hartenstein," who is the wrong woman.

In chapter thirteen, Kaylee meets Mrs. Hartenstein, who she believes is Lizzie Martin. Mrs. Hartenstein is hurrying off with her own small children. Kaylee tells her that her mother knew her in college. Mrs. Hartenstein asks the name of Kaylee's mother. Kaylee first answers "Bethany O'Shay," but then corrects herself: "Bethany Birdsall." But that is wrong, too. In her nervousness, Kaylee has used her grandmother's last name by her second husband rather than her mother's maiden name.

In chapter fourteen, the girls wonder why Lizzie Martin doesn't seem to mind the idea of reuniting with Mrs. O'Shay, but Kaylee's mother seems to be going out of her way to avoid any contact. The reason? Mrs. Hartenstein isn't Lizzie.

In chapter eighteen, Kaylee learns that Mrs. Hartenstein is not Lizzie Martin. And in chapter nineteen, we discover Lizzie's true identity when Mrs. O'Shay pleads with Miss Helen to help Kaylee dance again.

Acknowledgements

Thanks to My Lovely Wife Marsha, for your help with the manuscript and for your love.

Thanks to my daughter, Haley Marie, a daily inspiration to me through your Irish dance, your singing, and your incredible spirit and passion. And to my son, Josh, a gifted Irish dancer and soccer player, who constantly shows me how difficult it can be to juggle the things that are important in life.

Thank you to Kathleen O'Reilly-Wild, publisher of Feis America Magazine, for her continued support. Please visit her wonderful site at www.feisamerica.com.

Thanks to Mr. Terry Evan Williams for legal advice that proved immensely valuable in writing the courtroom action in this book.

Thanks to my special research assistants Breeanne Glavan, Katie Robinson, Maureen Robinson and Megan Sinclair.

Thank you to everyone who helped in ways big and small. Even if you were not named here, please know that I am enormously grateful for your contributions.

About the Author

Rod Vick is the author of the Kaylee O'Shay series that began with *Kaylee's Choice*. He has written for newspapers and magazines, has worked as an editor and has taught writing workshops and classes over the span of a quarter century. His short stories have appeared in a variety of literary magazines and have won both regional and national awards. Mr. Vick was also the 2000 Wisconsin Teacher of the Year.

Rod Vick lives in Mukwonago, Wisconsin with his wife, Marsha, and children Haley and Joshua. An occasional speaker at conferences and orientation events, he also runs marathons, enthusiastically supports his children's dance and soccer passions, and pitches a pretty mean horseshoe.

Rod Vick invites you to check out two other series he has written:

The Irish Witch Series
>   The Irish Witch's Dress
>   The Irish Witch's Tiara

The Coins of the Dagda Series
>   Dance of Time
>   Dance of Secrets

www.ingramcontent.com/pod-product-compliance
Lightning Source LLC
Chambersburg PA
CBHW031338040426
42443CB00006B/376